Blind People's Pragmatic Abilities

Blind People's Pragmatic Abilities

By

Jolanta Sak-Wernicka

Cambridge Scholars Publishing

Blind People's Pragmatic Abilities

By Jolanta Sak-Wernicka

This book first published 2017

Cambridge Scholars Publishing

Lady Stephenson Library, Newcastle upon Tyne, NE6 2PA, UK

British Library Cataloguing in Publication Data
A catalogue record for this book is available from the British Library

ISBN (10): 1-4438-1729-5
ISBN (13): 978-1-4438-1729-5

TABLE OF CONTENTS

INTRODUCTION

From time immemorial, comprehension has aroused the surprise and interest of a large number of scholars. In many concepts, models, approaches and theories, philosophers, logicians, linguists, psychologists and anthropologists (among others), attempted to explain the intricacies of the human ability to understand language. The relation between language and comprehension inspired, fascinated and astonished the great minds, and in equal measure it inspires, fascinates and astonishes new generations of scholars who do not persist in their efforts to study and elaborate on the nature of the two interwoven concepts.

The informal definition of comprehension proposed by Fauconnier (2005: 658-659):

> "Language is only the tip of a spectacular cognitive iceberg, and when we engage in any language activity, we draw unconsciously on vast cognitive and cultural resources, call up innumerable models and frames, set up multiple connections, coordinate large arrays of information, and engage in creative mappings, transfers, and elaborations (…). Crucially, we have no awareness of this amazing chain of cognitive events that take place as we talk or listen, except for the external manifestation of language (sounds, words, sentences) and the internal manifestation of meaning, experienced consciously with lightning speed. This is very similar to perception, which is also instantaneous and immediate, with no awareness of the extraordinary complex intervening neural events."

adroitly presents the complexity of the process and its dependence on a great diversity of information stored and acquired by each individual. As the author underlines, a great majority of the operations determining the human understanding of language are cognitively inaccessible. On the one hand this guarantees fast and effective communication, but on the other, it makes it extremely difficult (if not impossible) for the operations to be thoroughly analysed.

Furthermore, in order to visualise and support his stance, Fauconnier makes references to human perception, which just like comprehension, involves so many aspects and proceeds so insistently that it is impossible to be followed. However, perception and comprehension have much more in common than the quotation can account for, and the relation between them is not limited in the way the two can be characterised. Many scholars, presenting even more similar features, argue that the two entities are interdependent and cannot exist separately. Indeed, the role of the senses in comprehension is not to be overestimated and, although perception involves all of the senses, vision is arguably the most important sense for humans, providing them with imminent stimuli rich in contextual information. The logical consequence of the strong link between perception and comprehension is an equally strong correlation between context and comprehension, which is the subject matter of this book.

Despite incessant discussions and numerous attempts of delimitation, context remains one of the most imprecise, confusing and unexplained linguistic terms. As inherently pragmatic, context is assumed to be the key notion which differentiates pragmatics from other linguistic disciplines, in particular semantics. However, many other disciplines find it not only interesting, but also necessary to study different aspects of human communicative behaviour, with reference to the arbitrarily-understood context. Innumerable scientific publications propose different definitions of the term and enumerate a great variety of its features which, unfortunately, do not appropriately specify the nature of the context. The reason for this, according to Malinowski (1923:306), is that:

> "(…) the conception of context must be substantially widened, if it is to furnish us with its full utility. In fact it must burst the bonds of mere linguistics and be carried over into the analysis of the general conditions under which a language is spoken."

The study of context and comprehension seems futile without crossing the borders established by various disciplines, and looking at the two concepts from a much broader perspective than individual models, approaches and theories do. This perspective is successfully employed in pragmatics, which, as described by Nerlich and Clarke (1996:4),

> "(…) can be seen as keeping open the gates of enlightenment against narrow-minded dogmatism of all kinds. When the dogmatic linguist sets rigid limits to what language is, the pragmatician can invite him or her to look over the fence at other aspects of language, especially at how language is used in society".

Among pragmatic (i.e. context-dependent) theories of communication, Relevance Theory is the one which offers an interesting program based on the achievements of pragmatic theories and cognitive science, with due acknowledgement of other disciplines' contributions. Both comprehension and context comprise a scientific focus of the theory, which provides an eclectic insight into the two main issues discussed in this work. As a flexible model based on a well-evidenced cognitive mechanism, Relevance Theory (on the assumptions of which the discussion presented in the chapters of the book will rest) reliably explains various aspects of human communication and is open to new challenges, not yielding to problematic issues. Thus the aim of this book, is to apply relevance theory (and assumptions put forward by its creators Dan Sperber and Deirdre Wilson) to an empirical situation.

Although it is generally accepted that context plays a key role in comprehension, it is not yet known exactly how a hearer's interpretation depends on the contextual information which he or she is provided with. It is not clear which cues or which sources are contextually richer, and absolutely necessary for comprehension, and which are just assistive in the process. Finally, it is a mystery what effect a lack (or insufficiency) of certain contextual information has on interpretation and mutual communication between people, and to what extent failure in a communication process depends on an inability to compensate for missing information. Contemplating the questions and searching for satisfactory answers, it is imperative to examine how the comprehension of individual people (provided with different amounts of contextual information), changes in natural communicative situations. As the available literature suggests (e.g. Gibson 1986, Hampson and Morris 1996, Bruce et al. 2003), among all the senses, vision is assumed to provide humans with the richest and most accurate information. Hence the accessibility of visual cues, turns out to be of utmost importance for comprehension in communication. By the same token, it is well-justified to assume that visually impaired people, deprived of visual information, are likely to be less successful in comprehension processes, than sighted people.

In spite of extensive research and the growing interest of scholars in examining still new aspects of communication and comprehension, very little attention is paid to the investigation of blind people's comprehension of utterances in communicative situations. It can be easily observed that much greater concern is given to the analysis of mental disabilities and disorders such as autism, aphasia, or schizophrenia, which appear to have straightforward consequences on the comprehension of people suffering from these conditions. Since the effect which visual impairment may have on comprehension is not so evident, and the nature of the condition in both children and adults is very complex in itself, the problem seems to be overlooked or totally ignored in literature.

The main concern of this work is then to identify common ground between the pragmatic analysis of comprehension and visual impairment, as well as to show how the study of pragmatics can be enriched by the study of visual impairment. The following work consists of three chapters in which the first two chapters are intended to lay the theoretical foundations for the last chapter, which will present and discuss an empirical study investigating totally blind people on their ability to interpret situations on the basis of available contextual information. This final chapter is aimed at verifying the prediction that blind people might be less effective in comprehension than sighted people, or those who have greater access to contextual information in communication.

In chapter one of the work we intend to present arguments that the interdisciplinary approach of pragmatics, drawing from the achievements of various disciplines, gives an in-depth insight into human communication which other disciplines cannot offer separately. Comprehension is a cognitively complex process which embraces a great multitude of mechanisms, operations and aspects. Just as the functioning of our organism entails numerous complicated neural, physiological, and psychological processes which, despite enormous progress and research in medicine, psychology and other disciplines, has not been fully understood, comprehension entails a series of linguistic and non-linguistic processes, some of which are still mysterious. Consequently, the only way to present a comprehensible and possibly complete picture of human understanding in communication, is to look at it from the angle of not only linguistics, but also psychology, sociology, philosophy and other non-linguistic disciplines.

Next, we will present the leading models of communication. The relevance-theoretic model will be accepted as operational throughout the entire discussion presented in the book. The chapter will be also devoted to the analysis of different attempts of defining and delimitating the concept of context, contrasted with an original perspective taken by Relevance Theory. Concentrating on the definition proposed by Dan Sperber and Deirdre Wilson (1986/1995), we will discuss three main sources of contextual cues: perception, general knowledge and linguistic content. Firstly, we will concentrate on the role of senses in comprehension, paying special attention to the two main senses of sight and hearing, and show that they provide participants of the communication process with crucial contextual cues. As we will observe in the discussion, our understanding to a great extent relies on the visual stimuli to which we are exposed. These are not only objects or situations which are made manifest to us at a particular moment of communication, but also past representations formed in our memory for future reference. Subsequently, we will show that our general knowledge (which comprises innumerable past experiences, appropriately organised and stored in the mind), provides contextual information for the interpretation of utterances.

In discussing the linguistic content, we aim to demonstrate the presence of context at every stage of comprehension, thus following the relevance-theoretic heuristic of comprehension. In order to introduce the concepts and phenomena discussed in the subsequent chapters, the relevance-theoretic analysis of implicit and explicit utterances (as well as figurative language, which in the theory constitutes a separate category), will be presented. Since any theory of communication can be regarded as reliable only if it is able to account for both success and failures in the comprehension process, in the chapter we will present the analysis of potential problems in comprehension; those which lead to false interpretations or none at all.

Chapter two is aimed at reviewing the observations and findings concerning the comprehension of blind and sighted people. After introducing proper nomenclature related to visual impairment, the focus will be shifted to contrasting the pragmatic development of blind and sighted children, from early infancy to school years. The intention will be to identify potential problems and impediments in blind children's pragmatic abilities, which might have an effect on their comprehension of utterances in adult years. We will also aim to show how congenital blindness may influence the understanding of different concepts, and affect blind children's comprehension and communication. The second part of chapter two will look at the findings obtained from the studies comparing blind and sighted adults' comprehension. Analysing the data we will aim to identify the areas which failed to be overcome as blind children grew older, and which have serious consequences for blind adults' comprehension. We also intend to check if there are any differences between blind and sighted adults, which are similar to those found in blind and sighted children. Finally, throughout the chapter we will expose the areas which we believe call for particular attention and extensive research.

The last chapter presents an empirical study performed on blind and sighted adults with the use of research tools, and a procedure elaborated and tailored for this particular purpose. We hope that in the future this tool can be used as a standardised test, and possibly utilised to examine the comprehension of people suffering from other disabilities than visual impairment only. The intention of the experiment was to answer the question: will the lack of access to certain contextual information (as in the case of the blind), result in a distorted or inadequate understanding of utterances, or, in extreme cases, in an inability to arrive at any interpretation at all? Since the comprehension process embraces so many aspects, there is no other way to analyse it but by looking at its outcome, not its process per se. In other words, partitioning comprehension into individual mechanisms and operations is always doomed to failure, since as we have already mentioned many aspects of human comprehension are still unknown. If we want to learn of how people understand what is communicated, we need to analyse the final product of the comprehension process, i.e. interpretation. The study, as a starting point for further and more detailed research, was mainly to identify if blind adults, due to their impairment, are less successful in understanding utterances containing various pragmatic sub-tasks, than sighted adults, and if the interpretations in the two groups differed considerably. The findings, it is hoped, will shed some light on the way blind people understand utterances and dispel still present misconceptions concerning their abilities and disabilities.

CHAPTER ONE

CONTEXT AND COMPREHENSION: THEORETICAL CONSIDERATIONS

Introduction

Despite years of research and extensive investigation, communication between people remains a controversial domain. With the intention of making the process more intelligible, formal studies of language have gone to considerable lengths to reduce it to specific rules, principles and constraints; claiming that communication, just as mathematics or logic, should be analysed with similarly rigorous and rule-based methods. Although this approach could, at least theoretically, have guaranteed the feeling of greater empirical control over the process, it had one serious disadvantage: no matter how hard scholars tried to define the rules governing communication, each time there were unexplained aspects, thus making the proposals incomplete and adding only a small element to a complex jigsaw puzzle. The reason for this was straightforward: if one wants to understand communication, it is insufficient to perceive it solely from a linguistic perspective. It is also necessary to consider "invisible backstage cognition" (Fauconnier 2005:674), which is basically what pragmatics as a linguistic discipline encompasses.

Although the studies of language, discourse and interpersonal communication are age-old traditions, pragmatics is a relatively new discipline. For many years, in the realm of linguistics, pragmatics was regarded as the less important, uglier step-sister of semantics and syntax, merely a discipline which was not taken seriously and seldom welcomed into discussions about language due to its allegedly doubtful scientific credibility. Pragmatics, among other things, refers to human cognition, this automatically sparks controversy between metaphysicality and its questionable verifiability. These days the explanatory and descriptive power of pragmatics is consequently questioned. Also because of that, there have been many attempts to merge semantics and pragmatics into one discipline (semantics). This new discipline would be involved in explaining the relation between meanings of words and their use.

Despite its history, since it was separated from syntax and semantics in Morris' model of semiotics (Morris 1938/1970:6), a steady growth in this branch of linguistics can be observed. Nearly fifty years after Morris had coined the term 'pragmatics', Dan Sperber and Deirdre Wilson in 1986 published a book which can to this day be regarded as a breakthrough in the development of the discipline. The book, *Relevance: Communication and Cognition*, presented a theory which married previous achievements of pragmatics with philosophy, logic, sociology and many other scientific disciplines. Their work provides answers to fundamental questions, and lays theoretical foundations for empirical analyses presented in this book.

As stressed by linguists, the critical concept which distinguishes pragmatics from semantics and other disciplines, is context. As explained by Davis (1995, p.128):

> "(…) the distinction between semantics and pragmatics is, roughly, the distinction between (1) the significance conventionally or literally attached to words, and thence to whole sentences, and (2) the further significance that can be worked out, by more general principles, using contextual information".

In great simplification, context as understood in pragmatics is what determines the comprehension of utterances in a communicative situation. Yet defining the 'what' is not an easy thing at all. Highly imprecise, abstract and confusing definitions of context proposed in literature make it "one of those linguistic terms which is constantly used in all kinds of context but never explained" (Asher 1994, p.731), despite numerous attempts and intense debates. Just as pragmatics can be defined in various ways, in literature we can find numerous definitions of context which embrace various aspects, these play a role in the interpretation of utterances and in turn reflect different approaches to the nature of the context. Consequently, the fundamental task is to specify what the context really is before one tries to analyse its role and effect in communication, this will be our main concern in chapter one.

No matter if direct or indirect, verbal or non-verbal, spoken or written, implicit or explicit, every act of communication abounds in relevant contextual information. Nevertheless, communication is a dynamic process in which the topics under discussion, circumstances, attitudes, and not to mention utterances themselves change rapidly. As a result, the context appears to be allusive, intangible, and consequently indefinable. All the characteristic features of the context definitely make it an exciting phenomenon to study, as is evident in a large amount of available literature. However, hardly anything can be presumed when it comes to context. This undoubtedly daunting feature contributed to a lack of systematization in its study. In 1977 van Dijk wrote:

> "(...) we do not yet know how the representation of the context (and that of the text) is actually constructed during interaction[,] [w]e do not know how exactly information from perception is combined with all kinds of inferences, the actualization of frames, or how all kinds of input information is organized, stored, combined with existing knowledge, or with wishes, emotions, attitudes, intentions or purposes[;] [a]nd finally, we do not know yet how all this 'external' and 'internal' information is mapped onto representations of the social context categories and structures" (van Dijk 1977:229)."

For the present, the words seem to be up to date, since many of the questions still remain unanswered and call for exploration. Many attempts to give definite answers in the field are more based on guesswork than well-grounded findings. The following chapter is intended to demonstrate the influence of contextual information on the process of comprehension and provide a core of pragmatic findings about context and understanding, acknowledging contribution of other linguistic and non-linguistic disciplines.

The chapter is divided into four sections which have been arranged to facilitate systematization of the growing body of literature. The first section is an introduction to the scope of pragmatics as the discipline researching comprehension of utterances in the context. As pragmatics is interested in analysing communication; in section two the leading models of communication will be presented and discussed. Owing to the fact that the present work rests on the tenets of Relevance Theory, the ostensive-inferential model put forward by Dan Sperber and Deirdre Wilson will be given the greatest attention and will be accepted as operational in verbal exchanges analysed in the work. Section three is aimed at discussing linguistic and extra-linguistic elements which determine successful communication and which are heavily relied upon in interpretation recovery. As this book will endeavour to demonstrate, the perception and general knowledge of an individual, both exert a profound influence on the comprehension and interpretation of utterances, as well as decide how successful we are in the process. In the section attention will be also given to the content (linguistic input) of utterances during the interpretation process. Following the relevance-theoretic framework, the content provides the hearer with contextual cues, but since it does not fully determine a speaker's intention, only with the assistance of additional information derived from other sources can we truly comprehend and properly understand utterances. It should also be highlighted that communication is a complex process in which success cannot be warranted. There are various factors which have been known to affect the process, leading to miscommunication or misinterpretation. This will be our main concern in section four of the chapter.

Since communication embodies innumerable (direct and indirect) aspects, conditions and mechanisms, discussing all of them would hardly be possible and would definitely exceed the capacity of the work. Hence, this book will focus on the most important aspects which we regard as crucial for the further parts of the work. These will concern the presumable differences between blind and sighted adults in understanding utterances and the role of the context in the inferential processes discussed in chapter two and three.

Pragmatics – the study of language understanding and context

It is not easy to determine when pragmatics became a discipline and who was the first to find it worth researching. Although it is said to have grown out of the philosophical theories of Locke, Kant, Humboldt and other thinkers of the Enlightenment, the tradition of analysing speech, dates back to ancient times and can be found in the works of Plato, Aristotle, Protagoras and other Graeko-Roman philosophers (see Nerlich and Clarke 1996). Despite the age-long tradition and everlasting interest in language, pragmatics was not recognised as a scientific discipline per se until quite late, but the concepts which are now regarded as components within its scope, were studied in other disciplines popular at the times, like rhetoric, philosophy and logic.

Officially, the term 'pragmatics' was first introduced by Charles Morris who, undoubtedly inspired by Locke's semiotics, Peirce's philosophy of pragmatism (Recanati 2005, Levinson 1983) and logical positivism of the Vienna Circle (Nerlich and Clarke 1996), divided linguistic disciplines according to the relations of signs (words, expressions) to other signs, objects and persons into syntax, semantics, and pragmatics respectively. Pragmatics, or using Morris' definition, "the relation of signs to their interpreters", was understood as embracing "the biotic aspects of semiosis, that is, [...] all the psychological, biological, and sociological phenomena which occur in the functioning of signs" (Morris 1938:30).

Consequently, from the very beginning pragmatics was ascribed a challenging role. Not only was it to integrate the approaches of the other disciplines, but also with the aid of the approaches it was expected to explain many controversial and confusing phenomena. Additionally, taking into consideration the philosophical roots of pragmatics, it is apparent that the discipline goes far beyond linguistics and has an interdisciplinary character. Figure one shows that pragmatics is to be viewed as a melting pot drawing from numerous disciplines and effectively utilising multiple aspects, in an effort to describe and explain what communication and language really are.

Since the scope of pragmatics is extremely broad, it is well-justified to assume that it will be able to successfully explain the phenomena which other disciplines disregarded, found beyond their scope of interest or were unable to explain. There is no wonder that many scientific disciplines refer to pragmatics and draw from its achievements. Bearing in mind the mutual co-operation and effective contribution, it should not be of any surprise that in this work we will not restrain from referring to other disciplines when they may help us to better understand the peculiarities of human comprehension.

For decades, pragmatics was shaped by trends, tendencies, thoughts and theories of philosophers, logicians, anthropologists, psychologists and linguists. Among these great thinkers, there were prominent and influential figures such as Wittgenstein, Searle, Austin and Grice who contributed to studying language in real life situations. Natural and informal utterances, which arouse general interest nowadays, took the place of artificial (formal) texts which had been the object of research many years before (see Frege, Russell, Carnap, Tarski). The change opened up new possibilities of understanding and studying language, and communication which is not restrained, reserved, premeditated or flawless, but which is unpredictable, underdetermined, full of inaccuracies and challenging. Ipso facto, social and cognitive aspects, conditioning human communication and mutual understanding, came to be discerned and described as underlying pragmatic analyses; which integrated the aspects with a discussion of authentic language meaning.

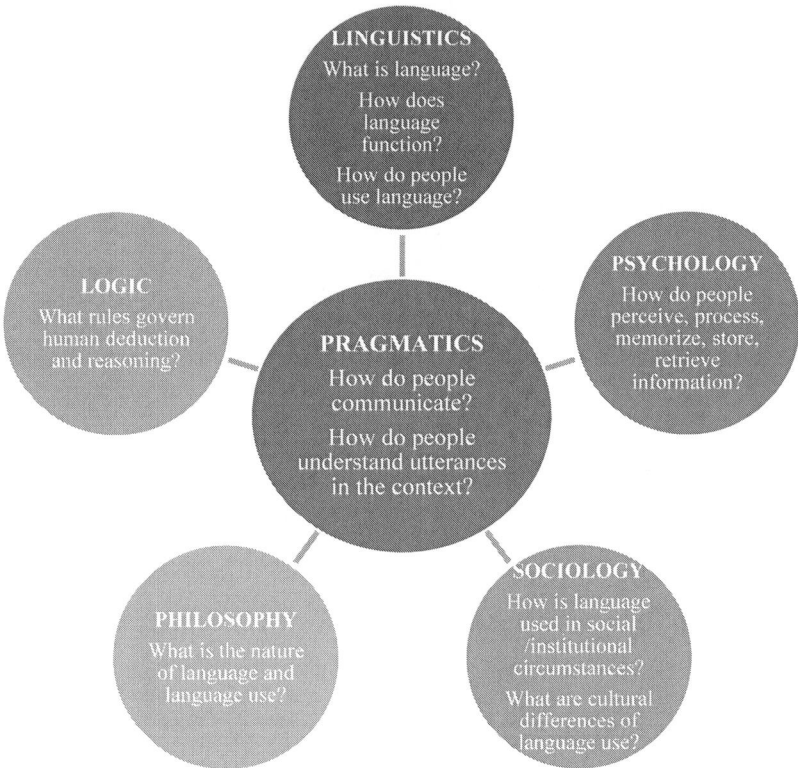

Fig. 1-1 The interdisciplinary character of pragmatics

   Be that as it may, the tolerant approach of pragmatics, welcoming and engaging other disciplines to join and co-operate in forming an integrated and complete picture of communication, has been criticised by some scientists who claim that pragmatics has no clear focus and like 'a garbage can' (Leech 1983) accepts and includes within its scope of interest, all the problematic aspects that other disciplines cannot or refuse to account for. Others maintain that it is an underdeveloped and unreliable discipline, claiming that "as a serious empirical discipline pragmatics is still in its infancy, clumsily attempting to grasp for its own meaning" (Givón 1989:1). But the bitter criticism has not prevented pragmatics from developing. On the contrary, as it will be demonstrated in the chapter, it has been the driving force behind its flourishing. The sign of its growing popularity is the immense interest displayed in the works of new generations of pragmatists, examining still new aspects of communication and aiming to prove that it is an adequately reliable discipline and has the potential to both describe and explain the way people use language to communicate.

In literature there are numerous definitions of pragmatics which vary across models, theories and approaches. In its broken down form, pragmatics, as described by Stalnaker (1996:79), "is the study of linguistic acts and the context in which they are performed". Hence, pragmatics, being interested in communication and language use, "concentrates on those aspects of meaning that cannot be predicted by linguistic knowledge alone and takes into account knowledge about the physical and social world" (Peccei 1999:2). Just as Peccei distinguishes between linguistic knowledge and knowledge of the world, Grice (1975) stresses the difference between 'sentence meaning' (i.e. literal/linguistic meaning) and 'speaker's meaning' as crucial for the understanding of the very essence of pragmatics. The same stance seems to be taken by Kempson (2002:396) who explains that:

> "[t]he starting point for studies in pragmatics is the mismatch, often a big one, between what words 'mean,' which is encoded in rules of language, and what speakers 'mean' by using them, which may be much richer."

The division between word, expression or sentence meaning, extracted from a situation and its context, and their meanings in the context; draw lines between semantics and pragmatics. Despite numerous attempts of separation and delimitation of the two disciplines, the issue still arouses many controversies, since in many areas they tend to either overlap or complement each other (Recantati 2005). What is more, many definitions of pragmatics emphasise contrasts with semantics in attempts to single out possible differences between the two similar disciplines. Gazdar (1979:2), for instance, explains that:

> "Pragmatics has as its topic those aspects of the meaning of utterances which cannot be accounted for by straightforward reference to the truth conditions of the sentences uttered. Put crudely: PRAGMATICS = MEANING – TRUTH CONDITIONS. "

Similarly, Kaplan (1989: 573-4) elaborates that:

> "The fact that a word or phrase has a certain meaning clearly belongs to semantics. On the other hand, a claim about the basis for ascribing a

> certain meaning to a word or phrase does not belong to semantics ...
> Perhaps, because it relates to how the language is used, it should be
> categorized as part of ... pragmatics ..., or perhaps, because it is a fact
> about semantics, as part of ... *Metasemantics.*"

Consequently, it is not clear if it is incumbent upon semantics or pragmatics to account for certain aspects of communication. In literature there are a lot of inaccuracies and it is possible to find many discussions touching on the problem (see Levinson 1983:1-34).

Referring to the first definition of pragmatics proposed by Morris and the interdisciplinary character of the discipline presented above, it should not be a revelation that pragmatics has the potential to explain the phenomena crossing the boundaries of linguistic and non-linguistic disciplines and takes on the challenge. We must also honestly admit that the in-depth account of linguistic phenomena is achievable only if we accept that the disciplines overlap and must co-operate to some extent. As described by Roberts (2005:197),

> "Semantics assumes that words do have basic meanings, and that a given
> syntactic structure corresponds with a determinate way of composing the
> meanings of its subparts. Pragmatics, on the other hand, studies utterances
> of expressions like ø attempting to explain what someone meant by saying
> ø on a particular occasion."

Thus, comprehension of language demands accounting for the interplay among all the branches of linguistics. As claimed by Guenthner and Schmidt (1979:vii) "we cannot hope to achieve an adequate and integrated syntax and semantics without paying heed to the pragmatic aspects of the constructions involved". Isolating pragmatics from other disciplines and the other disciplines from pragmatics, and claiming they are able to explain various phenomena on their own, we deprive ourselves of the possibility to thoroughly understand language and to make progress in this area. As argued in many works, pragmatics accompanied by syntax (e.g. Kempson 1975, Gazdar 1979, Huang 1994, Yus 1997, Carston 1998, Chierchia 2004, Wedgwood 2005), semantics (e.g. Moore and Davidge 1989, Manor 2001, Wierzbicka 2003, Ifantidou 2005, Attardo 2008) and phonology (e.g. Marek 1987, Akamatsu 1987, Clark and Lindsey 1990, Curl et al. 2006, Van Valin 2008, Barth-Weingarten et al. 2009) has the potential of shedding light on the linguistic aspects which have failed to be explained so far.

Parallel to the development of pragmatics, one can observe the unprecedented growth of such sub-disciplines as developmental pragmatics, lexical pragmatics, inter-language pragmatics, socio-pragmatics and clinical pragmatics, which draw from numerous non-linguistic disciplines and aim to explain still new phenomena. As the work will endeavour to show, pragmatics is the scientific discipline which with precision and an interdisciplinary approach is able to both describe and explain human comprehension and the role the context plays in the process.

Communication and comprehension

Etymologically, communication (from Latin *communico* – 'to share') is often defined in literature as an act of sharing information between people in order to reach mutual understanding. Traditionally, communication is also associated with verbal exchange and non-verbal behaviour which people perform for a purpose in social situations. A more precise and elaborate definition of communication was proposed by Puppel (2001:57) who, perfectly grasping the complexity of the process, wrote:

> "Communication by means of language may be defined as the summative effect of language and motor expression of language, with the added requisite of a receiver who shares with the source the knowledge of language rules in the narrow sense of phonology, syntax, and semantics, the knowledge of social world and of rules for using language in that world so that the speech is appropriate as well as grammatical, and the knowledge of the motor aspects of language expression."

Accordingly, language (understood as verbal expressions and gestural representations of people's intentions) is a tool of communication which can be used to trigger an effect, in response to a speaker's utterance. This is conveyed by the speaker (source) and experienced by the hearer (receiver), who both share linguistic, social and general knowledge. The effect of the tool in a social context is of general interest in literature and has been widely debated by innumerable disciplines. The key findings, assumptions, statements and principles specifying relationships among different aspects of communicative behaviour are referred to using the blanket term 'theory of communication'. Although not explicitly specified in literature and frequently overused, the theory is aimed at providing an integrated and unified model of how people communicate and what determines an effective flow of information.

Communication is a two-way process involving both the comprehension and production of utterances exchanged between people in the mutual act. Any model of communication must therefore account for how utterances are produced and how these are received and understood by the hearer. Additionally, as Turnbull aptly observed (2003:26) "(…) all models of talk must account for inter-subjectivity and subjectivity; that is, they must account both for shared understanding and for breakdowns in shared understanding". In other words, it is insufficient to try to describe and predict when communication is successful. Models of communication, apart from considering ideal circumstances, should be able to explain what has gone wrong when the communication does not lead to the expected outcome and the communicative goal is not achieved. The final challenge given to pragmatic models of communication is that they should allow "the integration of linguistic and non-linguistic forms of interpretation at all stages of the interpretation process" (Kempson 2002:396). Only then can an account of the process of comprehension be regarded as complete.

In accordance, pragmatics, attempting to meet the requirements expected of models of communication, aims at "providing a set of principles which dictate how knowledge of language and general reasoning interact in the process of language understanding, to give rise to the various kinds of effects which can be achieved in communication" (Kempson ibid.). It is also aspiring "to explain how the hearer of an utterance constructs a hypothesis about the speaker's meaning" (Wilson and Sperber 2005:615) on the basis of evidence provided, and speculates what effect the evidence has on the ultimate interpretation.

In the consecutive sections, we will present the Code Model and the Inferential Model - two leading models of communication which have been adapted from the study of psychology to the field of pragmatics and which present different perspectives of how communication works and what communication consists of. The final section will discuss the ostensive-inferential model put forward by Relevance Theory, which, in order to effectively describe communication, draws from the models previously discussed, claiming that elements of both of these models are involved in the process of comprehension.

The Code Model

The Code Model of communication was based on the assumption that communication involves the exchange of messages between participants, which can be likened to sending a telegraph or message using the Morse alphabet. Although the Code Model (or the Message Model) appeared in the 20th century, similar assumptions can be found from as early as the 17th century in Locke's philosophy of language. In his mechanistic approach, Locke, and later Hobbs and Bacon, believed that communication was based on "the conveyance of ideas from the mind of one individual to that of another" (Harris and Taylor 1997:129). A similar notion was demonstrated by Saussure (1916/1974:16) who claimed that "[l]anguage is a system of signs that express ideas, and is therefore comparable to a system of writing, the alphabet of deaf-mutes, symbolic rites, polite formulas, military signs etc." In the 1930s the same idea was included in a model of communication proposed by Shannon and Weaver (1949), two engineers who had been looking for a model applicable to any kind of communication (also non-human; see von Frish 1967). They put forward the General Communication Model which gave rise to the Code Model, now recognisable in psychology and linguistics (chiefly pragmatics).

In the model, communication proceeds according to the simplified paths presented in the diagram below (Fig.1-2):

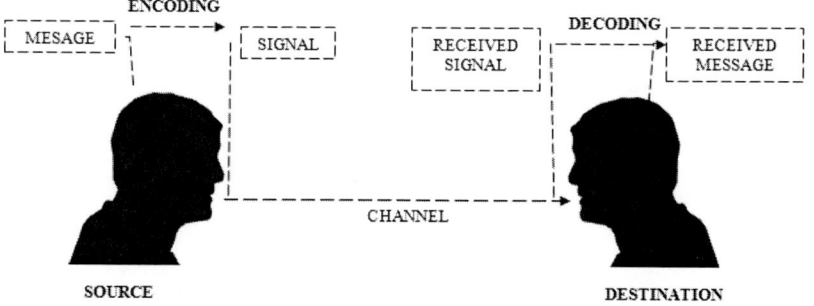

Fig.1-2 Shannon and Weaver's communication model

According to the model, the speaker (or 'source' using the terminology used by Shannon and Weaver) has a message to communicate. The message is encoded into a format which enables it to be sent, and after transforming it into the signal it is transmitted via the channel. The hearer ('destination') receives the signal and decodes the message. Consequently, the understanding of an utterance (message, signal) involves the reception of a signal sent by the source and a decoding of thoughts encrypted in the words of the speaker.

Despite great simplicity and superficial clarity, the model is not without major flaws. The main objection is that the communication process described by the model seems to be always successful in its attempts, and only noise causes disturbances and prevents communication. The model disregards situations where certain problems occur due to other reasons, such as the speaker's or hearer's incompetence. Ambiguous, underdetermined or incoherent utterances are not taken into account either.

Since the message sent by the source and received by the destination inevitably differ, the model, failing to mention it, does not take into consideration how complex the process of understanding really is (for discussion of the major problems in the model see Akmajian et al. 2001).

What is more, the model assumes that there is a binary relation between words and their encoded meanings, and between thoughts and words, whereas this is something the inferential model and other models of communication later refuted. As observed by Bach (2005:470):

> "Communication aims at a meeting of the minds not in the sense that the audience is to think what the speaker thinks but only in the sense that a certain attitude toward a certain proposition is to be recognized as being put forward for consideration. "

Hence, the relationship between a word and its meaning is not only one-to-one but one-to-many as the word can have different meanings, even many-to-many if we assume that words can build on different structures and have different meanings in the structures. There are innumerable ways of expressing thoughts through words. Out of a myriad of potential meanings, speakers must choose only the ones which meet their communicational needs and expectations, and hearers must choose to interpret those which are contextually sound.

Another objection to the Code Model is that, focusing entirely on how people understand each other, it disregards breakdowns in understanding which do occur, and more frequently than we often realise. Besides, the method of understanding utterances in the model has been abstracted from the context and social environment. This does not happen in real life situations and because of this the model cannot serve as pragmatically reliable or fully explanatory. On the other hand, as Sperber and Wilson (1986:8) claim "the code model is still the only available explanation of how communication is possible at all", and hence should be treated as a basic layout or formula for potential communication, on which more complex phenomena, mechanisms and processes can be built.

The Inferential Model

The Inferential Model, put forward by Grice, differs considerably from the Code Model described in the previous section. In *Logic and Conversation* (1975) Grice assumed that in communication people make use of commonsensical reasoning and make inferences to work out what their interlocutors intend to communicate. He observed that in the process of communication there is a distinction between the natural (sentence) meaning and non-natural (speaker's) meaning of an utterance. The speaker, according to Grice, communicates an utterance with an intention which cannot be rightly determined from the linguistic content alone. An understanding of any utterance requires a hearer's recognition of the speaker's intentions in order to produce an effect in the hearer. As Grice (1975:220) explains,

"[S] meant something by x is roughly equivalent to [S] intended the utterance of x to produce some effect in an audience by means of the recognition of this intention."

Schematically, the communication process in Grice's model proceeds in the way presented in Fig.1-3 below:

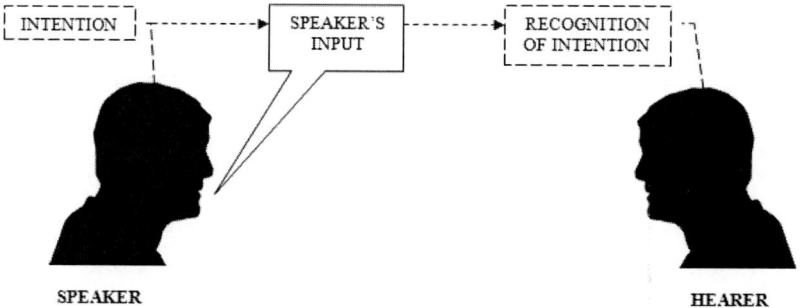

Fig.1-3 Grice's model of communication

In Grice's model, communication is a matter of co-operation between the speaker and hearer. As Grice (ibid. 274) describes,

"[o]ur talk exchanges … are characteristically, to some degree at least, cooperative efforts; and each participant recognizes in them, to some extent, a common purpose or set of purposes, or at least a mutually accepted direction."

It means that both of the participants engage in acts of communication because both of them anticipate some benefits. The speaker strives to communicate something and inform the hearer of his or her intention, which should in turn trigger an appropriate response or reaction. The hearer, on the other hand, wants to identify the speaker's communicative intentions and comprehend. Therefore, they both have similar immediate aims (as well as independent aims which at times may conflict) and their contributions to the conversation are mutually dependent (ibid. 277). The common and main purpose of any verbal exchange is mutual understanding between the participants, which can only be attained if the speaker's communicative intention is adequately recognised by the hearer. It is possible only if both the speaker and hearer follow the Co-operative Principle, which states that they should both "make [their] conversational contribution such as is required, at the stage at which it occurs, by the accepted purpose or direction of the talk exchange in which [they] are engaged" (ibid. 275).

The principle was elaborated on and developed into a list of conversational maxims[1], which, if followed, facilitate mutual understanding of the speaker and hearer in communication and, consequently, show the direction in which conversation should proceed in order to be effective. As stated by Bach (2005:471) the role of the maxims (or 'presumptions') is to "frame how the hearer is to figure out what the speaker is trying to convey, given the sentence he is uttering and what he is saying in uttering it". Maxims of quality, quantity, relation and manner were divided into sub-maxims which enumerated the 'dos and don'ts' of communication (see Table 1-1). In order to explain them, Grice introduced a few analogies of everyday activities (also included in the table), which as well as illustrating the maxims, presented the correlation between participants' expectations and contributions in a conversational situation. Satisfying the expectation, as further underlined in Relevance Theory, leads to the recovery of intentions and therefore, successful communication. Furthermore, the maxims do not let the balance of responsibility for the outcome of communication shift to the speaker. This is because it is not only he or she who should make his or her utterances adequately informative, brief, relevant and true. The hearer should also make sure that his or her contributions comply with the

---

[1] Grice in *Logic and Conversation* (1975) admitted that the maxims were derived from Kant's works. Yet also in Locke's philosophy of language we can find so called 'remedies' for language imperfections. As paraphrased by Taylor (1990:15-16), the 'remedies', which also bear resemblance to the Grician maxims, say: "(1) Use no word without knowing what idea you want to make it stand for. (2) Make sure your ideas are clear, distinct and determinate; and if they are ideas of substance, they should be conformable to real things. (3) Where possible, follow common usage, especially that of those writers whose discourses appear to have the clearest notion. (4) Where possible, declare the meanings of your words (in particular, define them). (5) Do not vary the meanings you give to words." Further commenting on the philosophy, he says: "from the individualist and voluntarist perspective adopted by Locke, language is subject to the control of the individual will. It is therefore improvable, and it is each individual speaking agent who is responsible for that improvement" (Taylor 1990:16).

communication principle; so as to facilitate maximally effective communication flow.

Table 1-1 Grice's maxims and their violations in common language

	MAXIMS		GRICE'S EXPLANATION (1975:276-7)	EXAMPLES OF VIOLATIONS OF THE MAXIMS
1	*Maxims of quantity*	✓ "Make your contribution as informative as is required. ✓ Do not make your contribution more informative than is required".	"I expect your contribution to be neither more or less than is required; if (…) I need four screws [to mend a car], I expect you to hand me four rather than two or six."	Kids are kids.
2	*Maxims of quality*	✓ "Do not say what you believe to be false. ✓ Do not say that for which you lack adequate evidence".	"I expect your contribution to be genuine and not spurious. If I need sugar as an ingredient in the cake you are assisting me to make, I do not expect you to hand me salt (…)."	A: This year we are planning to visit New Orleans. B: New Orleans is my city!
3	*Maxim of relation*	✓ "Be relevant".	"I expect a partner's contribution to be appropriate to immediate needs at each stage of the transaction; if I am mixing ingredients for a cake, I do not expect to be handed a good book, or even an oven cloth (though this might be an appropriate contribution at a later stage."	A: How is your work on the book? B: I wish I could be an artist.

| 4 | *Maxims of manner* | Supermaxim:
✓ "Be perspicuous".

Submaxims:
✓ "Avoid obscurity of expression.
✓ Avoid ambiguity.
✓ Be brief (avoid unnecessary prolixity).
✓ Be orderly." | "I expect a partner to make it clear what contribution he is making and to execute his performance with reasonable dispatch." | A: Let's get the kids something.
B: Okay, but I veto I-C-E C-R-E-A-M-S.[2] |

Unfortunately, hardly ever do participants of communication comply with the maxims. However, they could still be successful in the process, if only they are willing to cooperate. This brings one to the conclusion that while the maxims can be violated, the Cooperative Principle (CP) must be obeyed if the speaker and hearer are to communicate successfully. The following examples (1-4), presented in the table and repeated for convenience, present ordinary utterances in which the maxims are disregarded and only the CP is observed by the speakers:

(1)   *Kids are kids.*
(2)   A: *This year we are planning to visit New Orleans.*
        B: *New Orleans is my city!*
(3)   A: *Have you finished your new book?*
        B: *I wish I could be an artist.*

(4)   A: *Let's get the kids something.*
         B: *OK, but I veto I-C-E C-R-E-A-M-S.*

Analysing the utterance (1), it seems evident that the maxim of quantity, which says that the speaker should be neither more nor less informative than needed, is violated. Grice's theory rejected tautology as presented in (1), since according to the maxim, it is not sufficiently informative. It is self-evident that kids are kids, not for instance: sandwiches. From the perspective of truth-conditional theories of language, the utterance is meaningless and has no informative value, which is not necessarily true. Depending on the context, the utterance may

---

[2] the example taken from Levinson (1983:104)

be intended to produce reactions in the mind of the hearer and additionally to express the speaker's attitude which could not be otherwise achieved. For instance, in this situation the speaker may be attempting to excuse children's behaviour and criticise their childishness, as illustrated by (1a):

(1a)   Father: *Tom and Sally have been fighting all day.*
        Mother: *Kids are kids.*

The utterance in (2) violates the second maxim which stresses that we should not say what we do not believe is true. In the philosophy of language, false sentences were regarded as meaningless and empty. Hence, if the speaker in (2) says that New Orleans belongs to him and does not believe in it, we are faced with a self-contradictory statement called the Moors' paradox. Insofar as the speaker's proposition cannot be true and false at the same time, it seems obvious that his intentions are a far cry from the meanings of his words. The speaker in this case intends to say that he knows New Orleans very well, as if trying to engage the hearer in further interaction or hoping that the hearer will invite him to join them on the trip to New Orleans.

The next example (3) presents a further violation of Grice's maxims. This time the maxim of relation is disregarded by the speaker who does not give a proper or relevant answer to the question asked by speaker A. The answer that we would expect to get in this case would be 'yes' or 'no' instead of the one offered i.e.:

(3)   *I wish I could be an artist.*

As in the previously discussed examples, speaker B has a chance to communicate some extra information which would not have been conveyed if he had provided a simple negative answer. In this case the speaker wants to inform the hearer that he has not finished his book yet and he is fed up with writing. In this situation, the hearer would probably make some additional assumptions e.g. that the speaker has always dreamt of being an artist, or that he finds the profession more pleasant and relaxing than being a writer.

Finally, example (4) illustrates the utterance in which the speaker violates the maxim of manner, which puts an unnecessary strain on cognition. Instead of using the whole lexeme, the speaker spells out the individual letters separately. The intention of the speaker is to avoid using the word 'ice creams' in the children's presence in the fear that they would demand ice cream, which, for reasons unknown, they should not get. This and the other examples briefly discussed above, demonstrate that the restrictions enforced by the maxims would be impossible and unnecessary to engage in, which is one of the main objections to Grice's program. However, as pointed out by Warren (2006:109), Grice's maxims should not be treated as absolute mandates of success or failure in communication, but rather guidelines which, if disobeyed, may hamper or prevent mutual understanding and communication. For instance, the maxim of quantity, as Grice (ibid.) explains, informs that we should avoid over-informativeness because not only it is a waste of time, but may also lead to hearer's confusion and ultimately a lack of understanding.

At one time, the maxims came into severe criticism by some of Grice's successors, who claimed that the list was inadequate and should perhaps be further extended, while others believed that it should be reduced (Levinson 1983, Horn 2005). Still others maintained that the maxims were too vague and it was debatable whether they had any application within communication at all (see for instance Kempson 1975, Blakemore 1992, Grundy 2000, Sperber and Wilson 1986, McCarthy 1991). The maxims were also regarded as too idealistic and contrary to real life circumstances. Due to the fact that "much discourse is "telegraphic" in nature [;] [v]erb phrases are not specifically mentioned, entire clauses are left out, pronouns abound, 'you know' is everywhere" (Fromkin et al. 2007:156), during everyday conversations the maxims are rarely observed by speakers who seldom express precisely what they intend to communicate. However, contrary to the above objections, Grice seemed to be well aware of this fact. In his model, he introduced the terms 'implicature' and 'implicatum' which became foundations for modern pragmatic theories and which will be discussed in detail further on in the chapter. As explained by Bach (2005:471), "[Grice's] account of implicature explains how ostensible violations of [the maxims] can still lead to communicative success". In other words, the violations (or using Grice's nomenclature 'flouts') of the maxims trigger implicatures which force the hearer to engage in inferential processes to properly comprehend their meaning.

Despite criticism of the limitations introduced by maxims and other aspects of his theory, Grice's inferential model of communication gave rise to many theories and is undoubtedly one of the most recognisable and influential among classical pragmatists. His ideas became an inspiration or even a foundation for more modern theories, Relevance Theory is one of them. His works are eagerly discussed not only in linguistics, but in cognitive psychology, philosophy, sociolinguistics and many other disciplines.

The Ostensive-Inferential Communication Model

In the two previous sections we presented two different approaches to communication demonstrated by the Code Model and Inferential Model, in which communication is either a send-receive, mechanical process, or a conscious and commonsensical process. The model of communication proposed by Dan Sperber and Deirdre Wilson (1986/1995) presented in Relevance Theory is a compromise between the two former models and an integration of their assumptions. As aptly described by Jodłowiec (2008:24),

> "Relevance Theory is a psycholinguistic model which provides analytic tools to explain the nature of the mechanisms underlying human overt and intentional, that is ostensive, communicative behaviour".

According to the model, during the communication process, participants decode the linguistic meanings of utterances, which then sparks a chain reaction into the further and more complex process of drawing inferences about speakers' intentions. The ostensive-inferential communication is described as the process in which:

> "the communicator produces a stimulus which makes it mutually manifest to communicator and audience that the communicator intends, by means of this stimulus, to make manifest or more manifest to the audience a set of assumption {I}" (Sperber & Wilson 1986:63).

The stimulus (for instance an utterance) is processed and calculated by the hearer, who is in turn convinced of its relevance. This is consistent with the Principle of Relevance fundamental to Relevance Theory, which says:

> "every aspect of communication and cognition is governed by the search for relevance." (Wilson 1994:54)

Accordingly, it is the search for relevance which makes the hearer pay attention to what his/her interlocutor is saying and put in some effort to understand his/her utterances in a logical way. As hearers, we believe that the sole factor that the speaker wants to inform us of something, gives sufficient reason to assume that the utterance is relevant and in the event of this we are ready to make a cognitive effort to recover the speaker's communicative intention. It is necessary to realise at this point, that the term 'relevance' in the theory (contrary to how it is understood by van Dijk (1979)) is not a synonym of importance or significance, but is a psychological concept which ought to be understood as the property of an assumption to have some contextual effect (Sperber & Wilson 1986:122).

As argued by Wilson and Sperber (2005:609), utterances vary in degrees of relevance, which depends on inverse proportions to cognitive strain. As a result of this, the greater effort is needed in interpretation, the lower relevance of stimulus is thus achieved. In communication the hearer looks for an optimally relevant utterance, which keeps the balance between his/her effort and obtained contextual effect. Following the Communicative Principle of Relevance, "each act of ostensive communication communicates a presumption of its own optimal relevance" (1995:260) which, as explained by Wilson (1994:55), in the Principle of Optimal Relevance,

> "(a) achieves enough contextual effects to be worth the hearer's attention;
> (b) puts the hearer to no gratuitous processing effort in achieving those effects."

In other words, an optimally relevant utterance is one which exposes us (hearers) to some changes in knowledge and does not subject us to unnecessary mental effort in processing it. Bearing similarity to Grice's model, in particular the Co-operative Principle, communication can be compared to a barter deal in which both participants need to see some profit in the activity to be willing to engage in it. Both of them offer something and expect something else in exchange. The speaker wants to inform the hearer of some fact and convey it in such a way that the hearer understands his/her intention. The hearer 'invests' a reasonable amount of attention and processing effort in the hope that whatever the speaker is about to say will turn out to be contextually relevant and supply some worthwhile contextual insights. Our mental effort should then be compensated for and commensurate with the attained effect, be it strengthening, contradiction or negation of the old assumption(s) by new information. Hence, if the processing effort is high, the profits should be equally as great. As Mioduszewska (2008:70-71) explains:

> "relevance of a stimulus, for example of an utterance, is a balance between the cognitive gain it brings to the hearer/reader and the effort he must put in processing the stimulus to extract the gain. Every ostensive stimulus brings with itself a guarantee of its relevance to the hearer/reader and that is why he undertakes the effort to process it."

In recovering the speaker's intention, the hearer may choose from a wide array of possible interpretations. As stated by Levinson (1983:13), "there are at least half a dozen distinct and different kinds of meaning component or implication (or inference) that are involved in the meaning of natural language utterances". Probably if the hearer wanted to explore all the possibilities, and ultimately choose the most likely, it would take hours before s/he responded. This does not happen because of the speaker who, in order to facilitate the recovery process, gives hints as to the intended interpretation. Selecting appropriate lexical items and sentence structures, using varied intonation, stress and gestures, the speaker manipulates the hearer in such a way that s/he is able to make assumptions which will eventually lead to the desired conclusions. What is more, as suggested by Wilson (1994:58), our decision-making is influenced by the assumption that the interpretation remains consistent with the hearer's expectation of relevance. Thus, instead of going through all of the possible interpretations, we:

> "follow a path of least effort in computing effects: [t]est interpretive hypotheses (disambiguations, reference resolutions, implicatures, etc.) in order of accessibility [and] stop when [our] expectations of relevance are satisfied (or abandon)." (Wilson & Sperber 1986/1995: 613)

As it was said at the beginning of the work, Relevance Theory has had an enormous impact on the development and shape of modern pragmatics. Dan Sperber and Deirdre Wilson's model put forward in *Relevance: Communication and Cognition* (1986/1995), revealed very strong implications in the analysis of numerous linguistic issues, including the unexplored or problematic ones. As shown in a number of papers and as we aim to show in this book, Relevance Theory manages to successfully describe and explain various aspects of human communication, which suggests that it is well-justified to refer to human cognition in order to understand linguistic phenomena at the root – i.e. in the human mind. What also makes the theory unique is that neither does it lay down any artificial principles nor does it limit the way in which human cognition works.

Context

In interpreting the speaker's utterance, the hearer has to take into account numerous aspects which go far beyond linguistic meaning and which require from the hearer much more than just linguistic competence. The background knowledge, or context as it is more frequently known, encompasses a multitude of experiences (both past and current) which are manifested in such a great variety of mental representations, personal feelings and fixations that specifying the exact number of variables used in the comprehension of an utterance is extremely difficult, if not impossible. What is more, as long as the mysteries of human cognition remain unsolved, the notion of context, as "a psychological construct" (Sperber & Wilson 1986:15), will always be mysterious to a certain extent. Therefore, it seems inevitable that what has already been said and written about context is far from being complete. In this discussion concerning the interplay between context and comprehension, we do not aim to make up for that gap but, accepting that the context is one of the most mysterious terms in linguistics, we will strive to review major approaches to the context in literature and present our own understanding of the term, based on relevance-theoretic assumptions.

If, as it was argued at the beginning of the chapter, pragmatics originates from the philosophical, sociological, psychological, logical and linguistic traditions, context as a central concept must also have an interdisciplinary nature, which has weathered numerous changes in trends and shifts of focus over the years of analysis. Within a plethora of linguistic and non-linguistic works, assumptions, and statements about context, literature distinguishes two leading approaches, reflecting two different ways of understanding and analysing the concept. These have given rise to new approaches, all trying to define the nature of the context. The first was derived from the ethnographic and anthropological research of Malinowski (1923) who, inspired by the study of communication in a primitive nation, made the claim that language use is embedded in the context of situation and only the context can determine the meanings of particular words or sentences. As he explained,

"A statement, spoken in real life, is never detached from the situation in which it has been uttered. For each verbal statement by a human being has the aim and function of expressing some thought or feeling actual at that moment and in that situation, and necessary for some reason or other to be made known to another person or persons – in order either to serve purposes of common action, or to establish ties of purely social communion, or else to deliver the speaker of violent feelings or passions. Without some imperative stimulus of the moment there can be no spoken statement. In each case, therefore, utterance and situation are bound up inextricably with each other and the context of situation is indispensable for the understanding of the words." (1923:348)

According to Malinowski, the context determines not only the meaning of the statements, but also the acquisition and development of language. As he postulated, people have come to know language through using it in particular situations, which bears similarity to the notion of the performative role of language made known by Speech Act Theory. The context, in Malinowski's work, must be analysed from a wider, socio-cultural perspective, which is a significant departure from the notion of language as a formal system propagated by structuralism. Rejecting the so called 'arm-chair' approach to the study of language, Malinowski claimed that the context can only be analysed in a natural environment by a researcher who is part of and directly involved in unrestricted on-going social rituals. Although he was an anthropologist, not a linguist, his contribution to both the development of pragmatics and the study of context is substantial and undeniable. Even if in his works we do not find a precise and explicit answer as to the meaning of context and how it is manifested, after analysing Malinowski's approach and assumptions about language and context, one can conclude that they were ahead of his time and thus brought on the ever-present debates of these two concepts.

Many of Malinowski's ideas have re-occurred in subsequent works on context. The same notion of Malinowski's socio-cultural method of perceiving context was prevalent, for instance, in Goffman, Sacks, Silverman, Firth, Mey, Gumperz and Hymes. Duranti and Goodwin (1992) supported the idea that the linguistic content of utterances alone, is insufficient to analyse the context and Labov (1969) continued the notion of performative function of statements. Later, but still in the vein of Malinowski's ideas, we can observe the tendency to describe the context as a sum of parameters (or variables). Firth (1957), for instance, maintained that context consists of 'related [abstract] categories' which he divided into (a) relevant features (i.e. verbal and non-verbal actions of participants), (b) relevant objects and (c) the effect of interaction (Widdowson 2004). For Katz and Fodor (1963), context (or 'setting' to use their terminology) is understood as previous acts of communication, sociophysical factors and other aspects of 'non-linguistic' knowledge (Blutner 2005:488). Whereas, Halliday (1978) enumerated the field (goals of social interaction), tenor (relations between participants) and mode (channel of interaction) as crucial aspects of the context, which directly influence participants' grammatical and lexical choices in a verbal exchange. Another version of the contextual parameters was presented by Hymes (1974) who listed the parameters as the S-P-E-A-K-I-N-G acronym, where S stands for 'setting', 'scene' or 'situation', P means 'participants', E – 'ends' (goals), A – 'act sequence' (form and content of message), K – 'key' (tone, manner), I – 'instrumentalities' (channel), N – 'norms' (of interaction and interpretation) and G - 'genres'.

Regardless of the number of parameters mentioned by these and other scholars, the list embracing all the possible elements of the context is never finite and the context understood in this way could hardly be more abstract. Figuratively speaking, the approach regarded an act of communication as a movie frame and assumed that some parameters, more prominent and salient than others, determined comprehension on a particular occasion. Consequently, for any potential utterance spoken in a given situation we should be able to generate an exact list of the parameters, which in fact is hardly possible considering the myriads of possible situations and allusive nature of the context. What is more, the approach seems to assume that structurally, all the utterances consist of the same configurations of the variables mentioned above and it fails to account for the fact that utterances differ considerably. This limitation has serious consequences in the analysis of natural utterances, which do not always fall into the same pattern.

While the previous approach can be described as static and focused on determining the finite variables affecting the situation, the second approach concentrates on the dynamic nature of the context which is perceived as constantly changing (van Dijk 1977, Roberts 2005). The concept of the Dynamic Approach to Meaning is presented as a function, mapping from one context to another (see 'context change potential' in Heim 1982 and Stalnaker 1978) and updating as new things are communicated. Accordingly, it is a great simplification to believe that a communicative act equals only one context. In fact, the context projects onto another and there is not one and the same context throughout the whole conversation but it is updated over the course of communication by still new information. Following Lewis' famous metaphor (1979), Roberts compares context with a scoreboard "keeping track of the various types of information being shared in discourse" (2005:214) and claims that the dynamic context requires dynamic interpretation reaching from context to context and looking at discourse as a whole, instead of concentrating on isolated utterances. As originally proposed by Wittgenstein in *Philosophical Investigations* (1953), language is perceived as a dynamic game in which there are certain (individual and common) goals of participants who share common ground[3], accepted moves and points under discussion which the context consists of. Saying "context is action", Mey (2001:41) confirms the standpoint and presents numerous examples of how context changes in communication.

For instance, he reports an interesting German TV show in which two guests (former friends) initially address each other by the familiar *du*

---

[3] the term was introduced by Stalnaker (1978) and defined as a set of possible worlds shared between the speaker and hearer at a given point of conversation

('you') and switch to a more formal tone using *Sie* ('Mr'), as the discussion becomes more heated, and atmosphere becomes more tense and hostile. According to the author, the register has been altered because the context has also changed. The polite and friendly forms are no longer pragmatically possible and both of the participants, without previous agreement, turned to reserved ways of addressing each other, which betrayed their attitudes at that particular moment.

To illustrate the dynamic nature of the context, Mey discusses one more interesting example presented in (5) below:

(5)   *It's a long time since we visited your mother.*

As he explains, the meaning of the sentence alters depending on, when and how it was uttered and whom it was uttered by. Consequently, this sentence in (5) uttered by a spouse during a casual talk at a coffee table and the same one voiced by the husband in front of a hippopotamus enclosure at the zoo have different meanings, demonstrate different intentions and trigger different effects. In the former example the utterance could be understood as an initiative to visit the speaker's mother-in-law, while in the latter example, it is a bitter remark and an act of criticism, revealing the speaker's antipathy towards the target of his sarcastic utterance (mother-in-law). But, as we have already mentioned, differences in the meanings of utterances are not limited to the location in which they are said. In fact, there are so many elements that determine our understanding of communicative situations, that specifying what exactly leads us to come up with one interpretation, not another, and tracing how the interpretation changes as the context changes with on-going communication, is very difficult.

Considering the two major approaches to context presented above, there is one aspect in which pragmatists are unanimous: in order to pragmatically understand the notion of context, it is necessary to look from a greater perspective, rather than only looking at what the speaker says and the hearer perceives. As illustrated in (5), one utterance may mean and be understood in totally different ways depending on the available context. Consequently, any act of communication rests on numerous cognitive resources such as associations, connotations, mappings and elaborations. The subconscious cognitive mechanisms governing comprehension and interpretation of utterances and events, seem to be triggered by our competence and predisposition to collect, select and manipulate available contextual information (Levinson 1983:24, Assimakopoulos 2003:2, Carston 2005:634-635). From an overwhelming load of information, we concentrate only on the elements that are necessary for its appropriate interpretation. As stressed by Levinson (ibid. 23),

> "one needs to distinguish between actual situations of utterance in all their multiplicity of features, and the selection of just those features that are culturally and linguistically relevant to the production and interpretation of utterances".

To be able to do that, irrelevant information must be disregarded and only the contextually relevant must be considered.

As suggested in Relevance Theory, the selection of contextual information enabling comprehension and interpretation, must be relevance-driven and proceed according to the heuristics of relevance. Therefore, comprehension at each stage is oriented towards the identification of contextually relevant information, at the cost of reasonable (optimal) cognitive effort. Contrary to the static approach presented above, the context in the theory is not defined as a set of specific features inherent to a communicative situation and picked up by the participants of the situation. In contrast, Sperber and Wilson define the term as:

> "a psychological construct, a subset of the hearer's assumptions about the world"

and, as they further explain,:

> "[i]t is these assumptions, of course, rather than the actual state of the world, that affect the interpretation of an utterance." (Sperber & Wilson 1986:15)

The contextual assumptions are derived from various sources. General knowledge, common sense, the observation of the physical environment, preceding utterances, and also "expectations about the future, scientific hypotheses or religious beliefs, anecdotal memories, general cultural assumptions, beliefs about the mental state of the speaker" (Sperber & Wilson ibid.) are among those which may provide relevant contextual implications for a hearer's interpretation. Consequently, the context is not only confined to linguistic and social information, but also embraces our feelings, memories, beliefs, likes and dislikes, preferences, animosities and probably many more idiosyncrasies. Cognitive context propagated by the relevance-theoretic framework integrates linguistic, social and socio-cultural contexts with mental representations and assumptions, which Sperber and Wilson (1996) liken to an onion with a number of layers.

Similarly as in the dynamic approach, the authors give evidence to the fact that the contextual assumptions are constantly changing in communication, and they are not given, but actually chosen by individual persons according to their individual cognitive environment.

In a nutshell, understanding a single utterance in a context means having to tell crucial assumptions from less important or vague ones. The selection of appropriate contextual assumptions, being of key importance for interpretation, is a matter of individual beliefs, biases and preferences. As explained by Dewey (1931:215):

> "There is care, concern, implicated in every act of thought. There is someone who has affection for some things over others; when he becomes a thinker he does not leave his characteristic affection behind. As a thinker, he is still differentially sensitive to some qualities, problems, themes".

In consequence, it seems obvious that if the cognitive environment (knowledge) is different for individual people and if the contextual assumptions brought to bear in the process of interpretation differ among individuals to some extent as well, then the recovered interpretation must vary from individual to individual. How then is mutual understanding in communication possible? In general, an exact duplication of thoughts between the speaker and hearer is impossible and unnecessary in communication. What is both possible and needed for communication to be successful, is a mutual cognitive environment which is shared between the participants of communication and which consists of information being manifest (mentally representable, perceptible or inferable) and accessible (Sperber & Wilson 1986:41-43). It should be noted at this point that "the set of mutual contextual beliefs" is also defined as context in some circles outside Relevance Theory (see Bach & Harnish 1979:5, Bach 2005:470, Heim 1982 for extended version).

Summing up, just as in scientific disciplines critical concepts tend to be explained in many different ways which reflect evolution in certain areas, the notion of context has undergone numerous changes in pragmatics. Its scope of attending variables dwindled and expanded with new thoughts and theories. Yet the problem is that no matter how many variables are supplied, they are never finite, and fully sufficient enough to account for the context. Some of the parameters may seem so transparent and subconscious that they may go unnoticed in the considering and analysing of context. That is why in many cases the only thing to do is to follow our intuition. Any attempts at categorising, classifying or dividing variables did not bring any better results, either. Kaplan's (1989) objective context featuring the concepts of speaker, time and place (bearing resemblance to

Bach's narrow context), or Dewey's (1931) context, comprising (spatial and temporal) background and selective interest, only partially cover what context really involves. The imperfections stem from the fact that "context must contain information about what is salient at any given point in the discourse" (Roberts 2005:202), hence it must be updated along with a proceeding verbal exchange. Consequently, variables that have a voice in construing context at one moment, may not be taken into consideration in another.

Additionally, as observed by Ekiba and Maguitman (2001), over the course of communication, contexts overlap and are difficult or even impossible to determine. To thoroughly analyse a communicative act we have to consider what has been uttered in a particular situation, and in the past, as well as have the knowledge of what the participants know, think and feel at a particular moment, how these factors change as communication proceeds and how the environment influences the perception and state of mind of the hearer and the speaker. In all honesty, neither linguistic nor non-linguistic information can be fully sufficient in interpreting and comprehending utterances. As noted by Blakemore (1992:18):

> "the interpretation of an utterance may depend on the hearer's ability to supply certain assumptions from memory. These range from strongly evidenced assumptions derived through perception to guesses and hypotheses. They include memories of particular occasions and about particular individuals, general cultural assumptions, religious beliefs, knowledge of scientific laws, assumptions about the speaker's emotional state and assumptions about other speakers' perception of your emotional state."

All of these elements comprise cognitive context in Relevance Theory. Keeping in mind the classification of variables in the context discussed above, as well as the dynamic nature of the context, one can distinguish three sources which provide crucial contextual information and influence the understanding and interpretation of discourse. These are: perception, general knowledge and content of utterances.

Perception and context

Hobbs (2005:724) once said that "we are able to understand language so well because we know so much", and we know and understand so much because, as Foulke and Halten (1992:44) explain,

"(…) what we learn from the experience of the moment depends in part on what we have learned from earlier experiences (Brewer & Treyens, 1981); and what we have learned from earlier experiences depends in part on what we have learned from still earlier experiences (Hebb, 1949)."

The complex net of mental representations of the world (also known as 'concepts') construed on the basis of the multiple experiences collected in life, allows us to interpret other people's utterances and behaviour in communicative situations. Perception is a medium which by way of our senses, gives us opportunities to acquire knowledge. However, there is not only sensing or the reception of stimulus energy behind this complex process. Perception is a conscious and active seeking of the stimuli, to satisfy our needs for a certain purpose at any given moment. Consequently, we do not pay attention to all the stimuli available in these particular situations, but

"(…) our perceptual mechanisms tend automatically to pick out potentially relevant stimuli, our memory retrieval mechanisms tend automatically to activate potentially relevant assumptions, and our inferential mechanisms tend spontaneously to process them in the most productive way." (Wilson & Sperber 2005:610)

It is in evidence that perception is not one process but rather a collection of processes which embrace analysing, organising and integrating the acquired information, which facilitates its subsequent manipulation. In the relevance-theoretic framework, when we perceive a stimulus we presuppose that it is relevant and that it has the potential to produce some contextual effect. Convinced of the relevance, we pay attention to salient perceptual information only, ignoring additional and incidental clues which could distract or mislead our interpretations.

Experiencing multitudes of stimuli throughout life, each person constructs individual representations of their environment. In other words, due to the perceptual and inferential differences as well as differences in the physical environment, people do not construct identical representations of the world (Sperber & Wilson 1986:38). Everyone creates his/her own, very subjective interpretation of elements in their surroundings on the basis of perceived information. This information influences the person's understanding and thus interpretation of situations encountered over the course of their lives. The invaluable repository of the acquired information about the world cooperates with our perceptual mechanisms, so that each time we are faced with one of the familiar concepts stored in our memory, our perceptual mechanisms help us to identify the sensory stimulus we perceive as an already established concept. Milner and Goodale (1995/1998) call it 'perception for recognition' and, as they explain, it allows us to recognise familiar objects and save a lot of cognitive energy in the comprehension process. They also mention the second kind of perception which is 'perception for action', it involves determining the location of stimuli. As further argued by Haugeland (1993/1998), any perceived events or phenomena are inseparable from the context and in interpreting the situation we recognize them as one entity. This means that the context enables us to interpret what we perceive, just as perception supervises the selection of context. The interrelation and interdependence of context and situation, with all the elements that we perceive and analyse, is what determines our comprehension in any act of communication.

As it has already been said, the information needed for interpretation is derived from many different sources, and apart from the linguistic content of discourse, the hearer can rely on the cues provided by all of our senses: sight, hearing, touch, smell and taste. While visual perception and its influence on the understanding of situations and speech is a well-discussed issue in literature, less is known about auditory perception and other kinds of perception originating from the remaining senses. The reason for the immense interest in visual perception, demonstrated for instance in the works of Gestalt psychologists (Koffka, Köhler and Wertheimer), Bruce et al. (1996/2003) or Gibson (1979), is that visual stimuli provide us with clear and undeniable evidence for contextual assumptions and "assumptions derived through direct observation are held with strong conviction" (Blakemore 1992:14-15). As Blutner explains (2005:489), adopting Sweetser's standpoint (1990),

> "(…) vision and knowledge are highly related, in contrast to, say, smelling and knowledge or taste and knowledge, which are only weakly related for normal human beings".

The statement concurs with the popular assumption that senses other than vision provide us with somewhat impoverished sources of information leading to weaker associations, and visual perception is said to be favoured in the selection of context.

Undoubtedly, vision provides us with myriads of important cues, and plays an indispensable role in communication. The observation of a speaker's ostensive behaviour for example and consideration of elements in the environment, may decide about the appropriateness of a hearer's interpretation. As underlined by many authors (e.g. Mehrabian 1972/2007, Hinde 1972/1979, Patterson 1995, Wharton 2009), the ostensive behaviour of a speaker has the power to convey strong emotions, and observation of the behaviour is by no means less important or inferior to what is communicated verbally. Some authors hold that bodily communication simply has the function of sustaining and supporting verbal exchanges (Gordon et al. 1997), but in fact it is of much greater importance and has many more functions than we often realise. Let us consider the utterance (6), to observe how non-verbal communication may effectively substitute verbal communication and how the speaker may choose to refrain from verbalising her attitudes, emotions, feelings and/or intentions and instead manifest them using facial expressions, gestures or other non-verbal means:

(6)   Peter: *How was the press conference?*
         Mary: [WAVES HER HAND IN DESPAIR, SHAKES HER HEAD SIDEWAYS, AND IS CLOSE TO TEARS]

The observation of Mary's reaction provides clear evidence that something went wrong during the press conference. Although it does not give a precise answer as to what exactly happened, Peter will probably infer that the conference was a disaster. Since she is not saying anything, Peter will most probably assume that Mary does not want to talk about it, she has been shaken up and needs to cool down. Among other things, Mary's behaviour may also indicate that:

(a)   it was her first press conference,
(b)   she feels responsible for the catastrophe,
(c)   reporters were cruel and destroyed her confidence,
(d)   she will have to quit her job.

Recovery of the assumptions (a-d) will depend on Peter's background knowledge as well as other contextual cues, for example, the fact that Peter saw the conference on TV or they had had a conversation prior to the conference, during which Mary might have said that if the conference (e.g. promoting her new film) turned out to be a disaster and the film came under severe criticism, she would have to quit acting.

In a similar manner, non-verbal communication is often used when it is extremely difficult to find the proper words to describe the details of situations, or feelings. This, by saving cognitive efforts of the hearer, makes immediately evident what the speaker means. It might also be used if a speaker wants to conceal some fact from accidental overhearers or tries to be more polite or politically correct, by refraining from using offensive words. A good example of this situation, borrowed from De Brabanter (2009), is presented in (7) where the bracketed part of the utterance represents the type of ostensive behaviour demonstrated by the speaker.

(7)   *I didn't see the* [IMITATION OF FRIGHTENING GRUMPINESS] *woman today; will she be back this week?*

Imitating the woman, the speaker refers to the hearer's background knowledge, which allows him/her to identify exactly who the speaker has in mind. If the speaker does not know the name of the woman, his/her ostensive behaviour helps him/her to overcome the obstacle and make the hearer recover his intentions. Alternatively, knowing that saying (8),

(8)   *I didn't see the grouch/witch today; will she be back this week?*

instead of (7), sounds very impolite, the speaker takes steps to avoid disclosing his/her attitude towards the woman in fear that some overhearer might recover it and, for instance, repeat it to the woman herself, landing him/her in trouble. With his ostensive behaviour, the speaker protects his/her position and communicates the signal to the hearer only. Although more effort-consuming than explicitly communicated (8), (7) brings with itself a wide range of additional assumptions which compensate for the cognitive cost. The hearer is likely to recover, for instance, that:

(a)   the speaker does not want other people to know what his attitude toward the woman is;
(b)   the speaker has a low opinion of the woman;
(c)   the speaker wants to engage the hearer in backbiting the woman.

Gestures are then a universal means of revealing intentions and supporting hearers' recovery of intentions which are very often difficult to discover, only from the linguistic content of utterances. Newton and Burgoon (1990), analysing non-verbal cues which they grouped and matched with verbal strategies in communication, discovered that non-verbal behaviour is operational for many different intentions. One intention may consist of many non-verbal cues, which results in not one but many patterns for expressing a particular intention. The 'non-linguistic signs' provided by visual perception should by no means be ignored (Clark 1996) in interpretation, or depreciated in favour of the linguistic content of utterances, since, no matter if verbal or non-verbal, communication goes through the same pragmatic processes and should be treated equally (De Brabanter 2009). Therefore, in order to make the picture of interpretation complete, it is necessary to take into consideration how much crucial information is delivered by visual perception, and account for the fact in any discourse analysis.

It is also important to remember that the observation of the immediate environment provides us with rich contextual cues. For example, seeing someone dressed in black will naturally trigger the association that the person is going to a funeral. Since it is culture-specific, for instance for Sicilians it may also indicate that the person is going to a wedding and in other countries, in which other dress codes are adhered to, it may evoke neither of the associations. Various non-verbal signs and signals also help us to identify and interpret other people's feelings, emotions, states of mind and physical conditions. Using the example proposed by Wharton (2003) if we see someone shivering, we interpret that the person is cold, scared or unwell depending on other accessible contextual cues. Similarly, if we see that someone blushes, it makes us think that the person is embarrassed. The observation of natural behaviour makes us refer to our general knowledge and inferential mechanisms which help us to interpret situations. Intentional and communicative signals such us smiling, frantic gesticulating or pouting are there to convey information by which the speaker makes his intentions clear or more pronounced.

Even if we mostly rely on the information provided by vision, the role of other senses in making the conceptual representations of encountered experiences and selecting contextually relevant assumptions, is not to be denied. Let us imagine that we have never sniffed coffee or fresh bread, we have never touched a hot iron or delicate fabric, and that we have never heard a clock ticking or dog barking, how incomplete and impaired would our contextual knowledge be without the information? Hearing, smelling and touching not only supply the data for our general knowledge but also provide us with crucial information for the interpretation of on-going events. While the role of contextual cues provided by the sense of smell and touch is hardly discussed in literature, auditory perception and its relation to the comprehension process is more and more readily discussed. Among a great diversity of aspects embracing the issue, the importance of prosody for utterance interpretation, and the relation between pragmatic and phonological analysis have received much attention and have been discussed by many authors (e.g. Akamatsu 1987, House 1990, Fretheim 1996, Imai 1998, Wilson & Wharton 2006, Clark 2007, Couper-Kuhlen & Ford 2004, Barth-Weingarten et al. 2009). In the realm of pragmatic-phonology interface, special attention was paid to intonation which has been proven to be heavily context-dependent and to facilitate a speaker's context selection (Fretheim & Dommelen 1999, Hirschberg 2005, House

2006). One of the pioneering works touching on the subject was Bogusław Marek's *Pragmatics of Intonation* (1987), in which he presented an in-depth analysis of this interaction.

In his work, aside from other pragmatic theories and approaches, Marek focuses his attention on Relevance Theory as "the most promising model of utterance interpretation" (1987:168) and presents an interesting analysis which incorporates intonation into the model. On the basis of the relevance-theoretic assumptions, Marek claims that intonation (similarly to a speaker's behaviour) can be more, or less ostensive. As a result, the importance of intonation in the interpretation process varies and depends on the degree of ostensivness, which is established for each particular utterance. In accordance, intonation can be weakly ostensive (in the case of 'neutral' intonation) and have practically no contribution to the meaning of utterances, but also it may be highly ostensive and determine the choice of context. To substantiate his claim, Marek (1987:152), among numerous examples, analyses the famous exchange originating from Sperber and Wilson (1986) and presented in (9a)-(9c).

(9)   A: *Do you ever talk to Charles?*
         B: *I never talk to plagiarists.*

In the example, speaker B, using intonation, directs the hearer to a particular interpretation consistent with his or her intentions. Following directly from the principle of relevance, the intonation contour of speaker B's response, presented in (9a), serves to provide cues for construing contextual assumptions that Charles is a plagiarist and that the speaker never talks to him.

(9a) I N
           E
                V
                   E
                      R talk to plagiarists.

The same effect is achieved by the alternative version, presented in (9b):

(9b) I never T
               A
                  L
                     K to plagiarists.

As stressed by Marek, in both cases the word 'plagiarists' is deaccented, suggesting that it is 'given' (not 'new') information (Sperber & Wilson 1986) and that it should be treated as such by the hearer. Yet the information is not in the hearer's background knowledge and thus cannot be retrieved from this source. This leads the hearer to infer that the speaker wants to signal that it is generally known that Charles indeed is a plagiarist. The third version of the utterance discussed by Marek involves putting a heavy stress on the lexical item, as illustrated in (9c), which produces a contradictory effect implying that the speaker talks to Charles sometimes (Charles is not a plagiarist.), but he refuses to talk to people who are plagiarists.

(9c)   P
                                L
       I never talk to   Agiarists.

The following examples provide evidence that, unlike written texts devoid of the information, prosodic signals significantly reduce the processing effort and increase the relevance of utterances. In the effect, as Marek states (1987:160),

> "it is not only the presence of an unexpected intonational signal but also the absence of a signal that the hearer might have reasons to expect, that can decide on a strongly ostensive use of a particular fragment of an intonation contour".

This observation leads the author to formulate a principle of the ostensivness of intonation which says that:

> "[w]eakly ostensive intonational signals give rise to fewer contextual implications than signals which are ostensivly stronger" (ibid.132).

This claim seems to be confirmed by other authors in later works devoted to the analysis of the role intonation has in the process of interpretation.

Although the influence of intonation on interpretation was not of Sperber and Wilson's major concern in the first draft of their theory, with time the connection between intonation and pragmatic inference started growing in popularity. As Wilson and Sperber (1993) later explained, in Relevance Theory, intonation provides procedural information for interpretations of utterances, which means that certain prosodic variants "indicate, guide, constrain or direct the inferential phase of comprehension" (Carston 1992:162), reducing the processing effort of the hearer searching for an interpretation. For instance, interrogatives are typically pronounced with rising intonation, while falling intonation indicates declarative or exclamatory utterances. Indirect speech acts (e.g. suggestions or requests as illustrated in (10)):

(10)   *Why don't you be quiet?*

differ in prosodic structure from true interrogatives presented in (11):

(11)   *Can you lend me 50£?*

thus signalling the necessity of recovering non-trivial assumptions during the interpretation of an utterance (10), in this case not as a question, but a forceful way of reprimanding someone's noisy behaviour.

Going even further and relating their analysis to other prosodic inputs, Wilson and Wharton (2006) distinguish between signs and signals which, similarly to the ones present in non-verbal communication and described above, differ in functions and the way they are processed. As they explain, "signs carry information by providing evidence for it; signals carry information by encoding it" (ibid. 429). In other words, signs are pragmatically inferred representations of a speaker's state of mind or physical condition. If, for instance, a person is nervous, his/her tone of voice is naturally affected by the condition. On the other hand, signals, such as affective facial expressions or tones of voice, are intentional, and, the communicative expressions are determined by the hearer through decoding. Among the signs and signals, the authors identify natural signs and signals and linguistic inputs (like lexical stress, lexical tone) interpreted by the hearer as a combination of decoding and inference, as summarised in Fig. 1-4.

As the authors observe, the inputs may contribute to overt, covert and accidental communication, in each case creating certain impressions, conveying emotions/attitudes, or altering the salience of available interpretations. For instance, a speaker's tiredness, boredom or anger revealed in his/her tone of voice may not be overtly intentional and the speaker may do his/her utmost to prevent the hearer from recognising them. Other times the speaker may consciously and openly produce (or even exaggerate) prosodic input in order to trigger particular pragmatic effects. Consequently,

> "[w]hile neutral (or 'expected') prosody would cause the hearer least phonological processing effort, it would give him little guidance on the type of cognitive effects he was expected to derive. By contrast, any

departure from neutral (or 'expected') prosody would increase the hearer's phonological processing effort, but would thereby encourage him to look for extra (or different) effects" (ibid. 438).

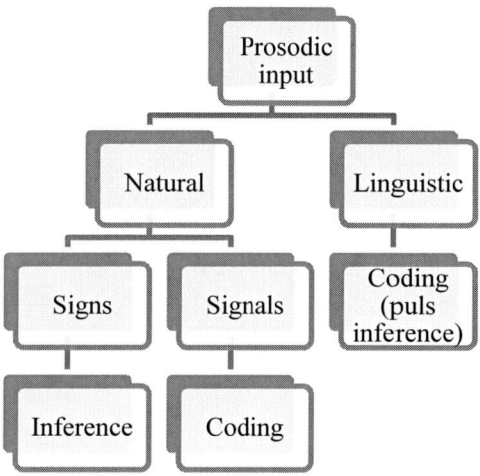

Fig. 1-4 Division of prosodic inputs (adapted from Wilson and Wharton (2006))

The overtly manifested signs and signals can be described and located on the showing-meaningNN continuum. As indicated in Fig. 1-5 below, natural signs, although not inherently communicative, manifest speakers' emotions or attitudes which contribute to hearers' interpretations. Linguistic signals as inherently communicative, are intended to convey a speaker's meaning (or meaningNN) in the most effective way.

Showing Natural signs Natural signals Linguistic signals MeaningNN

Fig. 1-5 The showing-meaningNN continuum (adapted from Wilson & Wharton (ibid.))

On the grounds that speech perception differs significantly from other forms of auditory perception, since it involves different cognitive processing mechanisms (Mattingly & Liberman 1990, Eyesneck & Keane 2000), stimuli that we hear and perceive as relevant (which are not utterances) very often play just as important roles as speech acts. Certain noises in our surroundings may be evidence to the fact that some action is being performed in close proximity to us and may trigger contextual assumptions. For instance, the noise of a car engine that we hear at a driveway outdoors makes us conclude that someone (expected or not) has just come. In the same manner, if we smell something burning we jump to the conclusion that it must be, for instance, meat in the oven that we have been baking for too long or an iron that we have forgotten to disconnect. Hence, the role of the senses and their assistance in construing the contextual assumptions are well-evidenced. As argued by Carston (2004:824) "most verbal utterances are a complex of linguistic, paralinguistic, facial, vocal gestures, which appear to function as a signal receiving a unified interpretation". Although generally we are not aware of the strong correlation between the elements, in analysing communication they should not be overlooked, since they all comprise what we understand of particular occasions.

According to what we have said, our knowledge consisting of registered perceptual stimuli, decides how effectively we utilise our pragmatic abilities, or in other words, how quickly and correctly we make inferences. In any context we entertain two kinds of information: (1) mental representations received through perception and stored in memory, and (2) input received in the moment. When, for instance, somebody says (12),

(12)   *Do you want to try it?*

and moves a spoon in our direction, we correctly infer that s/he wants us to taste, perhaps, the sauce that s/he is making. Speakers' ostensive behaviour, our recognition of smell, and the communicated utterance are all elements of the context, although not the only ones, which make us recover speakers' intentions. On the other hand, when somebody asks the same question in a shop when we are looking at a nice shirt, we know that the person is not asking if we want to taste it but is suggesting we put on the garment to check if the size fits. What makes it possible for us to distinguish between the two situations and at the same time two different contexts is our background knowledge, which comprises innumerable mental representations (concepts) we acquire, experiencing objects and events and which are then formed on the basis of information received from the environment by our senses (vision, hearing, touch, smell, taste).

Context and general knowledge

Generally speaking, context is a fine selection of information which is stored in mental structures and which is available at any given moment. This is more or less what pragmatists seem to agree with. However, the question is how the cognitive system recognises the cues necessary for interpreting an utterance in a situation and how it selects them for a particular purpose. Relevance Theory, which attempts to elaborate on this point, explains that context is not given, but chosen (or formed) at the onset of the comprehension process by each participant and modified as an interpretation of a particular utterance proceeds. This means that the context is not fully determined in advance, but its formation "is open to choices and revisions throughout the comprehension process" (Sperber & Wilson 1986:137).

During any communicative situation we have to deal with, not only one, but with numerous contexts which overlap each other. The previous context (derived from a previous verbal exchange in various communicative situations), constitutes background for newly derived assumptions, which during the communication process are adequately updated, reviewed and extended by still new information. To observe this, let us consider Mary and Peter's utterances in (13), taken from Sperber and Wilson (ibid.140).

(13)   Mary: *What I would like to eat tonight is an osso-bucco. I'm ravenous. I had a great day in court. How was your day?*
Peter: *Not so good. Too many patients and the air conditioning was out of order. I'm tired.*
Mary: *I'm so sorry to hear that. OK, I'll make it myself.*

As illustrated by the example, understanding utterances requires constant monitoring and updating of contextual cues, which in the end makes Mary in (13) change her mind. Although initially she communicated that she would be happy to eat out, having heard that Peter was not feeling well, she decided to prepare dinner at home. In the same situation it was also Peter who was expected to extend the existing context by interpreting Mary's utterance as a reaction to his own.

Extension of a context may also require going back in time to a situation which has a direct relation to the present exchange or adding information derived from the immediate environment. The utterances in (14) and (15) provide evidence for this assertion and illustrate an extension of the context. The situation is as follows: one day a mother accidentally discovers a packet of small pills in her teenage son's bag. She calls the boy and they have a conversation:

(14)   Mom: *Tommy, can you explain what this is and where you got it from?*
Tommy: *It's not mine. Someone must have put it in my bag.*

The mother, seeing some pills, immediately assumes that the boy is in possession of drugs and infers that he might have tried taking them as well. Observing the immediate environment (the mother holding the packet), the boy understands that with the imprecise 'this' the mother is referring to the packet of pills. Contrary to what might be ascertained from the linguistic content of the mother's utterance, she realises (or at least suspects) what the packet contains. The boy assumes that the mother expects him to make an excuse, which he does; claiming that the pills do not belong to him. This confirms the mother's inherent suspicion that these are drugs. A few days later, the mother, holding another packet of pills, utters the following words to the teenage son:

(15)   *And these aren't yours either, I suppose?!*

In (15) the mother extends the present context with the information from the past situation presented in (14) when she found drugs in her son's school bag. Referring back to the situation, she intends to communicate that this time she is not going to believe in her son's lies. In saying that and in showing the second packet of drugs that she found in her son's personal things, not only does she relate the previous situation to the new context, but she also wants Tommy to rise to the occasion by referring to the previous situation and make new assumptions updated by new contextual cues.

As we have previously underlined, the choice of context is determined by an individual's mental repository, which contains innumerable concepts derived from past 'perceptual experience' (Johnson 1987). Some concepts are established in early infancy before a child enters the production stage (Mandler 1992) and are developed as the child grows, while others are formed through experience at any time in childhood, adolescence or adulthood. In this way our general knowledge is constantly enriched by new concepts and these established concepts are enriched by still new information (Barsalou 1999). Therefore, knowledge can be viewed as a complex and expanding network of interdependencies and correlations between various concepts; which conjure up the conceptualisation of new elements. That is why the new information must be not only organized, but also reduced (van Dijk 1977) in order to be comprehensible and in order so that it can be used for future reference. Rosch (1975, 1977, 1978/1999) suggests that concepts are organised into categories according to the best examples known as 'prototypes'. For instance, unlike the less popular 'snake', 'parrot', or 'pony', the words 'cat' and 'dog' are categorised as typical pets, which gives rise to the so called 'typicality effect' in the field of comprehension (for 'typicality effect' see Rosch 1977, 1978).

However intricate knowledge seems to be, it is definitely neither accidental nor disorganised. As argued in cognitive linguistics, our knowledge is similar to a dictionary or encyclopaedia (Langacker 1987), in which each concept has its address in memory and three possible entries: logical, encyclopedic and lexical (see also Sperber & Wilson 1986:86). The components facilitate organization, storage and the future retrieval of concepts. The encyclopedic entry holds the information about a concept; its denotations, features, properties etc. The lexical, provides information about a word or phrase that expresses the concept in natural language, while the logical, stores the information about deductive rules. However, it is worth noting that not all of the pieces of information are equally accessible at every moment. In other words, not all of the data is entertained simultaneously and in a given situation only some of it is made available.

To make sense of the mechanism, consider the following example in (16):

(16)   *She must be **a saint** to tolerate his constant complaining.*

The whole utterance is made up of smaller constituents (concepts) which are structurally subject to deductive rules. Each constituent has its linguistic realisations (syntactic category, phonological forms) and a set of available assumptions and beliefs connected with it. Consider 'a saint' as one of such constituents in the sentence (16):

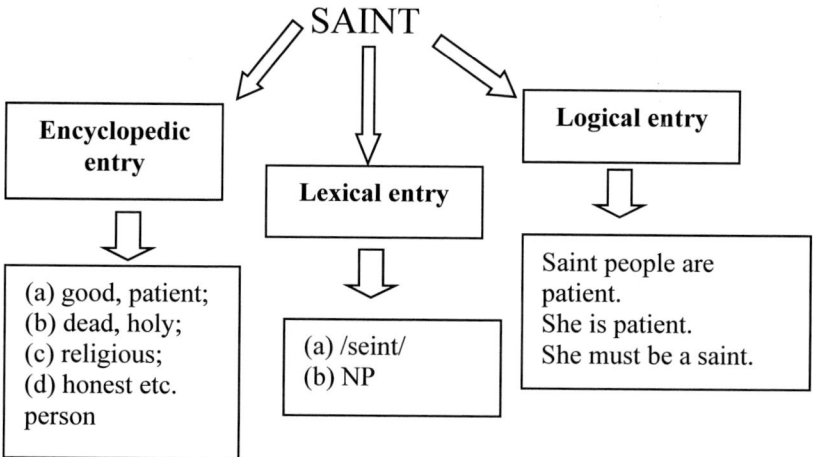

Fig. 1-6 Concept and its storage

As presented in the diagram (Fig. 1-6), under the address 'SAINT', apart from its syntactic and phonological realisation (lexical entry), and logical rules utilised in reasoning (logical entry), one can find a list of assumptions, connotations and beliefs concerning the concept. Obviously, the list will differ from individual to individual, which means that it may be extended by other assumptions, or, some of the assumptions (a)-(d) indicated in Fig. 1-6 may not be evoked at all.

Because concepts are not analysed as separate constituents, but in meaningful chunks, it is possible to refer to an appropriate assumption in an encyclopaedic entry following deductive rules. In our case, tolerating someone unbearable is straightforwardly connected with patience (16a), but not with being dead or honest, as illustrated in (16b)-(16d) below[4]:

(16a) She must be a patient person to tolerate his constant complaining.
(16b) *She must be a dead person to tolerate his constant complaining.
(16c) *She must be an honest person to tolerate his constant complaining.
(16d) ?She must be a religious person to tolerate his constant complaining.

The connection between religiousness and the ability to accept somebody's difficult behaviour may be weakly implicated and will therefore not be among the first associations. An interpretation of the utterance (16) that will satisfy our expectation of relevance, is namely that the woman ('she') has the patience of a saint for the man ('he'). This is determined according to the most accessible of assumptions, using the constituents and deductive rules without the need of examining all of the possible interpretations. Yet assuming that the speaker confines himself to one assumption would be gross simplification of the whole inferential process. Reasoning is hardly ever limited to one intended conclusion. Instead, one idea triggers another and one thought results in a series of new ones, which propels the process of communication and which also contributes to the fact that it is extremely difficult to follow a context as well as the factors playing a role in it. Communication is a dynamic process, and from this perspective we should try to understand the context not as a set of defined features (variables), but as a "chain of cognitive events" (Fauconnier 2005:658) which influences a speaker's behaviour and a hearer's interpretation.

---

[4] Anomalous sentences are marked with an asterisk '*', dubious sentences are marked with '?'

Apart from the encyclopedic organization of concepts, general knowledge is comprised of data structures stored in our memory and called 'frames', 'scripts' and 'schemata'. Although they can be assumed to "hinge on the apparent capacity of the human brain to represent and reuse knowledge of the world" (Taboada 2004:20), there are subtle difference in the scope of the constructs and in the way they are described by scholars. The term 'frames' (first introduced by Minsky 1977 and frequently used as a cover term) refers to slots which open access to other mental structures, so that the frame 'HOUSE' leads to another, like KITCHEN or BEDROOM, and in turn make other connections, e.g. with 'cooking' or 'sleeping'. Although also referring to the stereotypical knowledge and expectations, Schank and Abelson (1977) described the frame-like, culture-specific structures which represent typical actions and which facilitate the processing of encountered situations. For instance, eating out in a restaurant is saved in the mind as a set of potential activities connected with the event, such as choosing a restaurant, looking for a free table, talking to a waiter, choosing and ordering a meal etc. Being involved in the situation, observing it or reading about it, we automatically refer to this script without needing to interpret it from scratch. The organization of knowledge determines our expectations of relevance, which means that we anticipate what should happen next, what we are expected to do or say, or what someone may ask about or respond to in certain circumstances.

Although rather vague and intuitive term in literature, schemata are active and constantly developing conventional cognitive constructs which represent patterns of past experience utilised in perceiving, planning and making inferences in complex situations (see Coulson & Matlock 2009:104). As argued by Kintsch and van Dijk (1978), not only speech is controlled by schemata, but also text comprehension. The authors also made a claim that there is a difference in the comprehension of texts read with a certain purpose and the ones read for pleasure (see also Hayes et al. 1977). In the former, the reading task is controlled by special purpose schemata, while in the latter different readers were observed utilising different schemata in the task.

On the basis of the information which is stored and which comprises general knowledge, it is possible to interpret new information. To some extent understanding entails relating old information to new. The former is referred to as the background and makes new information (the foreground) more evident and salient (van Dijk 1979, Duranti & Goodwin 1992). The same view seems to be shared by Gibson (1986:73) who maintained that "[t]he essentials become evident in the context of changing nonessentials". The new information is then understood on the basis of background knowledge and, according to Relevance Theory, it should culminate in a strengthening, contradiction or abandonment of our previous assumptions; in order to be beneficial and compensate for our processing effort (Sperber & Wilson 1986).

Context and content

Understanding (or comprehending) alongside the production of utterances is the main competence of language use. To communicate in a language no matter whether native or foreign it is necessary to be able to understand an interlocutor's utterances and, on the basis of what is understood, formulate an appropriate response. In the inferential process, humans are expected to go beyond mere linguistic information provided by a sentence and engage general knowledge and commonsensical reasoning to figure out an interlocutor's intention. What is more, understanding has a substantial influence on speech production, since only if it is understood what the person has communicated, can another person respond appropriately and, essentially, prevent communication from failing. From both the psychological (cognitive) and linguistic point of view, understanding is a complex process which can be separated into numerous operations, not all of which have yet been thoroughly investigated.

Aside from mental abilities, past experiences, knowledge and contextual information derived from other sources, what counts most in the process is an utterance provided as an input for these complex thinking processes. It goes without saying that figuring out short, clear and explicit interlocutions is not as challenging or risky (taking into consideration the chances of misinterpretation) as processing long, ambiguous, and implicit ones. As speakers of language, we have at our disposal a wide range of tools and strategies, all of which we can use to best express our intentions and aid a hearer's comprehension. We can choose different words, syntactic structures, and out of the available elements we can build various sentences. The speaker, then, deciding about the semantic and syntactic content of his/her utterance takes the lion's share of responsibility for the hearer's recovery of intentions and thus, the success of the act of communication. Therefore, the speaker needs to calculate the risk of misinterpretation with the potential benefits of using either well-known words (which can be easily understood and processed by the hearer) or sophisticated and less explicit expressions, which, if more effort-consuming, may lead to an additional cognitive effect. Similarly, the speaker must decide if using complex sentence structures, instead of simple ones, will be more beneficial and if he or she can express his or her intentions in the best possible way which would not be otherwise achieved.

As it was pointed out by Grice and as it was suggested above, there is a great discrepancy between sentence meaning and a speaker's meaning, since a speaker's intention does not always correspond to what the sentence linguistically contains. Thus, it is our contextual knowledge which helps us to decide if somebody saying (17):

(17)   *It is cold outside.*

is trying to encourage us to take a sweater before leaving, or is asking that same person to close a window. Because everyday communication is spontaneous and focused on economy of expression, we hardly ever go into detail about what exactly we are driving at; believing that the hearer shares common ground and, even if provided with the bare minimum of information, can follow. Keeping that in mind, we supply a person with two types of information: (1) the information contained in the semantic structure of a sentence and (2) the information in pragmatic content which will be figured out from the structure, and we believe that these will be sufficient for the recovery of our intentions. Since, as purported in Relevance Theory, the semantic content of any sentence is underspecified and only partially determines the meaning of an utterance, we need to refer to the information provided by pragmatic inference. In communication we can distinguish two types of utterances (explicit and implicit), which differ in the amount of semantic and pragmatic information involved in their processing and which will be discussed separately for the sake of clarity. In this discussion we will try to show that the linguistic content of utterances (both explicit and implicit) and contextual information must cooperate if the hearer is to recover the intended interpretation.

In the relevance-theoretic framework the distinction between explicit and implicit content of utterances plays an important role and has been discussed at length (see e.g. Recanati 1989, 2004; Kandolf 1993; Carston 2002, 2005, 2009; Garrett & Harnish 2007, Capone 2009, Fretheim 2009). The term 'explicature', coined by Dan Sperber and Deirdre Wilson (1986), describes an utterance of which content is explicit or, more precisely, which they define as: "a development of a logical form encoded by *U*" (ibid.182). In the framework explicature is described as a two-layer entity which consists of linguistically encoded and contextually inferable information and the processing of which also requires two distinct processes in order to be successful: decoding and inference. In comprehension, the linguistic information undergoes a preliminary process of decoding and serves as an input for inferential processes. This involves the recognition of a speaker's intention on the basis of available contextual information. The fact that an utterance is explicitly expressed does not mean that a hearer can just pick up the signal and that it is sufficient for interpretation. In order to understand explicit utterances (just as in the case of implicitly communicated assumptions), inferential processes must come into play. As observed by Bach (2009:2),

> "(…) even if a speaker is being completely literal and means exactly what he says, that he means exactly what he says still has to be inferred. It takes more than decoding a sentence to figure out that a speaker is using it in a completely literal way".

To illustrate this claim, let us consider the following examples:

(18)   *What did you do on Saturday?*
(19)   *Can you pass me the salt?*

Both in (18) and (19) linguistic information does not fully specify what the speakers intend to convey. For instance, without any reference to contextual information it is impossible for the hearer to determine, among other things, what 'salt' the speaker in (19) is asking for, since there are various types of salt used for different purposes. It is also not immediately apparent which 'Saturday' the speaker in (18) is talking about and one could assume that to answer his/her question properly, the hearer would be expected to give a full account of all of the activities that he or she was engaged in on that day. Consequently, as will be argued, understanding explicatures (also the ones in (18) and (19)) requires adopting certain pragmatic procedures which, if relying on what is given in the sentence, make it possible for the hearer to draw conclusions about what is actually being communicated. As explained by Wilson (1994:39), the hearer must:

> "(…) decode the sense of the sentence uttered, and then disambiguate any ambiguous expressions, assign reference to any referential expressions, restore any ellipsed material, and narrow down the interpretation of any over-vague expressions. "

Pragmatic procedures (or sub-tasks) are highly context-dependent and are necessary for the comprehension of any utterance. Among other things, they involve free enrichment, reference assignment, disambiguation and incoherence resolution, which, although processed simultaneously during the inferential process, will be discussed separately.

As argued by Sperber and Wilson (1986), logical forms (or semantic representations) are never fully propositional, which means that they insufficiently determine the propositional content of an utterance. To be able to interpret speakers' intentions we need to complete the underspecified, decoded logical forms and left-out information, which in pragmatics is called 'enrichment'. The pragmatic procedure is described by many authors some of whom, instead of enrichment, call it 'saturation' (Carston 2005), 'expansion' or 'completion' (Bach 1994). Referring to the examples (18) and (19), as presented above, it is possible to observe that what is actually understood from the utterances is much richer than what is contained in the sentences. For instance, although it is not specified in the sentence, it is inferred that in (18) the speaker wishes to covey that s/he is talking about last Saturday; counting from the moment the conversation proceeds, not two weeks, months or years before. The person does not ask about all the activities the hearer performed on that day and most probably the speaker is not interested in details such as if the hearer brushed his/her teeth, got dressed, ate breakfast, lunch and supper, or went to bed late. Abstracting from the main purpose of the speaker's question, which can be clear with an insight into other contextual cues, it is possible to conclude that the speaker wants to know what the interlocutor was absorbed in for most of the day or if anything interesting happened. If there was unlimited access to necessary contextual information, it would be possible to tell if the speaker uttering the words just wanted to start a conversation and break the silence, boast about what s/he did on that day, encourage the interlocutor to confide in what the speaker knows the hearer did on Saturday, or if the person's intention was none of the above but something different. It is a general belief that understanding has a lot to do with mind-reading (Fodor 1983, Sperber & Wilson 2002, Bloom 2002, Papafragou 2002, Wilson 2005) and also taking into consideration an interlocutor's knowledge and his/her access to contextual information.

Similarly in (19), the speaker asks to pass him/her the salt not next week or next time he and the hearer have an opportunity to eat together, but immediately, which is not actually contained in the speaker's utterance. When the person says 'the salt', s/he probably does not think of a bag of salt from the kitchen or a shop nearby. In the situation, the hearer is expected to understand that the lexical item should be narrowed down to the ad hoc concept SALT meaning the 'saltcellar' which is standing on the table next to the person who is asked to co-operate. Hence, lexical items (like SALT) contained in sentences stand for many possible concepts (e.g. a bag of salt, bath salts, smelling salts, a saltcellar), which are specified in every context by application of the inferential processes governed by the principle of relevance. According to what we have said, the utterances (18) and (19) can be enriched in the way presented below in (18a) and (19a) where the enriched material has been put in brackets:

(18a)   *What did you [the hearer] do [last] Saturday [from today] [which was the most important/interesting]?*

(19a)   *Can you [the hearer] PASS [give] me [the speaker] the SALTCELLAR [standing next to you] [right now]?*

Specifying concepts expressed by lexical items does not always entail narrowing, as illustrated by the examples in (18a) and (19a). Sometimes it involves the converse process called 'broadening' (or 'extension'[5]), in which a concept is given more general meaning than it denotes. Approximations, category extensions and metaphors provide the richest data in order to observe the process (see Wilson 1994). As illustrated in example (20) below:

(20)   *Steven is a big brain.*

the concept of BRAIN denoting "an organ in a human body controlling all the processes, including thinking", in this particular sentence has an extended meaning, which stands for an extremely intelligent and wise person. What is more, depending on the context the utterance may have distinct effects and express, among other things, an awe and appreciation of somebody's intellectual abilities or, in contrast, may be ironical and pejorative which is visible in the following contrastive dialogues (20a) and (20b):

(20a)   *A: Steven has won the international mathematics contest.*
         B: Yeah, he is a big brain.

(20b)   *A: Steven tried to fix the cord but he didn't bother to disconnect it and now he is in hospital.*
         B: Yeah, he is a big brain.

Since the processes of lexical narrowing and broadening are also argued to enter within the domain of semantics (which is interested in what potential meanings can be encoded in a lexical item and how in relation to other lexical items the meanings are activated), lexical pragmatics investigates

---

[5] Schiffrin (1984)

how a literal/decoded meaning of a word is modified by the context. Relevance Theory, which also tries to account for the phenomenon, explains that appropriate concepts are chosen in a particular context and adjusted according to the hearer's expectation of relevance. Consequently, the meaning of a lexical item, underdetermined in the field of semantics, is a starting point for pragmatic processes which describe modifications in the currently used meaning.

Owing to the fact that utterances are hardly ever fully explicit, they need enrichment in order to be appropriately interpreted. Explicitness is a property that varies in degree and depends on the proportion of contextually inferable and linguistically decoded information. The utterances with which comprehension most refers to contextual information are less explicit than the ones which need enrichment (Wilson & Sperber 2005). What is more, explicatures in the relevance-theoretic approach may either be fully explicit or partially implicit, but regardless of this fact they undergo the same processing operations as implicatures. As Ariel (2002:365-366) puts it:

"(…) the similarity between the processing of what is said and what is implicated is due to the fact that both ambiguity and reference resolution (part of literal meaning) and the generation of conversational implicatures (nonliteral meanings) are inferential (performed in line with the principle of relevance)."

Wilson and Sperber (2005) also point out that we can distinguish basic explicatures and higher-order explicatures. The latter require from a hearer the ability to make inferences about a speaker's attitude, according to the proposition s/he is expressing and a recognition of the type of speech act s/he is performing (Carston 2002:119). Processing explicatures is then strongly linked and depends on the recognition of speech acts, these are among the most popular and widely discussed phenomena in the realm of philosophy, semantics and pragmatics (see e.g. Burkhardt 1990, Vanderveken & Kubo 1994).

According to speech act theorists[6] (Austin 1962, Searle 1969, Bach and Harnish 1979), to understand utterances means to identify them as speech acts which perform certain actions. As suggested by Austin, who was the precursor of Speech Act Theory, among speech acts we can distinguish locutionary acts (acts of speaking), illocutionary acts (acts of doing something in speaking) and perlocutionary acts (producing an effect in the act of speaking). Accordingly, within the theory, language use is not only

---

[6] for a more detailed discussion see Sadock (2005) or Levinson (1983)

saying, but also doing and introducing changes by way of speech acts. Consequently, an utterance contains information about what a speaker does or intends to do by expressing certain propositions, for instance promises, threats, warnings or requests. In short, to be able to comprehend an utterance as a speaker intended, we have to recover which speech act he or she is performing, recognise it from other possible speech acts and consider if the act complies with his or her intentions. In a natural conversation, questions are not always direct or intended to be answered, and threats do not always differ from promises. To resolve the dilemmas, various contextual cues need to be taken into account, as van Dijk (1977:211) comments,

> "Speech act comprehension is based on rules and strategies for so-called 'context analysis', in which (epistemic) frames play an important role in the analysis of social context, social frame, and interaction type".

The existence of higher-order explicatures suggests that utterances have not just one, but several explicatures, even if not all, or, just a few of them are entertained by the hearer at a particular moment. Following this way of thinking, the utterances (18) and (19) discussed above and enriched into (18a) and (19a), provide higher-level explicatures (18b)-(18e) and (19b)-(19e):

(18b)   S asks H what he did on Saturday.
(18c)   S asks for explanation what H did on Saturday.
(18d)   S wonders what H did on Saturday.
(18e)   S is curious what H did on Saturday.

(19b)   S asks H to pass the salt.
(19c)   S politely asks H to pass the salt.
(19d)   S orders H to pass S the salt.
(19e)   S impatiently asks H to pass the salt.

What is more, Wilson and Sperber (2005:623) comment that any of the explicatures "may contribute to relevance and warrant the derivation of implicatures", which implies that the two types of inferences are somewhat interrelated.

Apart from the underdetermined and incomplete information drawn from semantic representations, the hearer may come across ambiguous and incoherent utterances which s/he needs to resolve before the inferential processes are activated. It can be argued that if the speaker is to assist the hearer in the recovery of his/her communicative intentions, the occurrence of ambiguity and incoherence are instances of negligence on the part of the speaker and, following Grice's assumptions, a violation of the Co-operative Principle. It goes without saying that ambiguous and incoherent utterances expose the hearer to excessive processing efforts. Yet the fact that a discourse is full of inaccuracies and sloppiness does not have to dispute speakers' good intentions, since some intentions that we communicate are less perfect than the intentions that we have in mind and want to be recovered. For this reason, it is rather a matter of the imperfection of language and linguistic tools utilised to attain the desired purpose of communication than the speaker's malice and ill will that contribute to ambiguous and incoherent utterances. Against all odds, the hearer is determined to make sense of ambiguous and incoherent utterances on the basis of contextual information, general knowledge, commonsensical reasoning and developed strategies of utterance comprehension, because, s/he is convinced that what the speaker intends to communicate must be relevant.

As explained in the relevance-theoretic framework, ambiguity arises when an utterance has more than one logical form which triggers a number of possible interpretations. Thus, the semantic representation can be ambiguous in more than one way and must be "extended pragmatically to cover other referents or meanings" (Sweetser 1990:1). Although ambiguity resolution is found to be of interest in both the fields of semantics and pragmatics, and has been a subject of much debate (see e.g. Zwicky & Sadock 1975, Horn 1985, MacDonald et al. 1994; Asher & Lascarides 1995, Fredsted 1998, Jaszczolt 2001), there are still a lot of inaccuracies and the term seems to be very vague. As suggested by Jaszczolt (2002), first it is necessary to distinguish between structural ambiguity, in which a sentence structure offers alternative solutions and interpretations, and also semantic/pragmatic ambiguity in which alternative logical forms are related and provide propositions. In the first case, syntactic parsing alone is able to determine syntactic categories and the relations between them which make it possible to predict possible interpretations, but only pragmatic inferences enable a hearer to make logical anticipatory hypotheses consistent with a hearer's expectation of relevance and finally, recover which of the interpretations is intended by the speaker. The frequently cited quote by Chomsky (1965) presented in (21):

(21)   *Visiting relatives can be boring.*

is ambiguous as it yields two possible interpretations from one structure which can be paraphrased as (21a) and (21b):

(21a)   The act of visiting relatives can be boring.
(21b)   Our relatives who visit/are visiting us can be boring.

While from syntactic information only it is impossible to disambiguate the utterance, the ambiguity does not pose a problem for pragmatic analysis since the contextual information will eliminate the interpretation lacking in evidence. Hence, as illustrated by the following dialogue (21c),

(21c)   A: *I've heard that your grandparents arrived for the weekend.*
          B: *Yes, visiting relatives can be boring.*

if the speaker's intention is to complain about the visit of his/her relatives, one does not go through the two possible interpretations, but instead immediately chooses the one intended by the speaker after a quick search for relevance.
     Similarly, in the case of lexical ambiguity which is based on possible alternative readings of words, the hearer is able to work out the appropriate meaning of a lexical item on the basis of available contextual information. The classic examples of lexically ambiguous items are homonymy and polysemy, in which words either have the same form but different meanings (e.g. BANK), or a word has multiple related meanings (e.g. GET could mean 'take', 'become', 'understand', 'have' etc.). To illustrate the phenomenon, let us consider Cruse's (2001:245) example:

(22)   *We managed to get to the bank just in time.*

We can observe that the ambiguity in the sentence is caused by two possible meanings ('senses') of the word BANK, which may mean:

(a)   an institution providing financial service
(b)   place at a river or lake

As we mentioned before, the hearer in his/her interpretation is expected to narrow down a concept and, on the basis of contextual knowledge, select one meaning in this case, either (a) or (b). The context then filters out the other possible meanings and makes it possible for the hearer to resolve the problems of ambiguous expressions and finally infer whether the speaker got to his/her bank (meaning (a)) before closing time, or the speaker got to the bank of the river (b), where, for instance, s/he was supposed to meet with someone.

Horn (1985) and Sweetser (1990) made the claim that there is another type of ambiguity which is pragmatic. It occurs when words or phrases either have two distinct semantic values (meanings) or if despite one meaning they have more than one function. Horn (ibid.) observed that pragmatic ambiguity is most evident when analysing conjunctions such as *and*, *or*, *if*, and also in cases of negation as in (23a) and (23b) below:

(23a)   *She is not happy, she is sad.*
(23b)   *She is not happy, she is ecstatic.*

Wilson (1970) provided further evidence of pragmatic ambiguity discussing elliptical conditionals, where the difference between ordinary and concessive readings contributes to the occurrence of ambiguity:

(24)   *The Queen of England is happy, though she is not ecstatic.*

Sweetser (ibid.) also discussed the cases of modals in which ambiguity is caused by a discrepancy between a possible 'deontic sense' (expressing obligation) and an 'epistemic sense' (denoting probability), as illustrated by the examples (25a) and (25b):

(25a)   *John must be home by ten; mother won't let him stay out any later.*
(25b)   *John must be home by ten; I see his coat.*

The utterance in (25b), as a garden-path sentence, leads the hearer to follow a predictable route of reasoning until s/he discovers that s/he was mistaken and is forced to reinterpret.

Keeping all that in mind, we can say that pragmatic ambiguity resolution consists of determining the intentions with which utterances are expressed. It has already been said that general knowledge dictates how to make appropriate speech acts and how to interpret utterances as intended (direct or indirect) speech acts. Using Sweetser's example (ibid.), if we say (26),

(26)   *How're you?*

we may be intending to inquire about a hearer's wellbeing, greet him or start a conversation, obviously depending on the context of the utterance. What is more, as observed by Chen (1992), ambiguous utterances may be deliberate and may provide the only way to achieve a communicative goal.

To be more precise, the speaker may purposefully use ambiguous expressions; so as to retrieve two different meanings simultaneously and also to achieve additional contextual effect. It is often used for zeugmatic effect[7] in jokes and puns like in the following case (27) taken from Cruse (2002:246):

(27)   *The old man expires on the same day as his driving license.*

The understanding of the utterance in (27) rests on recovering more than just one reading of the verb 'to expire' to be activated in this particular context. In the sentence it is used to mean both 'to go out of date' and 'to die'.

As discussed in many papers, reference assignment may either cause or contribute to ambiguity in utterances. Both of the tasks: ambiguity resolution and reference assignment, together with enrichment and other procedures, are seen in Relevance Theory as sub-tasks of the inferential process. These tasks are driven by the principle of relevance and take place in parallel, rather than in sequence (Wilson & Sperber 1986). Understanding utterances involves determining and assigning references to co-referential expressions as they are spoken. As defined by Carlson (2005:76) "reference (…) is a kind of verbal 'pointing to' or 'picking out' of a certain object or individual that one wishes to say something about", regardless if the object or individual is in our immediate environment or not. Since there is a strong correlation between reference assignment and contextual knowledge (which plays a pivotal role in the procedure), understanding the following expressions (28)-(31) requires determining the object, time, place and person referred to, by assigning their appropriate referents.

(28)   *I like **this**.*
(29)   *I'll be back by **then**.*
(30)   *Let's meet at the **park**.*
(31)   *Did you tell **him**?*

Hence, what is meant by *this* in (28), what time the speaker precisely means by saying *then* in (29), which *park* s/he has in mind in (30) and which person s/he refers to in (31), can be interpreted only in the presence of appropriate contextual information, otherwise they become ambiguous.

---

[7] For further discussion and analysis of 'zeugma' see Cruse 1986, Solska 2008

As pointed out by Matsui (e.g. 1993, 1998, 2000), some utterances may require the assignment of 'bridging references', if an utterance lacks a direct referent, as evident in (32) below.

(32)   *I went to a restaurant. The wine list was exclusively French.*

In the example 'the wine list' must be connected with a visit to a restaurant, even though the relation is not explicitly made in the utterance. According to the 'restaurant' script of general knowledge, a hearer is expected to ascribe to the information that restaurants serve wine (usually more than one type) and all of the available wines can be found in a wine list. Without this knowledge, the hearer might get the impression that the speaker is talking about the restaurant for one thing and also a French wine list s/he could have seen on a website for sommeliers. It is worth noting that the speaker does not do his utmost to avoid confusing the hearer and does not specify what the utterance in (32) is about. A way in which the speaker could have specified is presented in (32a):

(32a)   *I went to a restaurant. The wine list [which I got in the restaurant] was exclusively French.*

In fact, the unnatural completion of the sentence in (32a) could be a cause of much greater confusion of the hearer, more so than the underspecified utterance. Following the principle of relevance, the hearer looks for the most contextually plausible interpretation of the utterance, which is why it is highly unlikely that s/he understands that the speaker is talking about a wine list on a web site. When presented with contextual information, the hearer determines that the former utterance sets the background for the next utterance, which hints that the speaker got the wine list in the restaurant, and thus ambiguity can be avoided.

Taking all this into account, it is evident that, (as stressed by Carlson (2005:81)) there must be a psychological mechanism behind linking understanding and reference assignment, and this notion seems to be supported by Kehler (2005), who based his categorisation of determining reference on the speaker's coherence needs and world knowledge bias. As he illustrated in the following example (33), utterances in which references are yet to be determined very often cause ambiguity:

(33)   *Carl is talking to Tom in the Lab. Terry wants to talk to **him** too.*

The problem with (33) is that the word 'him' is co-referential with more than one referent, which gives rise to two possible interpretations (33a) and (33b):

(33a)   Terry wants to talk to Carl, too.
(33b)   Terry wants to talk to Tom, too.

The situation, very difficult from the point of view of the approach presented by Kehler, results in an excessive processing effort on the side of the hearer, who if contextual information turns out to be insufficient for the resolution of the ambiguity and reference assignment, may abandon the process.

Although the ambiguity and incoherence of an utterance do not always have to exist together and the utterance may be ambiguous without being incoherent and vice versa, in general disambiguation allows incoherence to be avoided and the general thought is that the two processes are somehow interconnected. Asher and Lascarides (1995) hold that disambiguation is possible due to the hearer's search for coherence and that both of the processes are rooted in human cognition. However, it is thought that coherence is more extended and touches on many more aspects than ambiguity resolution or reference assignment (Hobbs 1979).

As defined by Kintsch and van Dijk (1978:365),

> "A discourse is coherent only if its respective sentences and propositions are connected, and if these propositions are organised globally".

They also underline the fact that the human cognitive system makes up for indirectly connected propositions and accounts for the missing sequence by utilising general or contextual knowledge. It proves that humans have a natural tendency to look for coherence in communication, which is well-evidenced in psychological research. Despite the arising of incoherent information in an utterance, they continue analysing it, this is because they assume that the information is relevant (Kehler 2005). This view is shared by the relevance theoretic framework, in which coherence is said to result from a search for relevance and is both necessary and sufficient enough for comprehension (Blass 1990, Blakemore 1992, 2001, Wilson 1998). As Wilson (ibid.) emphasizes, both the local coherence of adjacent segments of an utterance, and the global coherence of the whole discourse are governed by a search for relevance.

By modifying the available definitions of coherence and in an attempt to form a definition of the reverse phenomenon, we can say that an utterance is considered incoherent if it provides information, which is unconnected and/or contradictory (and in effect dubious), which hampers interpretation and comprehension. In the words of Relevance Theory, incoherence is a wasted processing effort. If our processing system comes across such an obstacle, it activates strategies which aim to restore coherence (Hellman 1995). To form an interpretation and eliminate incoherence, we have at our disposal various comprehension strategies which we employ in discourse analysis and which constitute our general knowledge and inferential abilities (see Kintsch & van Dijk 1978, Kehler 2005). Kehler (ibid.), for instance, identifies coherence relations (i.e. the structural relations between segments of discourse) in which, depending on the situation, cause-effect, contrast and/or resemblance, or contiguity relations must be identified in order to understand the discourse as coherent. According to this classification, the hearer presupposes that utterances are interdependent and the presupposition is satisfied only if the utterances remain within the boundaries of the relations mentioned previously. For instance, the hearer assumes that utterances are aimed at presenting a result of an action, which follows the causal sequence of utterances. In doing so, the hearer will infer that, in (34) below, Peter's getting soaked is an immediate consequence of his walking in the rain.

(34)   *It was raining and Peter got soaked.*

In processing the utterance we rely a lot on the sequence of the segments, which gives us a clear indication of what the connection between utterances is and in what temporal and causal sequence they take place (Halliday & Hasan 1976). That is why, changing the sequence of clauses (34) into (34a):

(34a)   *Peter got soaked and it was raining.*

can have serious repercussions when it comes to the comprehension of utterances and may lead to incoherence. It is natural to wonder if by any chance Peter did not get soaked earlier and if it was not due to something other than the rain.

Apart from cause and effect, the hearer may assume that subsequent parts of utterances are yet to reveal some contrasts or similarities. An example of the relation is exemplification, as illustrated by (35):

(35)   *He works too hard. Yesterday he stayed overnight at work.*

The sequence in this case does not play much of a role, but what matters is the relationship between the two clauses, which is broken in (35a) below:

(35a)   *He works too hard. Yesterday he ate plums.*

In (35a) the second sentence falls short of the hearer's expectation of further details or other comments linked with the earlier utterance, since eating plums has no correspondence to hard working whatsoever.

Finally, discourse coherence involves contiguity relations (in Hobbs (1990) called 'occasion') in which utterances progress in time. This is also illustrated by utterance (36) taken from Kehler (2005), in which the temporal sequence of utterances enables us to indicate how they are connected. It seems evident that the completion of one activity led to the other, which would not be so obvious if the order was changed.

(36)   *George delivered his tax plan to the Congress. The Senate scheduled a debate for next week.*

If any of the relations mentioned above are broken, the hearer does not immediately give up, even despite the obstacle. Convinced of the relevance of the utterance, s/he searches their contextual knowledge in the hope that it will allow him/her to establish coherence. This is a psychologically well-evidenced strategy for dealing with the problem. Therefore, the logical deduction and inferences must be assisted by contextual information, which provides strong evidence for one (consistent) interpretation over another. As mentioned before, it happens that the information received from the speaker seems contradictory, this contributes to incoherence and sometimes causes a break-down of communication. To avoid it, the hearer maximises the relevance of utterances, and in his/her interpretation of the speaker's utterances, not only needs to refer to common sense, but such aspects of the context as the speaker's tone of voice, behaviour and facial expression will also come in handy. Only by the virtue of contextual knowledge can appropriate conclusions be drawn and thus yield appropriate interpretations.

In the light of what was said before, the following dialogue should, at least at first glance, be seen as incoherent:

(37)   Jane: *Did you buy a dress for the party?*
        Mary: *What can you do in half an hour?*

The two speakers in (37) seem to be talking about two different things. On the other hand, in the presence of necessary contextual cues and presuming that in fact Mary's utterance is relevant, we realise that her utterance is not intended to be a true question and Mary does not expect any answer to it. What is more, knowing that half an hour for shopping is definitely not enough for an average woman, we discover that Mary not only wants to communicate that she did not buy any dress, but also gives a reason why she did not do so. This example perfectly illustrates Mann and Thomson's standpoint (1987, 1988), who claimed that the search for coherence is crucial to the understanding of implicit utterances.

As shown so far, natural language exchanges are specifically undetermined. Being aware of that, the hearer's role is to arrive at an interpretation of an utterance. If it were not for the context, (which provides the hearer with the needed unspoken information) the recovery of interpretations would not be possible. The context plays a decisive role in understanding both types of communicated assumptions, those presented and discussed in the work: explicatures and implicatures. The former has been described above along with pragmatic sub-tasks involved in understanding such as free enrichment, narrowing and broadening, reference assignment, ambiguity and incoherence resolution. Now attention will be paid to implicatures which, despite undergoing the same processing procedures as explicatures, require engaging general and contextual knowledge to a greater extent.

The term 'implicature' was first introduced by Grice (1957, 1975) in order to distinguish between the act of saying and implicating, in which speaker S saying p implicates q. Implicature in his theory is strongly linked to the notion of maxims and the Co-operative Principle, since the violation of the maxims contributes to the occurrence of implicatures. This means that, providing that both the speaker and hearer still observe the Co-operative Principle, the speaker disobeying the maxims wants the hearer to recognise and recover it as the non-trivial assumption. Constituting a speaker's meaning without being a part of sentence-meaning (Horn 2005:3), implicature provides much richer contextual implications than the speaker directly communicates. As summarised by Levinson (1983:113), implicatures according to Grice's theory, consist of:

"(i) conventional content of the sentence (P) uttered
(ii) the co-operative principle and its maxims
(iii) the context of P (e.g. its relevance)
(iv) certain bits of background information (e.g. P is blatantly false)
(v) that (i)-(v) are mutual knowledge shared by speaker and addressee".

Grice introduced a distinction between two types of implicatures, which he called conventional and non-conventional implicatures, in which he distinguished a class of conversational implicatures. While the concept of conventional implicatures (which are said to be calculated on the basis of the conventional meaning of the words, like particles: *but, still* or *even*,) has been a matter of dispute and with time its importance started to decline, non-conventional (i.e. context-dependent) conversational implicatures are the subjects of innumerable discussions. In the category of conversational implicatures Grice differentiated generalised implicatures and particularised implicatures which, as summarised by Recanati (2003), differ in the amount of contextual information necessary to calculate them. As explained by Levinson (ibid. 126),

> "(…) generalised conversational implicatures are those that arise without any particular context or special scenario being necessary, in contrast to particularised implicatures which do require such specific contexts."

Among generalised implicatures, the sub-types of scalar and causal implicatures, as presented by the examples (38) and (39), received special attention (see Gazdar 1979, Horn 1972, 1989; Hirschberg 1985, Chierchia 2004, Belletti 2004):

(38)   ***Some** children are spoilt.*
(39)   *The keys are on the fridge, I **believe**.*

In producing the utterances (38) and (39), the speaker conveys the assumptions (38a) and (39a), encoded in the meaning of 'some' and 'believe':

(38a)   Not all children are spoilt.
(39a)   I'm not sure if keys are on the fridge.

The types of inferences are also included in the processing of other quantifiers (e.g. *a few, all*), verbs of ranking (e.g. *know, believe; love, like*), numerals (e.g. … *two, three* etc.), modals (e.g. *might, must*) and connectives (e.g. *and, or*), which indicate that the speaker has reasons to use one in particular, not the other.

Generalised and particularised implicatures in Grice's theory are also characterised according to certain characteristics which facilitate their calculation, among which, Grice identifies cancelability (i.e. the instance of being made explicit by adding a clause to determine a speaker's preference of interpretation) and undetachablity (i.e. the irreplaceablity of any other utterance in which something could be expressed and produce the same effect). Although in Relevance Theory there are many references to Grice's assumptions, the two theories differ in what is understood by implicature. First and foremost, Relevance Theory rejected the dichotomies and the features of implicatures characteristic in Grice's account. Consequently, in Relevance Theory implicatures are not the violations of the maxims (which have not been borrowed from Grice either), but inferences calculated on the basis of explicatures. As explained by Wedgewood (2005:45):

> "Implicatures are different to explicatures in that they are drawn over explicatures (not logical forms) in interaction with contextual assumptions, but the nature of the inferential reasoning involved is just the same in the derivation of both explicatures and implicatures – that is, driven by the Principle of Relevance."

Hence the main difference between the two types of assumptions, lies not in their structure, but in the way they are derived.

A well-known example, taken from Sperber and Wilson (1986) and repeated in (40) below, allows explicatures and implicatures to be better understood and a clear distinction between the two types of assumptions to be made:

(40)   Peter: *Would you like a cup of coffee?*
         Mary: *Coffee would keep me awake.*

In the conversation, Peter's communicative intention is to offer Mary the cup of coffee. Although he explicitly expresses his intentions, Mary needs to make certain 'improvements' to his utterance in order to understand what he intends to say. Accordingly, she infers that the proposal is due now, not tomorrow or in two weeks' time, even if it is not specified in Peter's utterance. Among other things, she is expected to have conceptualised COFFEE as a drink which gives a boost of energy. To be able to cooperate, Mary and Peter must share mutual knowledge, but at the same time each of the two participants possesses his and her own individual contextual environment which is based on previous experiences, and which enables them to make idiosyncratic assumptions in the situation. Although it is not explicitly expressed by Peter, his utterance carries the presuppositions that he is going to make coffee or that he would like to have a coffee. Additionally, depending on the available contextual cues, Peter's utterance may be either understood as explicature or may be derived as implicature. As illustrated in (40a) below, Peter is tired of

listening to Mary who cannot stop talking and, hoping for a short break, he
offers her a cup of coffee.

(40a)   Mary: *Did I tell you about Ann and Sam's new apartment? Well,*
          it's marvellous. They bought it 2 years ago... well, almost bought
          it... Sam had had to take a loan and Ann had been working
          overtime. Anyway, the apartment...
          Peter: *Would you like a cup of coffee?*
          Mary: *Coffee would keep me awake.*

Alternatively, Peter might be a habitual gossiper. When Mary visits him
and tells him some news, he intends to encourage her to reveal more facts,
just as in (40b) below:

(40b)   Mary: *Hi, Peter. Here are the documents you asked for. OK. I*
          will be running now. I'm so tired after the scandal with Jane...
          Peter: *Would you like a cup of coffee?*
          Mary: *Coffee would keep me awake...*

Certainly, the scenario may be still different, which ultimately will have an
effect on the general interpretation of the situation.
    Focusing our attention on Mary's response, we observe that she does
not give a proper answer to Peter's question. Instead of yes or no, she
replies that coffee would keep her awake. Similar to the examples
presented in (40a) and (40b), Mary's utterance may express different
intentions and produce different effects depending on the context. This
comprises of, among other things, previous utterances of Peter and Mary,
prosodic features of her utterance (see Marek 1987:153-157 for the
discussion on the example and interesting perspective on how intonational
cues change interpretation of her utterance), and her ostensive behaviour.
For instance, if it is already late, Mary with the utterance may intend to
communicate that she will not fall asleep afterwards, which is to be
interpreted by Peter as a refusal. However, if Mary is, for example, in the
middle of doing something urgent for tomorrow, Peter by offering a cup of
coffee, offers her help. Consequently, Mary's response in this context
would actually be not only an acceptance, but also an appreciation of
Peter's help.
    Although more challenging, taking into consideration the processing
effort, implicatures provide additional contextual effects which, if
explicitly communicated, would not be obtained. In (40) the extra effect is
not only an answer plus an explanation of Mary's decision contained in

one utterance, but also an additional (weak) implication derived from the answer. For instance, if the contextual cues lead to the interpretation of Mary's utterance as a refusal, one could make an extra assumption that she is already bored or tired with the conversation. If her utterance is an acceptance of Peter's offer, we may assume that she is a hard-working and conscientious person. These weak implications are merely some of many possible assumptions which can be drawn during the process of interpretation. It does not mean that the hearer entertains all of them and perhaps more. The weak (related) inferences are drawn from background (contextual) knowledge and the speaker may not realise that s/he has triggered them in the hearer. This is due to the fact that "speaker meaning and hearer meaning are hardly ever identical" (Jodłowiec 2008:23), just as their contextual knowledge differs. The hearer may follow the weak assumptions or stick to the one which he finds most relevant, but regardless of his/her choice, implicatures, regardless if strong or weak, require the engaging of inferential processes in order to discover the intended implications in any context. Nonetheless, it should be noted that only the context provides the speakers in the dialogue with sufficient information which allows them to recover the intentions of the other person and interpret them as intended. Hence the dialogue, may stand as an example that implicatures "conform to our expectations that exploit our encyclopaedic knowledge in order to derive more global, non-truth functional aspects of interpretation" (Blutner 2007:45).

At the end of this analysis concerning the understanding of explicitly and implicitly communicated utterances, the processing and comprehension of irony and metaphors will be briefly discussed. The discussion may as well be extended to other forms of figurative language and humour, such as sarcasm, hyperbole, litotes, meiosis and synecdoche, which, in spite of producing different effects in a discourse, comply with the same principles of processing utterances. Although many people believe that metaphor and irony should be attributed to the study of literature and literary terms, surprisingly enough we readily implement them in daily communication due to their expressive force. Taking into consideration their sophistication and the fact that they are used with special purposes, some people believe that the interpretation of these figures of speech must be based on different and more complex mechanisms than the processing of other utterances. It can be also tempting to treat them as a breach or exception from the general standard procedure of working out the meaning of utterances, since their recovery entails a certain amount of flexibility in the understanding of concepts. A similar notion was demonstrated by Grice (see also Kumon-Nakamura et al. 1995) who believed that irony and metaphor violated the maxims of conversation (especially those of truthfulness), and that in their processing (being a two-stage process), understanding literal meaning precedes processing contextual information. In the process the literal meaning provides unsatisfactory and incompatible information for the interpretation of the utterance and, in consequence, inferential processes must be activated. However, psychological research shows that the comprehension of figures of speech requires neither processing at any extra level (Gibbs 1986) nor any violation of the doubtful (from the relevance-theoretic point of view) maxims or conditions. In fact, the comprehension of these types of utterances is said to be a one-stage process and no different from the processing of other utterances (Sperber & Wilson 1986).

In Relevance Theory, metaphors and irony, it is argued, fall into the same category and are analysed in the same way as non-figurative utterances. In the theory, utterances can be descriptions of an actual or desirable state of affairs or, as in the case of figures of speech, interpretations of an attributed or desired thought. Sperber and Wilson explain that:

"(...) metaphor involves an interpretative relation between the propositional form of an utterance and the thought it represents [and] irony involves an interpretive relation between the speaker's thought and attributed thoughts or utterances" (ibid. 231).

Among various stylistic devices, metaphor is one of the most frequently used figures of speech. As observed by Chandler (2009), metaphor is so popular that now it is often used as a general term referring to other figures of speech, such as metonymies or similes, which are regarded as special forms of metaphors. As described by Davidson (2000:333):

"[m]etaphor is the dreamwork of language and, like all dreamwork, its interpretation reflects as much on the interpreter as on the originator. [...] So too understanding a metaphor is much a creative endeavor as making a metaphor, and as little guided by rules."

This non-conventional definition of a figure of speech demonstrates that not only production but also the comprehension of a metaphor (and other stylistic figures alike) involves a creative and indirect use of language. Lakoff and Johnson in their seminal publication *Metaphors we live by* argue that human thought is fundamentally metaphorical, and that "the essence of metaphor is understanding and experiencing one kind of thing in terms of another" (1980:5). To illustrate the mechanism, let us return to example (20) and repeated below:

(20)   *He is a big brain.*

As we have previously mentioned, interpretation of this utterance entails an elaboration (broadening) of the concept, labelled in our encyclopaedic knowledge as BRAIN (organ, object) which is juxtaposed with an unrelated concept: HE (person). The metaphor in (20) forces the hearer to think of the used concept in some other than the accepted and common way (brain = organ), and to explore any possible additional implications derived from the utterance. The derivation of the two concepts compared in the metaphor (called *topic* and *vehicle*) is vital for metaphor comprehension.

As argued in the leading psychological models of metaphor understanding, the comprehension of the language devices is based on establishing common properties or relations between the topic and vehicle, through the means of analogy (see Gentner & Bowdle 2002), or category inclusion (see Glucksberg & Keysar 1990). As stressed by Bortfeld and McGlone (2001), the comprehension of a metaphor is conditional on the context, which determines the choice of salient properties necessary for the discovery of metaphor and its interpretation. In an appropriate context, the utterance (20) may be taken as an implication that the person ('he') is intelligent, talented, clever or sly. The metaphor can be interpreted in various ways by different people. Due to the differences in contextual and general knowledge among them, people attribute distinct properties to concepts. There is also a difference in processing novel metaphors, which are generally processed as comparisons, and the frequently used metaphors, which with time become conventionalized, are stored in our encyclopaedic knowledge with an acquired (secondary) meaning (Gentner and Bowdle ibid.).

A similar procedure is applied to the processing of, for example, metonymies. The only exception is that while metaphors represent the relation: 'X is understood in terms of Y', in metonymy 'X stands for Y', as illustrated by Evans and Green's (2006:182) example presented in (41) below:

(41)   *The ham sandwich has wandering hands.*

As the authors explain, in this case 'the ham sandwich' is not to be understood as a food item. In the example above, the entity is associated with some other entity, specified as 'having wandering hands'. Instead of a real ham sandwich, it refers to a customer who ordered it and who, as reported by the waitress uttering the sentence, behaved improperly. As observed by Lakoff and Turner (1989), the understanding of a metonymy is possible because both of the concepts (in the above case 'the ham sandwich' as the vehicle and 'the customer' as the target), belong to the same domain (restaurant) in a hearer's cognitive structures. The interpretation of a metonymy is heavily dependent on the accessibility of contextual cues, which make it possible for the hearer to interpret 'the ham sandwich' as an indirect way of referring to a person.

As stressed by many authors (e.g. Gibbs 1986, Barbe 1995, Yus 1998, Attardo 2001, Wilson & Sperber 2007, Giora & Fein 2007) and as revealed in numerous experimental data (e.g. Dews & Winner 1999, Ivanko & Pexman 2003, Pexman 2008, Sak-Wernicka 2010), context also plays a prominent role in the derivation of irony and other figures of speech. Tone of voice, facial expression and body language, together with other key aspects of context, determine the comprehension of utterances and their appropriate interpretation. Additionally, the context provides the information about the attitude expressed by irony or metaphor, this is because these figures of speech express many different and sometimes contradictory emotions.

Humour is ubiquitous in speech and its presence in communication is hard to be ignored. Due to a great variety of its forms and functions, humour is frequently and readily used in social situations to express manifold intentions, attitudes and emotions ranging from friendliness to jealousy and despise. However, no other form of humour is discussed so readily and obtains such an immense interest as irony in literature, including Relevance Theory (see e.g. Sperber & Wilson 1986, Giora 1998, Attardo 2000, Wilson 2006, 2009, Padilla Cruz 2007, Bromberek-Dyzman 2010, Hirsch 2011). In this framework, irony is claimed to be a second-order interpretation in which the speaker expresses "a thought about an attributed thought, as well as an attitude of dissociation from it" (Curcó 2000:268), this is called 'echo' (or 'the echoic effect'). As further explained by Jorgensen (1996), this type of "humour offers a way to attack another person while denying responsibility for the attack". The aim is to ridicule a speaker's utterance and attitude, and/or to express disapproval towards them. The echo may be direct and involve a repetition of the content of the speaker's utterance in the hearer's response, like in (42) below.

(42)   Mary: *I promise I won't be late this time.*
         Peter: *You surely won't.*

Alternatively, the effect may be attained in an indirect way, as shown in a previously discussed example (20b) and repeated here as (43).

(43)   Mary: *Steven tried to fix the cord but he didn't bother to disconnect it and now he's in hospital.*
         Peter: *Yeah, he is a big brain.*

As described by many authors, what is characteristic about irony is its diachronic nature in which words contradict intentions (Curcó 2000, Solska 2005). The utterances in (42) and (43) illustrate this phenomenon and in both of the cases the speaker says one thing and thinks another. Accordingly, in (42) Peter seems to confirm that he knows Mary will be punctual this time. In fact however, he intends to communicate that he does not believe in it at all and he is convinced that Mary will be late as usual. In the next example, the speaker ridicules Steve's mental abilities, which at first glance may be mistaken by the speaker's intention to express admiration to Steve's intelligence. Consequently, understanding irony involves a detection of the mismatch between literal and ironic meaning. This also involves a recognition of the speaker's attitude, thus following the principle of relevance. As explained by Yus (2000a, 2000b), the realisation of the incompatibility of an utterance to provided contextual information, facilitates irony detection. This follows the criterion of optimal accessibility to irony, which he put forward and which says:

> "[t]he processing effort required for the interpretation of the intended ironic meaning of an utterance decreases in proportion to the decrease in the number (and quality) of incompatibilities (detected by the addressee) between the information supplied by the inferential integration of simultaneously activated contextual sources (…) and the information provided by the proposition expressed by the utterance."

To sum up, metaphor and irony have been analysed in many literary and linguistic works, which tend to treat the rhetoric figures as extraordinary expressions which deserve special analysis. In Relevance Theory the use of creative language is regarded as no different than any other non-figurative utterance, as it undergoes the same processing mechanisms. Yet, as in the case of any utterance, comprehension of the figures of speech demands from the hearer contextual knowledge, in the absence of which these figures of speech may be misunderstood, misinterpreted and lead to miscommunication.

Misunderstandings and communication failures

Even if all the necessary conditions of successful communication seem to be met and both the hearer and speaker are willing to participate, the outcome of the communication process cannot be predicted in advance and the success of communication can never be taken for granted. As stressed by Sperber and Wilson (1986:45):

> "(…) failures in communication are to be expected; [but] what is mysterious and requires explanation is not failure but success".

Taking into consideration the individual differences in general knowledge, perceptual abilities, context selection and utterance comprehension discussed in the chapter, not to mention cultural[8] or generic[9] aspects, this assumption seems to be well-grounded. Additionally, if we realise that there are a large number of factors which have to be tuned at the same time in the context, we start to wonder how communication is possible at all. Due to the fact that problems in communication are no less mysterious than communication itself and they are "not always obvious, but often latent or so obscure that they are difficult to recognize" (Rehbein 2006:62), many theories avoid discussing them. Nonetheless, as we stressed at the beginning of the chapter, any pragmatic model of communication must be able to account for adverse situations, detect possible problems and elaborate on communication failures. The ostensive-inferential model of communication proposed by Relevance Theory and presented in this work, does not evade discussion on the issue. It describes and explains possible reasons for misunderstandings and also strategies of dealing with them. The problem of miscommunication is growing in popularity among researchers, who come to find various ways of describing communication failures with the aid of Relevance Theory, at the same time as referring to human cognition.

Generally speaking, in the communication process the hearer and speaker are responsible for communicating their intentions in the most effective and effort-saving way, so as to avoid mutual confusion and problems with interpretation. However, in making decisions about how to communicate intentions, "communicators take risks and sometimes fail, and addressees expect such failures to occur occasionally" (Sperber & Wilson 1986:159). A reasonable amount of confidence allows hearers, to

---

[8] For further discussion on cultural aspects of miscommunication see Bührig and ten Thije (2006)

[9] For further discussion on the relation between gender and miscommunication see Coupland et al. (1991)

eliminate minor errors in communication (such as slips of the tongue and misused words) which might be misleading for interpretation, and allows them to continue processing utterances without disruption or without the need to ask for additional explanation or correction. It also prepares them for more serious problems, the elimination of which requires taking special steps, or else communication will be in jeopardy. The most obvious sign of such a situation would be when communication is suspended for a short while, and the confused hearer has to take a step backwards in order to search for additional information necessary for the processing of an utterance. Also, he or she would need to utilise available processing strategies so as to make necessary repairs and arrive at a sensible interpretation (for negotiation and repair in miscommunication see Drummond & Hopper 1991, Bohus & Rudnicky 2008).

Although in literature we can find many different terms referring to problems with communication, such as misunderstanding, misinterpretation, miscommunication and a few more, in the relevance-theoretic framework there is no clear distinction between the terms. Outside Relevance Theory, McRoy (1998) distinguishes between 'misunderstanding,' which involves missing the intended interpretation, and 'misinterpretation', which reveals the differences between speakers' and hearers' beliefs about the world. Traum and Dillenbourg (1996:37) define 'miscommunication' as "action failure (the speaker fails to produce the intended effect), misperception (the hearer cannot recognize what the speaker intended to communicate), or both". As we can see, the definitions seem to overlap, and grasp entirely or at least to some extent, the same elements which affect communication. Hinnenkamp (2001:222) conflates the terms by saying that:

> "What all types of misunderstandings seem to have in common is the illusion of understanding".

Due to vagueness or the lack of differentiation among the mentioned terms, in our discussion we will apply our own definitions for the sake of coherence and clarity. Accordingly, each time we use the term 'misinterpretation' we will mean the inability to convey an interpretation (for instance when two interpretations are equally relevant and consistent with a hearer's expectation) or the conveying of an interpretation in another way than was intended. 'Misunderstanding' will be treated as a term referring to processing problems (such as reference identification or ambiguity resolution failure, etc.). 'Miscommunication' (interchangeably with 'failures in communication') will be regarded as an umbrella term embracing any of the possible problems which could lead to a break down in communication.

As we have already stressed, at any stage of communication something may go wrong. One or both of the participants may be blamed for it, or at times failure may be brought about by other factors beyond their control. Contrary to the Code Model which predicted that only noise could hamper successful communication, Grice's inferential model and Sperber and Wilson's ostensive-inferential model, admit that there are numerous factors which may lead to problems in communication, some of which are more apparent than others. Since the factors may affect communication collectively or individually, it is hard to decide what exactly has led to communication failure in a particular situation. By observing everyday acts of communication, we notice that failures occur more frequently than we realise. However, the vagueness and fleeting nature of these factors leading to miscommunication, explain why the issue does not get due attention and lacks systematisation. One of the efforts to describe problematic communication was taken by Mirecki (2002, 2004), who classified some, as he admits, failures in communication from the perspective of Relevance Theory (see Fig.1-7 below).

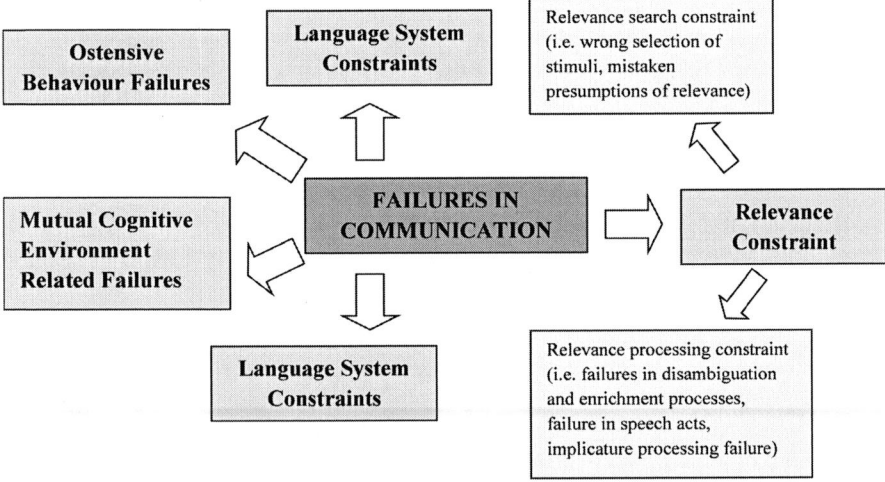

Fig. 1-7 Failures in communication (adapted from Mirecki (2004))

The classification of communication failures presented by Mirecki (ibid.), provides evidence that, directly or indirectly, they all are contextual in nature and boil down to the inability to retrieve contextual (linguistic or non-linguistic) information from one or many sources. Elaborating on this assumption, Bou-Franch (2002) claims that misunderstandings are either external and caused by factors such as noise or foreign language use, or participant-related and associated with a speaker's or hearer's capacity. As the author explains, misunderstandings may be caused by a speaker who suppresses contextual information essential for interpretation, or who uses ambiguous utterances. Also, a speaker may overestimate a hearer's ability of interpretation. On the other hand, a hearer may not be listening and may fail to interpret a current utterance because s/he is still absorbed with processing a previous utterance. Additionally, a hearer may not notice that the speaker has changed the topic, or may face linguistic problems in communication such as the inability to interpret an intonational contour. Finally, as Bou-Franch (ibid. 335) mentions,

> "an addressee may understand the meaning of the utterance but may reach some sort of deficient, partial understanding due to lack of cultural knowledge needed for a richer interpretation".

To sum up, miscommunication stems from a dissonance between the context envisaged by the hearer and that which is used by the speaker (Sperber & Wilson 1986). It emerges as a result of:

> "(1) misinterpreted ostensive behaviour of the speaker and misplaced intentions,
> (2) the lack of a mutual cognitive environment between participants,
> (3) wrong choice or processing of stimuli,
> (4) ill-formed linguistic input,
> (5) adverse environmental conditions" (Mirecki 2004).

As a result, not only a lack of contextual cues, but also an inadequacy of access may lead the interpreter to wrong assumptions. For instance, among other things, a speaker's ostensive behaviour and access to visual cues, which normally play a pivotal role in interpretation may in some cases cause misinterpretation. The fact that we see someone wearing black garments, sometimes contrary to our expectations, does not have to mean that one of the person's relatives has just died. Also, if we see a man and a woman eating out together, this is not necessarily evidence that they are in a relationship. Many a time our initial interpretations turn out to be impossible in certain situations, when this happens we are forced to look back over previous interpretations and find some more suited to the situation.

McTear (2008) further advocated that speakers' misconceptions about the world (including the so called 'pragmatic overshoot'[10]) may seriously contribute to miscommunication. Tzanne (2000) earlier reported that analysing the relation between context and misunderstanding, indicated that the roles of participants in communication were also important to the occurrence of misinterpretations. Also, apart from the main participants and audience, she elaborated on the role of a bystander who overhears an utterance and enters a conversation with mistaken assumptions. She also mentioned the case of 'intentional misunderstanding', when a hearer pretends not to understand and teasingly misleads the speaker.

In the light of what we have said, the real results of communication, being a complex process, can never be guaranteed. Mirecki (2008) went even further, claiming that human communication actually starts with misunderstanding and turns into successful communication, further misunderstanding or communication failure. The problem is that since there are no two identical interpretations, and that the thoughts of a speaker are not duplicated by the hearer, we can assume that what for one person may be a faulty interpretation, for another may be just another option that he or she conveys on the basis of his or her individual world knowledge, contextual information, linguistic and cognitive abilities. Hence the question remains when we talk about a misinterpretation and when it is simply a different interpretation which we did not entertain but someone else did. What should be classified as communication failure, or the inability to entertain any interpretation at all, and which is an additional assumption made during the inferential process?

It should be noticed that even if communication takes a turn for the worse, hardly ever do participants give up. Mostly they are determined to make the necessary repairs to sustain communication. Since our inferential abilities are geared towards maximizing the relevance of stimuli, even if at the cost of excessive mental processing, we look for any interpretation to satisfy our expectations, those which are consistent with available information. Additionally, as noted by Sperber and Wilson (1986:85):

> "[a deductive system is] a tool not only for working out the consequences of adding a new assumption to an existing representation of the world, but for guaranteeing the accuracy of any conclusions deduced from initially accurate premises (...) [and] exposing inconsistencies, and hence, inaccuracies, in any existing representations."

---

[10] a term introduced by Carberry (1986) indicating discrepancies between a speaker's and a hearer's view of the world

If faced with a problematic utterance (detected by the deduction mechanisms), a hearer tries to discover what led him or her to puzzlement and at which stage the problem could have occurred. Also the speaker whose utterance caused the confusion, understanding that what s/he said might have caused the problem, usually tries to recover what has led to such a state, makes corrections to provide the hearer with necessary information which was previously unavailable, or paraphrases his or her utterance. The strategic mechanisms employed in communication and described by Relevance Theory are based on the search for relevance, which governs both problematic and non-problematic communication discussed in this chapter.

Summary

The psycholinguistic model put forward by Relevance Theory rests on the assumption that communication (i.e. both comprehension and production) is tied to the search for relevance. This approach, drawing from a time-honoured tradition of linguistic and non-linguistic disciplines, provides a broad perspective on different facets of communication. Despite some criticism, the theory is presently among the most popular in the realm of pragmatics. Its contribution to exploring the nature of human communication is acknowledged in other disciplines within the theory of communication. Within the models presented in this work, Relevance Theory is the one which describes the mechanisms and processes co-operating together and controlling the effective flow of information, without evading discussion on problematic communication. Meeting the requirements imposed on fully explanatory and descriptive models, Relevance Theory attempts to find complete answers to pressing questions concerning language use, discourse analysis and interpersonal communication.

The theory expounds a seminal view on context which, as a central concept for all pragmatic theories and models, is not given with a situation in which the utterance or conversation is set, but is construed in the mind of an individual person on the basis of world knowledge, linguistic content, perceived phenomena and other available contextual cues. In this chapter, we intended to present the role of contextual information in the recovery of an intended interpretation. Throughout the discussion, we presented arguments that the comprehension of utterances is heavily context-dependent at each stage. Since our prior experience plays a significant role in the interpretation process, the conceptual organisation of an individual's knowledge was discussed. With presenting the information provided through senses, we intended to demonstrate how important perceptual abilities are for comprehension. Finally, our attention in the chapter was focused on the analysis of different types of utterances, in which the amount of inferable contextual cues varied. Having discussed the pragmatic sub-tasks involved in the comprehension of explicitly and implicitly communicated utterances, we turned our attention to figurative language and humour, and briefly presented their understanding on the basis of metaphor and irony.

This chapter was aimed at showing that access to contextual information derived from different sources, determines successful interpretation. Keeping that in mind, it is well-justified to ask if, at the absence of contextual cues, people are still able to interpret utterances. To be more precise, if blind people who have no access to visual information can understand utterances equally well and in the same way as sighted people. Before we try to answer these questions, in the next chapter we will first introduce the necessary nomenclature and present major findings concerning blind people and their pragmatic abilities, in comparison to the pragmatic abilities of sighted people from early infancy to adulthood.

CHAPTER TWO

BLINDNESS:
IMPLICATIONS FOR THE ANALYSIS
OF CONTEXT AND COMPREHENSION

Introduction

Despite the increasing application of pragmatic theories, including Relevance Theory, to the investigation of disorders and limitations in human communication, our understanding of the connection between visual impairment and comprehension is still very limited. Pragmatic impairment, being the domain of clinical pragmatics, is mainly associated with cognitive dysfunction caused by brain damage or injury[1], and discussed with reference to Asperger syndrome and autism (Happé 1993, 1995; Papp 2006, Loukusa 2007, Chevallier et al. 2009), schizophrenia (Livingston 1998, Gernsbacher et al. 1999; Langdon et al. 2002) and aphasia (Christiansen 1999). Nonetheless, according to Perkins' (2007) definition and classification, visual impairment falls into the category of secondary pragmatic impairment, that is caused by sensimotor dysfunction, which limits communicative choices in the sensorimotor system, and in consequence affects cognitive and linguistic abilities. The author states that visual perception plays a key role in inferential processes and its impairment may lead to problems with conveying the adequate interpretations of a situation. This is a result of restricted access to contextually relevant information.

In literature on the subject, we come across numerous confusing terms referring to this complication. For the sake of clarity, it should be specified that the most general term embracing any form of blindness (i.e. partial and total blindness) is visual impairment. When we refer to a person born blind, we use the term 'congenital blindness'. If a person lost his or her vision later during his or her life, the person is referred to as 'adventitiously

---

[1] In Perkins' terminology 'primary pragmatic impairment' (2007:108)

blind'. Conventionally, if we talk about an 'early-blind' person, we mean that s/he has been blind since infancy or early-childhood. The term 'late-blind' is greatly imprecise and may imply any period or age at which vision was lost, this could range from childhood to adulthood. Due to the fact that these terms will be used extensively in this and the subsequent chapter, the same nomenclature will be used over the entire span of the work.

Visual impairment has a profound impact on a person's development and functioning, these depend on, among other things, the severity of the impairment, the age of vision loss, the family and educational background, as well as personal and psychosocial aspects. If a person is congenitally or adventitiously blind, the facts that s/he lost vision gradually or rapidly, early or later on in his or her life, can have a critical effect on adult performance and comprehension, and may tell us a lot about which abilities might have been affected by the vision loss. Due to a large number of factors corresponding to visual impairment, visually impaired people differ from each other in the way they develop. Keeping in mind and accepting possible variations among individuals, we will attempt to analyse prior studies conducted on blind and/or sighted people (children and adults), and consider what effects blindness (congenital or acquired) may have on comprehension and communication.

The following chapter is intended to present critical points of current knowledge, and methodological approaches to the development of pragmatic abilities, which lead to competent language use as adults. As we argued in the previous chapter, context, as understood by Relevance Theory, is a set of individual assumptions about the world derived from general knowledge, linguistic input and perception. Accordingly, it is well-justified to assume that visual impairment encompasses all the three areas, which stems from the fact that not only are visually impaired people provided with perceptually impoverished information (for instance, the emotional states of a speaker, observable in his/her facial expression, gestures and body language), but also being born blind or blinded in childhood, their cognitive and linguistic development was marked by the impairment, and proceeded differently than in cases of sighted children. In other words, we assume that visually impaired adults may demonstrate certain problems with the comprehension of utterances, resulting from limited access to context, however their linguistic competence is not inferior to that of the sighted.

With presenting selected aspects concerning the pragmatic development of children (up to 7) with normal vision, and indicating the critical abilities achieved in particular periods, we would like to draw attention to the fact that vision lost at a particular stage of development, may affect certain abilities developing at certain times. Since only some aspects of pragmatic development can be marked by vision loss in people who are not congenitally blind but lost vision in childhood, and who have some prior visual experience, we assume that in some communicative tasks or situations, adventitiously blind people may be at an advantage, if compared to totally, congenitally blind people. In order to present certain limitations and difficulties in blind people's comprehension, we will compare the pragmatic development of sighted and visually impaired children, highlighting significant differences and developmental impediments. The discussion is aimed to preface the subsequent discussion on the comprehension of blind adults, and the ways in which they account for insufficiency, inadequacy, and a lack of contextual knowledge. In the literature review we will focus our attention on various aspects (also those discussed beyond the scope of linguistics) which influence comprehensive language use in communication, such as conceptual knowledge, non-verbal communication, extra-linguistic features of speech and implicitly communicated utterances.

Developmental pragmatics

In the previous chapter, we argued that pragmatics is the study of language in context, whose primary goal is to investigate the linguistic and extra-linguistic aspects of communication and the impact of the context on the process. As aptly summarised by Roberts (2005:217):

> "the domain of pragmatics includes phenomena at the edge of linguistics proper, the outcome of the interaction between purely linguistic structures (syntactic, phonological, etc.) and more general cognitive capacities and attitudes (inference, perception, belief, intentions, etc.)".

The broad and interdisciplinary perspective of language and communication provided by pragmatics, even if criticised in some circles, has grown in popularity. There has also been an emergence of pragmatic sub-disciplines, which cover the issues on the border of pragmatics and other linguistic and non-linguistic disciplines. Clear evidence of the growth of interest and research in pragmatics, is provided by the increasing popularity of developmental pragmatics, which, as described by Kasper and Rose (2003:68),

> "(...) addresses the "acquisition of the knowledge necessary for the appropriate, effective, rule-governed employment of speech in

interpersonal situations" (Ninio & Snow 1996:4), including the acquisition
of communicative acts and their realizations strategies, politeness, social
marking, and conversational ability".

This sub-discipline, preserving the interdisciplinary character of pragmatics,
aims to describe and explain the occurrence and development of pragmatic
abilities in children, toddlers and adolescents. Developmental pragmatics
also aims to determine the occurrence and development of mature
comprehension and the production of language which is

> "peculiarly fine-tuned to context, (…) shaped by the interaction between
> cognitive and cultural constraints of a given communicative situation (e.g.,
> shared knowledge, social status of interlocutors), on the one hand, and
> discourse-internal constraints on the organization of linguistic information
> (e.g. global text construction, online processing of speech production), on
> the other" (Berman 2004:15).

Along the same lines, in order to account for how children learn to use
language communicatively and investigate critical stages in language
acquisition, developmental pragmatics needs to look at the growth of a
human being from the perspective of psychological, cultural and linguistic
factors, which influence and shape a child's development.

Despite the growing interest, there is still a call for further research in
developmental pragmatics and a need for the updating of old. Since rapid
changes occur in the development of children, there is a constant need for
studies conducted on different age, gender and language groups in various
countries, in order to investigate the different aspects of communication.
Considering that past empirical studies also lack systematisation and
consistency, and the results obtained from the experimental work become
outdated in a relatively short time, data produced more recently very often
differ substantially, to the less contemporary. Children, it is noted, acquire
certain linguistic abilities quicker and earlier than in the past. The reasons
for this progress may be found in the many social, cultural and educational
aspects of present children's lives.[2] Thus being aware of that, as much as
possible, our discussion will concern and be based on the state-of-the-art
literature, found in these aspects.

In the following section, we will briefly discuss the development of the
pragmatic abilities critical for communication, with the intention of
contrasting it to the development of pragmatic abilities found in visually

---

[2] Since the analysis of historical-comparative research is not the main intention of
the chapter, although it is definitely needed and beneficial in developmental
pragmatics, for the sake of clarity, it will not be discussed in the work.

impaired children later on. We believe that a child's pragmatic development determines its future comprehension abilities. Therefore, it seems well-justified to assume that the process of pragmatic development in blind children proceeds differently than in the case of sighted children. If a child is congenitally blind (lost vision in infancy or late childhood), the consequences of the vision loss on the child's pragmatic abilities and development may be different and more, or less recognisable. Analysing the process in reference to the differences between sighted and non-sighted children on the one hand, and sighted and non-sighted adults, on the other, we can expose potential problems in language comprehension which are crucial for the analysis of the empirical part of the work.

Following Yule (1996:3-4), by the term 'pragmatic abilities', to which we will refer frequently in the following sections, we will understand:

> "(…) the ability to deal with meaning as communicated by a speaker or writer and interpreted by a listener or reader, and the ability to interpret people's intended meanings, their assumptions, their purposes or goals, and the kinds of actions (e.g. requests) that they are performing when they speak."

In a nutshell, the term refers to the ability to use language in any given context, thus understood as the ability to speak, understand and respond appropriately, as well as the ability to provoke verbal exchange using language in a communicative way, by means of available linguistic tools. Blaye et al. (1999) describe these abilities as "changes in the pragmatic landscape", enabling greater flexibility and adaptability in thinking. The term 'pragmatic abilities', covers comprehension and production, when both are performed in an appropriate context. The distinction we make brings to the mind the notions of competence and performance (introduced by Chomsky 1965, 1968), where competence signifies a speaker's linguistic knowledge and the tools necessary for comprehension. Performance on the other hand, denotes the product or realisation of a speaker's knowledge (production). Comprehension and production are the fundamentals of communication, they both involve developing pragmatic abilities, cognitive mechanisms and strategies, all of which progress constantly over the course of children's lives and are perfected as the children grow up.

In chapter one, we argued that general knowledge, perceptual information and linguistic input are the main sources of contextual assumptions. Since pragmatic abilities signify the recovery of a speaker's communicative intentions in a context, we believe that the abilities are determined and developed by experiencing the elements of the world supplied through the senses and by linguistic prompts a child is provided with by care-givers. Many factors can influence the comprehension of a speaker's utterances and behaviour in a particular context. As these factors often overlap and are difficult to distinguish, many of the pragmatic abilities naturally achieved in a child's growth go unnoticed. These are outrun by other more easily observable or prominent achievements, like progress in motor or kinaesthetic abilities. Consequently, many pragmatic abilities may be wrongly attributed to later stages of development, even though they might start to develop earlier.

To be able to understand children's development of pragmatic abilities, we need to take into consideration many factors. A child's cognitive, linguistic, and perceptual abilities along with emotional, motor, neural and social skills, play a significant role in the process of development, and make a complete and full-scale picture of a child's pragmatic development. As we tried to prove in chapter one, comprehension involves going far beyond the semantic information provided by words or phrases. It is a complex process of selecting relevant data from other sources, a sentence alone may not be able to provide for this. It entails relying on our own knowledge, intuition, feelings and beliefs. 'When children start to utilise this information', and 'how they come to understand utterances fully utilising contextual knowledge', will be of interest to us in the next section.

The development of pragmatic abilities in sighted children

As argued by some scientists, children do not come into the world unequipped with knowledge. DeCasper et al. (1994) claim that new-born infants recognise and are familiar with language, which is probably due to the fact that as they develop in the uterus, they can hear their mothers speak (Clark 2005). Another explanation for this phenomenon is offered by the nativist approach of Chomsky (1965), Lenneberg (1967) and McNeill (1968), who claim that children do not have to learn how to acquire language due to an innate biological endowment. The inherent knowledge is language-specific and contains general cognitive notions from which a child constructs linguistic principles (for more detailed discussion see e.g. Lightbown & Spada 1999, for comparison with other theories of language acquisition see Puppel 2001). The nativist approach also holds that this innate ability enables children to communicate, even from the earliest (pre-linguistic) period of their lives, even if they cannot yet express their thoughts in words. This assumption seems to be supported by Wilson and Sperber (2005:625), who maintain that due to innate endowment, children do not have to learn what ostensive-inferential communication and language really are, but they do need to learn how to use language for ostensive-inferential communication. The observations of deaf infants making different sounds in early periods of their lives (Brain & Mukherji 2005), and utilising gestural language despite a lack of verbal and gestural input from parents (Goldin-Meadow & Feldman 1977), provide further support to the claim that humans have a biological tendency to develop language communicatively.

However, it is still open to debate exactly which aspects of language are innate in a child's development. Reddy (1999), Trevarthen (1982) and Vedeler (1991), for instance, claim that children are born with communicative intentions. Plunkett and Schafer (1999) stress innate phonological discrimination abilities, and Kuczaj (1990) highlights innate lexical acquisition constraints. It seems evident that children come into the world equipped with some knowledge or at least 'disposition' (Becker 1990:11), and an ability to acquire knowledge in the relatively short periods of their infancy and childhood, but what they do know exactly remains a mystery for linguists and cognitive psychologists.

Locke (1996:280) once declared that:

> "the developmentally significant things that the infant needs to learn about spoken language are written on the faces, voices, and gestures of those who talk."

The material provided by visual and auditory perception is the main source of information for analysis and imitation, both which underlie the development of speech and communicative behaviour. Before a child is ready to pronounce its first words, it relies a lot on verbal and non-verbal stimuli in order to learn how to comprehend, interpret and use language for different purposes. As argued by Breheny (2001) and Tomasello (1995), concept formation and extension (emerging when a child is around 9 to 12 months), determines communicative development. A child, apart from receiving various signs and signals, utilises gestures, facial expressions and vocalisations to communicate its own intentions (Dromi 1999). Having observed that they are recognised by caregivers, children realise that their communicative goals have been achieved and thus the behaviour is reinforced.

Early (pre-verbal) communication is possible only if a child and the parent(s) establish 'joint attention', which is attempted by children as young as one year old (Clark 2001, 2005). In the relevance-theoretic framework, a mutual cognitive environment is a prerequisite for successful (verbal and non-verbal) communication. Although joint attention is by some regarded as evidence of mutual knowledge and also the developing of social-cognitive skills (e.g. Tomasello 1995, Clark 2005), Breheny (2001) maintains that the notion is too far-fetched and does not necessarily need to involve any of them. However, it ought to be acknowledged that, even if not yet fully communicative, the ability to establish joint attention with parents or caregivers is definitely the first sign of a child's communicative behaviour and interest in social contacts. Although parent-child interactions are initially unbalanced and dominated by the parent who initiates and engages any communicative situation, the child observes that its reactions trigger different (verbal or non-verbal) types of parental behaviour.

Besides, children are observed to associate different types of behaviour with particular feelings and emotions. For instance, they recognise the smiles of other people and in response they smile back. We assume that they associate this facial expression with safety, calmness and joy. If somebody frowns, children get surprised or scared, which indicates that the non-verbal stimulus arouses anxiousness, confusion, or fear. By observing parents and other people, they learn to treat people's ostensive behaviour as contextual information. This also gives the child an opportunity to associate different types of behaviour with various situations, and recognise other people's intentions, feelings and needs in various situations. As a result, many children by the age of two can understand what various gestures mean and what intentions they express (Tomasello et al. 1997). What is more, a study by Spencer (2001) performed on children (aged 3;1-5;11), shows that they rely on ostensive behaviour to a large extent, and divide their attention between verbal and non-verbal cues. The participants, if presented with either verbal or non-verbal cues exclusively, could not understand utterances or understood them literally. However, if provided with both verbal and non-verbal cues simultaneously, they understood intentions correctly. These findings showed that gestural communication is no less important or inferior to verbal communication, and plays a significant role in the process.

Apart from the visual stimuli provided by people's body language, and through observation of the surrounding world, a new-born child is attracted to various voices and sounds. The information supplied by auditory perception is of great importance in concept formation, since it allows the child to associate sounds and noises with various activities or objects, and categorise them accordingly. Additionally, sound recognition may turn out to be critical for appropriate interpretations, since it may give clear and strong evidence which will enable one to draw conclusions. Wilson and Wharton (2006) explain that the sound of a gunshot is a sufficient and relevant signal that someone has fired a gun. Although ordinary sounds do not always carry relevance, from early infancy auditory perception is of major significance in the development of pragmatic abilities.

Generally speaking, auditory perception involves the reception and analysis of any sound supplied through the sense of hearing. However, it should be noted that speech perception, as a special type of auditory perception, provides information which differs from that derived from sounds and noises. It requires engaging both cognitive and linguistic mechanisms for the analysis of the material provided. Technically speaking, speech is a complex system which poses challenges to human comprehension. It is not precisely known when and how children come to understand the speech produced by adults, but as pinpointed by Clark (2003), children need to break up individual words from the fluent flow of other people's speech, as well as account for variance among language speakers and work out systematic sound patterns. Speech as a source of information and means of communication contains ambiguities, inconsistencies and understatements, hence its understanding requires developing certain strategies of working out and tolerating the unknown and the difficult.

Surprisingly enough, despite the challenging task, just after birth very young children are able to distinguish their native language from other languages. It was observed that children if confronted by new (visual or auditory) information, demonstrated a higher sucking rate. This observation allowed Mehler et al. (1988) to demonstrate that neonates are able to tell their language from other foreign languages. In other studies it was noticed that very young children observe prosodic properties of language-specific speech (such as stress patterns (see Jusczyk et. al 1993)), and show preference for the prosodic properties present in recognising their own native language. Allen (1983) stresses that children aged between 3 and 5 make significant progress in stress acquisition, the results are that by the age of 7 they use stress systems on the same par as adults (see also Smith et al. 1982).

Although a child starts to express its needs and intentions very early through reflexive behaviour and vocalisation (as we argued above), it is not until the child reaches 12 months of age that it starts to pronounce its first words (Barrett 1995). In producing these words, children show a sensitivity to suprasegmental phenomena, and as stated by Lenneberg (1967:279):

"The first feature of natural language to be discernible in a child's babbling is contour of intonation. Short sound sequences are produced that may have neither any determinable meaning nor definable phoneme structures,

but they can be proffered with recognizable intonation such as occurs in
questions, exclamations or affirmations".

Snow (1999) supports the view claiming that even very young children are
able to distinguish different types of utterances by utilising acoustic cues.
To illustrate this ability, Goodluck (1991) refers to the example given by
Klima and Bellugi (1973), who observed that young children tended to
omit inversion in questions, as illustrated in (44):

(44)   *The skunk was black?*

By uttering the grammatically incorrect sentence in (44), the children
retained the rising intonation typical for interrogatives, which suggested
that from the earliest years the children were sensitive to prosody and that
they observed intonation in speech.

Despite the fact that the first signs of intonation acquisition are to be
observed before a child reaches the age of two, the process is said to
continue throughout the school years (Goodluck 1991, Menn & Stoel-
Gammon 1996). At that time the child has numerous opportunities to
observe the phenomena in different contexts, and learns to use prosody to
express particular (concealed or overt) emotions and attitudes. They also
learn to produce direct or indirect speech acts, and to stress more
prominent elements (information) in an utterance. A study by Grassman
and Tomasello (2010) performed on a group of two-year-old children,
shows that children at this age use prosodic stress to distinguish between
old and new information. The experimenters verbally described and
showed pictures to the children. Different objects were first introduced as
'new' information and some time later they appeared again as 'given'. It
turned out that the children spent more time looking at the referents of the
words which were stressed and new to the context.

A sentence-imitation task created by Bonvillian et al. (1979), which
was carried out on a group of three-year-olds, demonstrates that children
rely on intonation to increase their comprehension when given a mentally
challenging task. The researchers also observed that normal (rather than
flat) intonation at a normal speed (rather than too fast or too slow),
facilitates stronger recollection of knowledge. Choi and Mazuka (2003)
observed that children at the ages of 3 and 4 utilised prosodic information
in order to resolve ambiguous sentences, but only if they involved word-
segmentation. Even older children (5-6 years old) failed to resolve the
structural ambiguity involving phrasal grouping. This observation was
confirmed by Snedeker and Yuan (2007), who observed that syntactic
ambiguity is particularly difficult for children aged between 4 and 6.

Finally, Crystal (1999) listed other prosodic features (e.g. tone, pitch, pause and rhythm) which children utilise to derive meaning in their first years of life. However, as indicated by Choi (2003), the initial high sensitivity to prosody (observable in infants) changes into a more selective use of these features in the processing of language in preschool children.

The general thought is that the first stage of a child's development is highly dominated by perceptual experiences. We could say that the pre-linguistic period (or, using Piaget's (1951) terminology, the sensorimotor stage) prepares children for the use of language, and presents them with a myriad of new contextual cues, as a result of which children collect the experiences and form their own mental representations of the world. In this period children rely heavily on sensory stimuli, these are provided through engaging with different activities, in which they use all possible senses. As aptly observed by Adams (1972:10):

> "It appears plausible to think of the child's actions as manipulation of that part of the world presented to the child at any one time and to think of language as conferring on the child the ability to transcend the 'here and now'."

The 'here and now', as the first (physical) context for a child in the early period of its life, becomes the micro-world in which the child learns to understand communicative situations and engage in their first attempts to communicate with adults and other children. Since "language acquisition cannot take place in the absence of shared social and situational contexts because the latter provide information about the meaning of words and sentence structures" (Bradsford 2000), social contacts have an enormous influence on a child's pragmatic development.

By participating in various recurrent social situations, a child organises its world knowledge in the form of scripts, these facilitate the interpretation of situations. The studies by Hudson and Nelson (1983) and Hudson and Slackman (1990), show that children as young as four utilise scripts to interpret events. What is more, when presented with a story containing a 'birthday party' script, in which the order of some events was changed (the opening of the presents was before the giving of the presents and the eating of the cake was before blowing out the candles), the children noticed the mistakes and made necessary repairs. Among the tested age groups, the younger children (4 to 5) were observed to rely on schemata to a greater extent than the older children (6 to 7), who were more flexible in their application. This was related to the fact that the younger children's knowledge was much less developed than the older children's, which limited their inferential abilities and forced them to resort to better established knowledge. Nelson and Gruendel (1986) also claimed that even three-year-olds have well-developed scripts for more familiar routines, and seem to be aware of generality, sequence and central activities of events. However, they tend to disregard the context of the task in which the script is used, which suggests that a cognitive context provided by scripts is preferred.

Other than the scripts (or schemata and frames), children organise their acquired knowledge according to certain categories. Testing four and five-year-olds on their categorising abilities, Lecacheur et al. (1999), presented the subjects with small, plastic models of different pieces of furniture painted in red, yellow and blue. Some of the children were asked to place the objects in a cardboard house, and the other in three plastic bags. The study revealed that all of the children considered the context in performing the task, with the result that all the children in the first group sorted the pieces of furniture according to where they should be located in the house, and all the children in the second group sorted them by colour. At the end of the task, all the children were asked to sort out the objects again on a piece of cloth. Most of the children in the second group maintained their mode of sorting while children using the schematic mode exhibited a disorganised way of sorting.

In another study, Blaye and Bernard-Peyron (1996) observed that in groups of five, six and nine-year-olds, while performing a free sorting task involving eighteen drawings which could be organised taxonomically or schematically, both types were utilised in all age groups. However, the older children were more flexible in switching between categories on request, which adds evidence to the hypothesis that the ability to categorise develops and matures with age. As observed by Slackman et al. (1986), script organisation also changes with age. This is manifested in verbal reports provided by preschoolers and children at school age, among whom the younger children are more sensitive to the temporal order of events and report fewer component events, as opposed to older children.

As we attempted to show, the first period of a child's life is not a passive one. In fact, it is a period of extensive mental work, during which the child absorbs a large number of various stimuli received from different sources, and via all the available senses. The opportunity to experience and perceptually explore the surrounding world (which is essential for normal conceptual organisation), is enormously important in a child's pragmatic development. Having discussed the pivotal role of the senses in children's development, we will focus our attention on the early production and comprehension of utterances in young children.

Very young children are observed to attempt communication with other people from the beginning, and they consider context in the interpretation of other people's utterances and behaviours (Donaldson 1978 and O'Neill 1996). At first, they rely extensively on physical context, but as they grow up they make use of the knowledge they have already acquired (Leinonen 2003). This suggests that the ability to use contextually relevant information is age-related and improves as children grow older. As commented by Clark (2005:571-572):

> "The ability to make inferences in context appears critical because it affords children a basis for interpreting the speaker even when their knowledge of language is still minimal. It also provides a basis for any coping strategies that children rely on in the earliest stages of mapping meanings onto words (Clark 1997), and so helps them accumulate information across contexts as they start to fill in details about meanings for different words and constructions".

As the available literature indicates, even when children are two years old, they are able to make inferences and understand various utterances on the basis of contextually relevant information. This is provided that the utterances are communicated in a simple and comprehensible way. As described by Siegal and Surian (2009),

> "From the age of 2 years, children work hard to use a wide variety of cues (including mention of action, intonation and form of question) to guide their responses in conversation (Shatz 1978; Shatz and McCloskey 1984). They use their understanding of language to increase their knowledge of the world of people and objects and they use their knowledge of the world to increase their understanding of language".

By that time, children's use of language and comprehension is nearly equivalent to that of adults, which makes them 'capable communicators'. However, "they are more prone than adults to misunderstanding, miscommunications, irrelevancies" (Breheny 2001). Due to lower linguistic proficiency and underdeveloped strategies of comprehension, they fail in linguistically and cognitively demanding tasks such as incoherence or ambiguity resolution (Trueswell et al. 1999). Regardless of this fact, studies show that, as illustrated by the following example in (45) given by Ervin-Tripp (1970:82), children no older than two can correctly understand indirect requests:

(45)   *Why don't you put it in the wastebasket?*

By the age of three they can also understand some implicatures, as the dialogue (originally presented by Ervin-Tripp (1977:182)) in (46) below indicates.

(46)   A: *Mother (in car): I'm cold.*
          B: *Child (3;3): I already shut the window.*

However, the study by Noveck (2001) suggests that preschoolers have problems with interpreting the scalar implicatures introduced by modal verbs, quantifiers and connectives. Her experiment reveals that children aged between five and nine years old, fail to evaluate statements like (47)-(49) as true or false.

(47)   There *might* be a parrot in the box (or something else).
(48)   *Some* giraffes (but not all) have long necks.
(49)   Every farmer cleaned a horse *or* a rabbit (but not both).

As she explains, the poor performance of the children in this task is due to the fact that "younger, albeit competent reasoners, initially treat a relatively weak term logically before becoming aware of its pragmatic potential", and hence in comprehension they "are more logical than adults" (Noveck, 2001:165). This observation seems to be confirmed by Gualmini et al. (2001), who tested young children as to their understanding of utterances with *or/and* connectives, using the truth-value judgement task.

However, the experiments performed by Papafragou and Musolino (2003), and Papafragou and Tantalou (2004) do not lend support to this claim, and show that children in the early years (4;1-6;1) are sensitive to scalar implicatures in utterances, and possess the pragmatic-inferential abilities necessary for computing them. The researchers also argue that instead of focusing on the truth-condition of the utterances (which was the case in the studies previously discussed), the children should be asked to focus on pragmatic infelicity, which would much improve the results. In other words, they claim that the children would do much better, if presented with stories in which scalar implicatures were included. A study by Papafragou and Tantalou (ibid.) provides confirmation for this prediction. In their experiment they presented children with short scenes in which animals performed certain tasks. The children were asked to either award them with a prize if the animals completed the assignments, or refuse the prize if the task was left unfinished. For instance, the experimenter asked a toy parrot if it had wrapped all of the presents. When the parrot answered (50):

(50)   *I've wrapped some.*

the child was expected to refrain from giving the award to the parrot, since its response implied that not all of the presents had been wrapped. If however the experimenter asked the bear if he had drunk the milk and it answered (51):

(51)   *I drank it and I liked it.*

the child should have awarded the bear with a prize, having understood that the bear completed the task. Since "the success with scalar inferences depends crucially on the semantics of individual scalar terms and is subject to context effect" (Papafragou & Musolino 2003:256), the findings provide empirical evidence that children consider contextual information in the comprehension of utterances from early years.

Two experiments performed by Miller et al. (2005) provided further confirmation of the findings previously indicated. They showed that children aged between 3;6 and 5;5 do understand scalar implicatures with the word '*some*'. They also discovered that contrastive stress plays a significant role in the process and that children treat the unstressed '*some*' differently to the stressed one. In the first experiment, the experimenters presented the subjects (divided into three groups) with pictures of faces, illustrated in Fig.2-1.

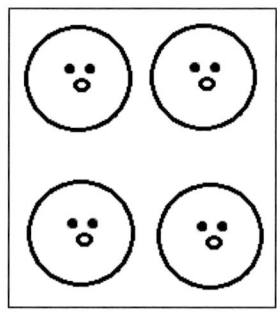

Fig.2-1 The Direct Instruction Task (adapted from Miller et al. (2005))

Each group was asked to follow the instructions, exemplified in (52a)-(52c), in which the word '*some*' was either unstressed and presuppositional (52a), stressed and presuppositional (52b) or unstressed and nonpresuppositional (52c).

(52a)   Make some faces HAPPY
(52b)   Make SOME faces happy.
(52c)   Make some HAPPY faces.

The dependent measure was the number of times in which the subjects did not act upon all the faces. The subjects, similarly to the adults who also took part in the study, treated the last instruction (52c) as not having a scalar implicature, this was contrary to the two previous ones which were interpreted as containing scalar implicature.

In the second experiment involving a Picture Matching Task, children were given three pictures, presented in Fig.2-2.

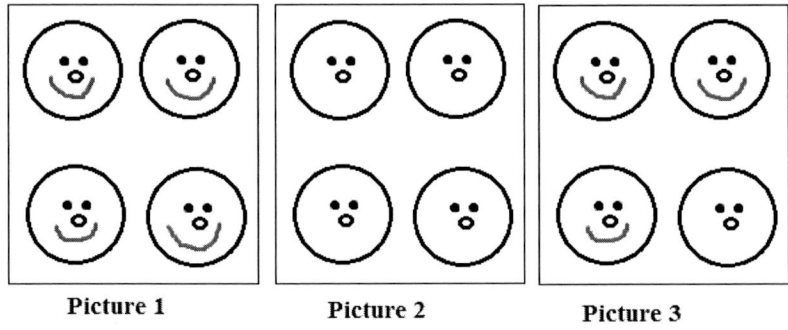

Picture 1   **Picture 2**   **Picture 3**

Fig.2-2 The Picture Matching Task (adapted from Miller et al. (2005))

The children were asked to indicate in which picture Pete (a toy introduced in the study) *made SOME faces happy* or *made some faces HAPPY*. The subjects were expected to choose Picture 3 in which only some faces were drawn, and reject Picture 1 and 2 in which either all or none of the faces were made happy. The experiment confirmed the results from the previous experiment, showing that children's interpretations of scalar implicatures did not differ from adults' interpretations, and depended on the prosodic features of the utterances.

As children grow older, their cognitive and linguistic abilities improve along with their conversational competence, which is "based on their developing sensitivity to linguistic and extra-linguistic context" (Siegal &

Surian 2009:304). Despite the fact that children by the age of 3 display a mastery of the lexicon and grammar of their native language, some findings show that certain complex inferential comprehension tasks are correctly performed only after a child enters school. For instance, although "the ability to understand simple forms of irony is normally present from around the age of 6" (Wilson 2006), it is only later that children can readily use and appreciate sophisticated ironic utterances and humour. As shown in an experiment by Hancock et al. (2000), younger children (at the age of 5 and 6) cannot yet correctly identify the intentions of a speaker using irony for compliments rather than criticism. This is illustrated by the following example (53).

(53)   *You sure are a bad basketball player.*

Dews et al. (1996) report that children tend to rate ironic criticism as less aggressive than literal criticism. Winner (1997) argues that even before children can understand irony they are able to interpret metaphors. An experiment by Andrews et al. (1986) confirms this claim, showing that six and eight-year-old children, when asked to interpret utterances like (54) below:

(54)   *There sure isn't any pepper in the soup.*

in two different contexts (i.e. either as a metaphorical statement referring to two children who are too tired to play, or as an ironic statement uttered by a customer in a restaurant who was served soup heavily seasoned with pepper, even after he had specifically requested no pepper), were more correct in understanding the metaphor than the irony.

What is more, it is argued that overextensions of concepts demonstrated in a child's early language, are their first attempts to use metaphor. 'Scar' meaning 'a streak of skywriting', 'crust' as 'street curb' or 'fire engine in my tummy' as 'stomach ache' (Winner ibid.), are just a few illustrations of the unconventional uses of words. By some they are taken as metaphors and by others as examples of misuse. Distinguishing between the two is extremely difficult and hence the subject raises many debates. Nonetheless, many authors claim that metaphoric abilities are present in preschool years and continue to develop into school age.

An experiment by Bucciarelli et al. (2003) performed on children aged 2;6 to 7, proved that the comprehension of different tasks involving speech or gestures (including irony and humour), increases with age and depends on children's mental representations and inferential processes. In the study, the children were shown videotaped stories in which direct and simple indirect requests, simple deceits, simple ironies or complex indirect requests were introduced. The simple direct and indirect requests were equally easy between the age groups, and complex indirect utterances were more difficult for all of them. Children in all of the groups performed equally well in the interpretation of speech acts and gestures, which implied that the way utterances were communicated did not affect their comprehension to the same degree as underdeveloped linguistic and extra-linguistic knowledge. Similar results regarding the comprehension of indirect speech acts, ironies and metaphors, were obtained by Shatz (1980), Gelman and Greno (1989), and Papafragou (1998), who gave evidence that comprehension is age-related and is still developing in preschool children. Therefore their success in pragmatic tasks cannot be guaranteed.

Clear evidence of progressing inferential abilities was found in a study by Bezuidenhout and Sroda (1998), in which children aged 2 to 6 were tested on their ability to assign reference as intended by a speaker. In the experiment, the children were asked to put the ball into *the* box. It was not specified which box the experimenter had in mind, since there were two boxes at close proximity. The most noticeable one for the child was not visible to the experimenter and the less salient box was visually accessible for both of the persons. Up to the age of 4, the subjects mostly chose the box which they found the most striking, while older children considered the perspective of the experimenter in the task. Most of the older subjects assumed that the experimenter must have meant the box that s/he could see, rather than the other. A child's success in the task pointed to its competence in the 'false-belief' task, and the ability to determine a speaker's intentions. As commented by Wilson (2000:423), the experiment reveals the typical developmental shift from naive optimism, when a child acknowledges a speaker's supremacy and competence and "makes characteristic mistakes in comprehension (in disambiguation and reference assignment (…))". Then comes cautious optimism, when the child considers the possibility of a speaker's incompetence or lack of knowledge. This transition coincides with the acquisition of the first-order 'theory of mind', which underlies comprehension in any communicative situation.

As we have tried to show so far, comprehension involves knowledge of the world which children acquire from infancy, plus their ability to draw inferences from people's utterances and behaviour. But 'to comprehend' also means to possess the mind-reading abilities to recognise the beliefs, needs and intentions of other people, without which no communicative situation can be successful. As illustrated in Piaget's Class Inclusion Task

(Inhelder & Piaget 1964), most children below the age of 8, having been shown a bunch of flowers (consisting of five tulips and three daisies), and asked if there were more tulips or more flowers, mistakenly chose tulips. Although the researchers concluded that the children who failed the experiment had not yet mastered classification skills, the children's performance might indicate that they in fact had already developed mind-reading abilities. The children, assuming that the examiner intended to check how well they could count or if they could discriminate between two kinds of flowers, answered according to their expectation of relevance (Politzer 1993). It would be a sheer oversimplification to assume that in failing the experiment children demonstrated a lack of logical thinking, this is because adults are also sometimes deceived by their expectations of relevance during communication. A good illustration of this is a series of 'Moses illusion' experiments (Natsopoulos 1985, Bredart & Modolo 1988, Sanford & Graesser 2006), in which a great majority of the adults who were asked the question in (53):

(55)   *How many animals of each kind did Moses take on the ark?*

answered that Moses had taken two animals of each kind, ignoring the fact that it was Noah not Moses who had taken animals on the ark. All of the respondents were aware of this fact, but processed the question according to what they thought the experimenter might have intended to find out.

One of the most recognisable studies investigating the development of mind-reading ability was performed by Happé (1993), who tested children in three age groups (up to 4, 4 to 6, and 6 to 7). Every child was given a standard false-belief task in which they were asked to watch Sally and Ann playing a ball. Sally put the ball away in a covered basket and left the room. While Sally was away, Ann moved the ball from the basket to a covered box. When Sally returned, the child was asked (56):

(56)   *Where will Sally look for the ball?*

In order to answer the question, the child had to consider not what s/he knew but where Sally thought the ball was hidden. The child passed the test if they pointed to the place where Sally had left the ball.

In the second part of the experiment the child was asked where Ann thought Sally would look for the ball. To answer correctly, the child had to understand that Ann thought Sally assumed that the ball was in the covered basket where she had originally put it, and not in the covered box. The results of the experiment showed that the first age group of children (up to 4) could not yet attribute mental states to other people and had not yet acquired mind-reading abilities. The second age group passed the first task but had problems with the second, and children between the ages of 6 and 7 passed both of the tests. However, Bloom and German (2000) argued that the children's performance in the experiment was hindered by the fact that the subjects were expected to display reasoning about the false-belief task rather than to solve the false belief task as such. This contributed to an overload of processing and posed additional difficulties. Nonetheless, due to the fact that mind-reading abilities require higher-order inferential processes, only older children are said to be able to rationalise about other people's states of mind.

In conclusion, the discussion (centring on the progress of a child's psycholinguistic mechanisms that govern early comprehension), provides evidence that the assessment of pragmatic abilities in early and late childhood is extremely difficult and burdened with inaccuracy. The data presented above provide a selective and representative treatment of the subject, which may not apply to individual children. Each child develops in their own way, hence idiosyncratic features at all levels of development are to be anticipated. From a substantial body of literature covering early language acquisition and with the aid of selected findings, we have attempted to substantiate our claim that context is the effect of perceived experiences which allow pragmatic abilities to be developed and perfected. The role of the senses in the process is not to be overestimated and forms a pervasive theme in literature. Excluding any of the senses from cognition could have serious consequences on a child's pragmatic development, in the next section the importance will be placed on vision and its significance, not only in concept formation but also in on-line utterance comprehension. As we said at the beginning of the chapter, the development of pragmatic abilities proceeds differently in the cases of visually challenged children. Therefore, it is important to remember that if little can be taken for granted about sighted children's development, even less can be asserted with reference to the development o blind children.

The development of pragmatic abilities in visually impaired children

Throughout infancy and childhood, "cognitive, motor, affective, communicative, and perceptual development are completely interwoven" (Warren & Hatton 2003:440). In the chain of the developmental dependencies and correlations vision, which "is the primary system of sensory input for human beings (…) [and] the basis for the majority of human learning" (Fazzi & Klein 2002:107), appears to be the link unifying and integrating all of the elements. Visual perception and the growing ability to comprehend perceived stimuli pertains to the development of psychological, social, physical, sensory and linguistic abilities. The relation between vision and cognition is discussed by many researchers, mainly with reference to the multiple functions eyesight has in cognitive processes. The study of children with visual impairments helps to illuminate the role of vision in cognitive development, which governs natural language use in communication.

Visual impairment can affect various areas of development and "may have very different consequences for the development of individual children" (Lewis 2003:38). Taking into consideration the channels through which blind children acquire knowledge, it seems obvious that certain differences in their development are to be expected. However, some visually impaired children overcome developmental milestones normatively, which implies that visually impaired individuals do not fall into one homogeneous group. The dissimilarities mainly result from different causes of vision loss, the severity of impairment, concomitant disabilities, children's age and, finally, parents' attention and assistance in the development and adaptation of their children.

In general, when discussing the development of visually impaired children there is a tendency to go to extremes, unduly underestimating or overrating their abilities which is probably caused by a lack of, or shortage of unequivocal data. All things considered, analysing the pragmatic development of visually impaired children it is more appropriate to refer to recurring or possible impediments. These may temporarily or permanently hamper their communicative skills but do not necessarily represent a developmental delay in the whole group. While certain problems are severe in some children and do not occur at all in others, many difficulties are overcome easily and early, while the others require greater attention. The difficulties should by no means be analysed as failures or delays, but rather as cues which allow us to better understand how blind children perceive and understand the world around, how they account for gaps in knowledge, and what strategies they employ in communication.

As observed by Frampton et al. (1969:173), the way that blind children use language reflects the problems they come across in acquisition and production. "The motor problems, the lack of experience, the disordered perception, the inability to organize what they [have] experienced, hostility, withdrawal from reality, insecurity, anxiety, immaturity, compulsive drives, and egocentricity" may all be observed in blind children's behaviour and speech. Language is a tool which exposes and

detects conceptual and linguistic difficulties and offers numerous problem-
solving strategies, this is particularly important in the case of blind
children.

Since a child's early development is dominated by the need to explore
the world around, everything that is in a child's immediate environment
and which the child observes, manipulates and examines, plays an
important role in the growth and formation of mental representations. The
opportunities to engage different senses in the process, help to construe a
complete and integrated picture of the world which is necessary for a
child's normal functioning. Vision is the medium through which the child
obtains immediate access to the elements in the surroundings and, as
argued by Finnello et al. (1992:34),

> "[it] is a key motivator for activity, for it provides consistent information
> about the environment and immediate feedback for and verification of
> other sensory experiences".

However, vision is not to be seen merely as a stimulus motivating children
to explore the surrounding world. As underlined by Dunlea (1989), vision
also plays a prominent role in a child's early linguistic development and
prepares them for competent language use in adult life. Therefore, we can
expect that the differences in the ways blind and sighted children acquire
information about the world, could lead to discrepancies in their
conceptual knowledge. Along these lines, Lowenfeld (1981:68) explains
that:

> "Blindness imposes three basic limitations on the individual:
> (1) in a range and variety of experiences.
> (2) in the ability to get about [mobility].
> (3) in the control of the environment and the self in relation to it."

These limitations have a tremendous effect on conceptualisation and point
to further problems in the cognitive development of blind children. These
will be discussed in the present and next section of this chapter.

As we argued above, following the views of Finnello et al. (1992),
visual access to the immediate environment encourages small children to
experiment with various activities aimed at exploring the world. Many
visually impaired infants however, are observed to display little interest in
objects and the external world in the first 12 to 18 months after birth
(Adelson & Fraiberg 1974, Fraiberg 1977, Bigelow 1995, Preisler 1995,
1997). As a result, it is also generally thought that various concepts may
be formed later in their development, of course this is when compared to

sighted children. Since visual perception is a spontaneous and automatic process, the acquisition of new concepts is performed effortlessly by children with normal vision. The touch which blind children utilise to a great extent in forming mental representations, can be characterised as an active and conscious seeking of the energy of stimuli (Dunlea 1989:10). Deriving information through this medium entails investing greater cognitive effort, in which case blind children might need more time and be slower in construing concepts than their sighted peers. This suggests that tactual information is not immediately made manifest and in some cases achieves lower relevance than visual stimuli.

Additionally, in construing their representations of the world on the basis of senses other than vision, children are provided with incomplete and impoverished data, and this could affect their comprehension and result in the occurrence of gaps in their knowledge. Many of these gaps remain undetected until adulthood or even sometimes throughout life. For instance, due to fragility, overall dimensions or possible danger, many objects (such as a fly-too small, a plane-too big, or boiling water-too dangerous) are unavailable for tactual exploration and even if a child can learn to associate the concepts with certain sounds (e.g. an insect buzzing, an engine roaring or a kettle singing), they are conceptually meaningless and incomplete without the possibility of seeing them. Aside from the potential limitations, "the experience that blind babies have of objects will be sequential and much less extensive than sighted children's visual experience" (Lewis 2002:51). While children with normal vision perceive an object as an integrated whole and can embrace all of its elements at once, visually impaired children examine it piece by piece, which may be a reason for their dissimilar understandings of various concepts.

Visual terms pose challenges to the imagination of blind children, and they understand visual concepts differently to the way most sighted people may expect. Contrary to what some sighted people may think, words denoting visual perception such as 'to see' or 'to look' are not empty or nonexistent in blind children's knowledge. In evidence, Landau (1983) described a blind girl who used to stretch her head and arms upwards or downwards when her parents told her to look up or down. The visual concepts of seeing or looking are generally understood by blind children as 'haptically explore' or 'haptically be aware of' (Landau and Gleitman 1985). Mills (1988:62) also mentions that some blind children use the word 'to see' when they actually mean 'to hear'. The following situation presents evidence for this:

"Lisa (3;3) is playing with her mother and other adult on the floor. The
tape recorder is running. Lisa had previously asked about the noise it made.
She starts to move away from the game.
Mother: *Where are you going?*
Lisa: *I can't see it.*
Mother and adult do not understand. Lisa moves so that her mother is no
longer between her and the tape recorder and orientates herself so that she
has binaural input but with her back to the tape recorder.
Lisa: *Now I can.*"

It appears that the way blind children understand words denoting visual
perception, mirrors the way in which they derive information and refers to
the senses they utilise most, these are touch and hearing.

While 'seeing' is an involuntary state and 'looking' is a more
conscious act for sighted people, the two acts are understood by blind
children in the same way as active and conscious exploration, both which
require some effort. Blind children's reliance on physical context
embraces the "here and now" which is accessible via tactual exploration,
this reliance is also visible in the way they understand certain concepts. It
is no wonder that blind children, having no access to information beyond
that of limited physical context, treat sighted people's ability to see the
surrounding world as the equivalent of clairvoyance. The following words
of a young blind girl explaining what 'to see' means to her, provides
confirmation for this presumption:

"It is like telling the future - because you know now that there will be a
tree, and I will know later, when I come up to it and touch it." (Marek
2000)

In these words can be found the very essence of how the concept of
'seeing' is understood and represented in the mind of a blind child. They
also demonstrate that touch is for visually impaired children what vision is
for the sighted: touch provides context for activities, without which they
would be meaningless and abstract. Tactual contact with an object is
evidence that the object exists and is within reach, hence its relevance is
automatically high and cognitive effort is adequately reduced. This
observation has strong implications in blind children's early education,
during which they should be provided with as many opportunities as
possible to 'watch' various objects with their hands.

From the first moments of their lives, children are also sensitive to
sounds and voices in their surroundings and are observed to turn their
heads in the direction of those sounds. In particular, blind children during
their childhood learn to depend on hearing and pay attention to auditory

stimuli much more than sighted children do. An experimental study by Ashmead et al. (1998), testing blind children, adolescents and adults (aged 6 to 20 years old), and sighted adolescents (12 to15 years old) on spatial hearing abilities, provides evidence for this claim. In the experiment, all of the blind participants proved to have greater skill in locating the distance and direction of sounds than the blindfolded, sighted group. This suggests that blind individuals learn to rely on auditory stimuli extensively, and in matters of hearing ability they are superior to the sighted.

It is interesting to note that from the perspective of a sighted person, many objects do not emit any sound at all, thus making them an unreliable source of information for a blind child (see Dunlea 1989). A contradictory view is presented by Marek (1999) who explains:

> "Not many sighted children would drop a lemon on the table to hear what it sounds like, and check that against the noise made by a potato or an overripe tomato. Sounds guide us towards a dropped coin, or draw our attention to an oncoming bus, car, or to the tapping of raindrops on the windowsill. Unless we are waiting for a bus, or a friend who is to give us a lift, engine noises will barely be noticed. Likewise, in order to check whether or not we are going to need an umbrella, we tend to look outside rather than prick up our ears to hear whether it is raining. Not so when you are blind".

This points to the fact that hearing may provide crucial information about various concepts, those beyond a child's reach in a both literal and figurative sense. In the same manner, auditory information may provide contextual implications in numerous situations. An engine roaring may provide clear evidence that the person who we have been waiting for has arrived. Rain pattering against the roof or windowsill indicates that it is actually raining. A knocking on the door signifies that someone is on the other side and expects us to open up. The ability to recognise and interpret this information is crucial for effective comprehension, that is why the various sounds which a child experiences in infancy and childhood are so incredibly important, especially in the case of blind children. However, taking into account the true nature of sounds which fade away very quickly, and "do not specify the characteristics of objects that are readily appreciated by vision and touch, such as shape, size, texture and colour" (Foulke & Halten 1992:45), hearing provides blind children with conceptually and contextually incoherent information unless accompanied by information from other senses.

In all honesty, little is known about blind children's perception of speech and the means by which they acquire phonology. Blind children's reliance on and sensitivity to auditory stimuli (which compensate for the lack of vision), may suggest that they are more dependent on the prosodic features of speech than sighted children (for similar view see Pérez-Pereira & Conti-Ramsden 1999). However, it is also speculated that the lack of vision may affect the discrimination, acquisition and articulation of some sounds (see Mills 1987, Hoff 2005). However, a study by Lucas (1984) in which blind and sighted children (aged 5 to 7) were tested on their ability to detect mispronounced words in stories, seems to contradict this statement. The blind children performed better in the task than sighted children, which means that their auditory perception is better developed. Although the matter definitely requires in-depth research and further elucidation, generally it is assumed that blind children do not differ from sighted children in the development of sound discrimination (for further discussion see Warren 1994 and Vihman 1996).

In literature, the impact of parents' speech on blind children's comprehension and production of language received much greater attention. In particular, differences in the language used by the parents of sighted and visually impaired children were of higher importance to researchers. Kekelis and Andersen (1984), Landau and Gleitman (1985), and Andersen et al. (1993), analysed the language spoken by parents of blind children. They discovered that the language contained more imperatives, wh-questions and labels, but fewer declaratives, descriptions and explanations in comparison to the language used by the parents of the sighted children. The parents of the blind children also initiated more topics, but mostly referring to their children's activities rather than to their environment, which in contrast was a recurring characteristic in the language used by the parents of the sighted children. The investigators assumed that the language used by the parents had a profound effect on their children's linguistic development, and might point not only to conceptual but also to linguistic differences between blind and sighted children.

Indeed, the assumptions of the influence of parents' language on children's linguistic abilities seem to be confirmed, and characteristic differences between blind and sighted children's early language can finally be observed. For instance, as reported by Pérez-Pereira and Castro (1992), visually impaired children use hardly any words to describe objects, even fewer words to describe other people's actions than of their own, and more labels for objects than for general categories. Some classification problems were also observed by Friedman and Pasnak (1973), Hatwell (1985), Dunlea (1989) and Dimcovic and Tobin (1995), who all investigated the abilities of different age groups in classification tasks.

One of the earliest experiments investigating the verbal and tactual classification abilities of visually impaired subjects (aged 6 to 14), was performed by Friedman and Pasnak (ibid.). The findings revealed that the younger age group with some functional vision, made fewer errors in the tactual classification task than the totally blind children. Interestingly however, they observed no major differences in the verbal classification task between the two groups. Additionally, no significant differences occurred in the group of the older participants (aged 14), with or without residual vision.

Hatwell's study (testing congenitally blind and adventitiously blind children), confirmed the previous results and revealed the advantage of the latter group in several classification tasks. Dimcovic and Tobin, in turn, compared sighted (blindfolded) and visually impaired children (6 to 11 years old) in a series of odd-one-out tasks. These involved selecting an object, different with regard to shape, size, area or position, from the four presented. The tasks turned out to be very challenging for the visually impaired children, of whom only the two oldest participants performed the tasks successfully. The sighted children, who also found them difficult, did much better in the tasks. This indicates that vision plays a significant role in the categorisation and classification of objects. Additionally, it should be noted that even though the blind children achieved worse results when challenged with the objects, they performed much better if the tasks involved the selection of strange words, which again suggests their dependence on auditory stimuli.

Apart from the classification and selection of the concepts mentioned above, vision has been proven to play a pivotal role in the process of early language development. Dunlea (1989), analysing the role of visual information in the emergence of meaning, considered sighted and visually impaired children in their comprehension of the semantic relations of words. The study revealed serious difficulties in the latter group, which, as the investigator suggested, points to problems with "the schematization of events perceived in the world" (Dunlea 1989:90) and a delay in the acquisition of semantic concepts. Among other things, Dunlea argued that the blind children used fewer semantic relations. For instance, they were observed to avoid talking about new information that had references to the location of objects or actions (i.e. the relation 'action/state + location'). The blind children were also observed to persistently use the 'entity + attribute' relation, as if they were unable to separate the entity from the attributional features with which the objects were associated. Over the course of the study, the blind children were also reported to speak in self-centred ways using the 'agent + action/state' relation, this was contrary to the sighted children who referred mostly to the actions performed by other people rather than just themselves.

As further attested by Andersen et al. (1984, 1993) and Miecznikowski and Andersen (1986), Dunlea's experiment revealed the blind children's tendency to use stereotypic and formulaic speech. What is more, she maintained that due to a lack of access to visual information and with no opportunities to observe the social context in which words are used, the process of lexical extension is seriously restricted. Consequently, the blind children's speech was observed to be less creative and lacking in idiosyncratic terms (invented by the children themselves), which definitely had an effect on the development of their linguistic abilities. Harris (1992:115) offered an explanation of this tendency, saying:

> "For, although the blind children acquired new words at roughly the same rate as sighted children, they did not show the same pattern of development. In comparison to sighted children, the blind children's use of words was rigid: They were generally very unwilling to extend their initial use of words either beyond the scope of their own action or to unfamiliar objects. This makes them very different from sighted children who (...) very rapidly extend their use of individual words."

Dunlea's experiment touches on a subject which is scarcely discussed in literature, which places it among very few studies investigating the role of vision in early linguistic development. Despite this fact, some scholars have criticised the study and demonstrated a dissimilar view. Landau (1995) and Norgate (1996), for instance, claimed that the study was methodologically dubious due to the fact that the techniques used in the experiment did not allow for the manipulation and recognition of objects. These as we know provide crucial information about concepts, specifically for children with visual impairment. By the same token, Pérez-Pereira and Conti-Ramsden (1999:100) question the research saying that the children:

> "have many limitations in talking about visually perceived actions performed by others at a distance, visual qualities of objects, locations of actions, or identifications of entities, unless these actions and entities are accompanied by information that can be perceived through senses other than vision".

This brings us to the conclusion that the assumption that blind children demonstrate delayed or inadequate concepts, is in fact too far-fetched. Foulke and Halten (1992) explain, and we lend support to the view, that:

"it is by the way of perception that both those who see and those who do not see acquire the information they need (…) and carry on the activities in which they engage; but to a considerable degree, the sense data they process in order to acquire this information are different".

In light of these words, it is crucial to understand that blind children do not necessarily perceive the world around wrongly, but simply differently. In other words, they perceive the world as much as their visual limitations and sensory compensation allow them to.

Considering the limitations and differences mentioned above, it is well-justified to assume that blind children's conceptual knowledge is different and that the vocabulary they use is much poorer than that of sighted children. For instance, blind children are observed to use fewer words for concrete concepts, functions and qualities of objects. The studies by Kephart et al. (1974) and Murphy and Vogel (1985) also revealed that the blind children did not use as many words to describe different objects as sighted children, and that they tended to omit elements to which they may have been oblivious. For example, Kephart et al. observed that, blind 5 – 7 year-old children (when asked to describe what a child looks like), mentioned only some body parts and disregarded others (for instance, ignoring fingers and ears). What is even more important, as the investigators mentioned, the children could not understand even the basics of how the body parts were connected. Murphy and Vogel in turn discussed the case of a boy who did not know that his house had walls, probably because he had never explored the house around. The same observation was confirmed by Kephart et al., who observed the same peculiarity among blind children describing a house. In the experiment, the sighted children were reported to most frequently mention walls and roofs, this was contrary to blind children who focused on the element which they had access to and could touch most frequently, this is the door (see Fig.2-3).

Since the children frequently had opened or knocked on the door, but never touched the roof, their immediate association with the concept HOUSE was the door, while the retrieval of other less accessible elements was much more difficult. Additionally, some blind children might not realise that inner and outer walls (especially when some are smooth and the others are rough to touch) are just the same, and that the walls in the kitchen are shared with other rooms.

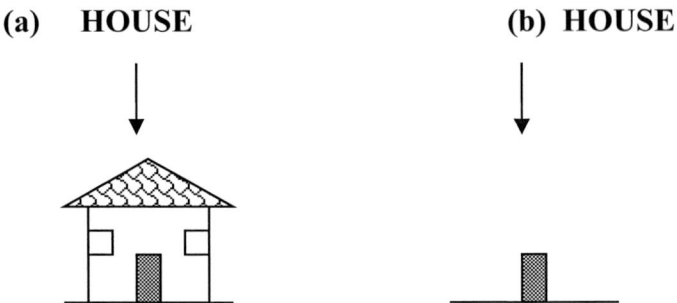

Fig.2-3 Differences in understanding the concept HOUSE between a sighted child (a) and a blind child (b) (based on the study by Kephart et al. (1974)).

Another interesting example was presented by Gibbs (1981), who described a six-year-old girl who wanted to touch a ceiling in the garden with a very long stick. The girl assumed that if there was a ceiling in the house which, as she had been shown by sighted adults, could be touched with a long stick, there had to be a ceiling in the garden. From sighted people's explanations that the sky and clouds are high above, she also inferred that she would need a very long stick to reach the ceiling in the garden. There is no doubt about the fact that the child's assumptions were carefully thought over, logical and made perfect sense, even if they were false. They also exposed inaccuracies in sighted people's explanations and an inability to help a blind child understand certain concepts and the laws of nature. This example shows that, since the comprehension of spatial relations requires not only the 'here and now' accessible to blind children by touch, but also the synchronising of different elements and utilising background knowledge about the physical world (which in the case of blind children is very limited), understanding certain concepts is particularly problematic.

Due to lack of vision and the differences in general knowledge resulting from visual impairments, blind children frequently come across concepts which they cannot understand. This ultimately leads to the occurrence of certain gaps in their knowledge, which if undetected, in due time may result in comprehension problems not only in childhood and adolescence, but also in adulthood. A good illustration of this happening is an example offered by Chapman (1978). The author refers to the utterance of a visually impaired child who, having heard a cow bellow, asked:

(57)   *Which horn did she blow?*

In a similar vein, the dissonance between already acquired knowledge and new information makes blind children ask innumerable questions, such as the following (58)-(61) taken from Blagden and Everett (1992) and Marek (1999):

(58)   *What colour is the wind?*
(59)   *How can you see a big mountain through a small window?*
(60)   *I know how fish swim but how do they walk?*
(61)   *If you can see me through a closed window, why can't you see me through a wall?*

These intriguing and thought-provoking queries not only reveal inconsistencies and inaccuracies in blind children's cognition (caused by inaccessible visual concepts), but also they show how the children having limited knowledge and access to the environment can analyse, assume, conclude and perform logically and pragmatically complex operations. Furthermore, these questions point to the difficulties that blind children face in the comprehension of visual concepts, among which one of the most problematic is the concept of colour (as illustrated by (58) above).

Neither touch nor any sense other than vision alone can provide comprehensible information of what colour really is. Since "one cannot feel colours" (Millar 1986) and since colours cannot be heard or felt, but at the same time nearly everything can be described, characterised and categorised using colours, being familiar with the concept of colour turns out to be an important part of world knowledge. For blind children colour is a permanent property of an object, understood in sensory terms and frequently associated with other, more tangible features. That is why, when a blind child feels a breath of wind across their face (as illustrated in (58)), automatically they assume that it must have colour.

The same tendency was observed by Urwin (1981), who gave an example of a four-year-old girl associating 'dark' with a cold and damp coal shed. Even more interesting associations of white as 'a wedding dress', blue as 'the sea and a warm beach' and green as 'freshly cut grass' were presented by Marek (1999). Analysing the associations, it seems evident that the way blind children understand colours is connected with their first experience of particular objects described by sighted adults. As a result, individual blind children can give different examples of objects falling into a given colour-category, but the most accessible, tangible and/or appealing achieve the highest relevance and become the strongest association.

Children also deduce the meanings of visual concepts, associating them with the contexts in which they heard sighted people use them. Faulty or incomplete mental representations (e.g. DARK standing for 'damp, cold' as illustrated by Urwin's example), if not verified in other contexts and appropriately explained, impinge on the occurrence of misunderstandings in communication and the possible construing of other faulty concepts. As illustrated in the following sentences (62)-(65), the misunderstood concept of DARK hinders the accurate interpretation of utterances:

(62)   *I don't like clothes in* DARK (*damp, cold) *colours.*
(63)   *It's getting* DARK (?damp, cold).
(64)   *The* DARK (*damp, cold) *man is very handsome.*
(65)   *The man was standing in the* DARK (*damp, cold).

The word 'dark' can refer to many different things, have different meanings and also different syntactic functions. In all of the cases above (62)-(65), 'dark' has little to do with coldness and even less to do with dampness, hence a mistaken understanding of the concept can distort interpretation.

In the same manner, blind children not only assume that whatever they can feel has colour, but they also project this assumption onto abstract notions. The examples presented above show that the concept of colour is only partially understood by blind children, and presents them with manifold problems since the concept is very broad. Not everything has one colour and objects can change colours (e.g. unripe fruit). Different parts of objects can differ in colour, and colours can have different shades. One can distinguish warm and rich colours (unlike *hot and *poor colours), but they have nothing to do with emitting heat or earning money. Awareness of that requires extensive knowledge of these concepts and can be obtained through detailed explanation from the sighted.

The example (58) presenting a blind child's difficulties with understanding the concept of colour, also involves understanding of other problematic concepts. These are transparency and perspective (also shown in (61) and repeated below).

(61)   *If you can see me through a closed window, why can't you see me through a wall?*

Explaining the concept of perspective without referring to 'looking through something' or referring to colour (both of which are understood differently by the blind), seems very difficult or even impossible.

Additionally, the questions (58) and (61) demonstrate that "mistaken assumptions are sometimes very well evidenced" (Sperber & Wilson 1986:39) and carefully thought over, but still vision is the missing element which allows the assumptions to be verified. As explained by Lewis (2003:56), "vision can provide a context for events which helps [a] child make sense of them". From the perspective of the blind child who asked the question in (61), it is illogical that a parent cannot observe them playing in another room inside the house, but can see them playing outdoors looking out of a window, which is similar to a wall in touch.

Another example of a well-grounded (but false) assumption is repeated in question (60) below,

(60)   *I know how fish swim but how do they walk?*

in which the child logically infers that if people and animals (for example dogs) can both walk and swim, fish should also be able to do it. Never having observed a fish swimming himself/herself, the child has come to this conclusion on the basis of the 'well-established knowledge' which gave rise to the anomalous/faulty representation in the first place. This can be depicted in the following way presented in Fig.2-4.

Fig.2-4 The visualisation of the concept of FISH formed by a blind child (Sak-Wernicka 2009)

The lack of necessary information does not allow for the assumption to be either strengthened or rejected, and leads to the occurrence of dissonance. The words of the child in question are in line with the words of de Beaugrande and Dressler (1981:93-94) who noticed that:

"Humans are evidently capable of intricate reasoning processes that traditional logics cannot explain: jumping to conclusions, pursuing subjective analogies, and even reasoning in the absence of knowledge".

It seems evident that the lack of knowledge and visual access does not stop blind children from trying to understand unfamiliar (and challenging) concepts and from forming their own mental representations. The extraordinary ideas they offer about different elements of the surrounding world also prove that they are not naive, incompetent and do not take everything for granted, but on the basis of established knowledge they try to form new concepts and make new assumptions. By asking questions like those illustrated above, it is evident that blind children need information explained properly to them in order to verify their previous assumptions, those perhaps which would not be detected or explained otherwise.

Another problematic concept for blind children which we would like to briefly discuss is presented in question (59). Having no or limited access to very small objects (like insects, dust, grains or drops) and bigger objects (e.g. buildings, machines, planets), the children are oblivious to what size they really are and cannot make actual mental representations of the objects. However, apart from the problematic objects, in their surroundings there are elements which they are familiar with and which they have explored thoroughly. With reference to only these objects they try to understand the unfamiliar and unexplored elements of reality, as illustrated in (59) above, and repeated below for convenience:

(59)   *How can you see a big mountain through a small window?*

The child, who could feel around the window, concluded that in order to be able to see something through the window the object must fit the size of the window, unaware of the perspective which is accessible only through visual perception. The dissonance between the old and new assumption appears when the child is told that a mountain is bigger than a window, and realises that the window cannot embrace the mountain. Perspective is a sensation received by our eyes and processed by our brains. Blind children, having no access to this information, will find it difficult to understand the concept of and the various utterances in which it occurs.

Aside from colour, perspective and transparency, there are other concepts which involve visual perception and which may be misunderstood by people with visual impairments. A detailed comparative study of blind and sighted children (aged between 7 and 9) conducted by Jaworska-Biskup (2009), demonstrates further differences between the two groups in comprehension and exposes gaps in blind children's understanding of visual and spatial concepts. The two groups were asked to perform a series of tasks, which among other things involved making word associations with concepts (such as *grey, pale, sparkling, checked etc.*), explaining the elements of nature and processes (like *rainbow, lightning, dust, mist, sky and mould*), and finding similarities and differences between concepts (for example: *needle/bee, leaves/petals, fireworks/lightning*). Although the blind children offered numerous associations with the concepts (most of which were similar to the sighted children's), some of their ideas were too vague or imprecise (e.g. *a yellow egg* or *a sparkling pen*). Additionally, they frequently used stereotypic speech and had problems with explaining what certain expressions (like *a pale face*) meant. As reported by the experimenter, the major gaps in understanding concerned the concepts presented in Table 2-1.

Table 2-1 Gaps in knowledge and erroneous responses provided by blind children (adapted from Jaworska-Biskup (2009)

STIMULUS	RESPONSE
red	*window*
yellow	*a kick*
grey	*grapes*
silver	*shoes*
golden	*shoes, car*
blue	*screen*
tan	*a person is fried, chocolate is tanned, a tanned person is black and yellow*
wrinkles	*hollows, appear when you have a long bath, when you are angry, only old people have them when they are 50 years old, spots on the face, I have many wrinkles, my hands are wrinkled*
vein	*pumps the heart*
striped	*a man can have stripes when he is angry*
sparkling	*smile*
star	*triangle in the sky, grey, small, like a lamp*
rainbow	*dark circle, small circles in the sky, appears in the afternoon and in the evening, colourful sticks*
sky	*similar to the earth*
mist	*similar to sky, a kind of meadow, like a curtain*
plane/bird	*the difference between a plane and a bird is that a plane cannot fly into the bird and a bird can fly into the plane*
dust	*like sand, powder*
lace	*something worn by a king*[3]

---

[3] The study was performed in the children's native language (Polish). The word 'koronka' (lace) was confused with 'korona' (crown).

The study also showed the effect that age had on the performance of the children, among whom the oldest children performed the most successfully.

Other than the concepts discussed above, Hall (1982) presents still other concepts which are problematic for blind children, and can be classified according to the following categories summarised in Table 2-2.

Table 2-2 Problematic concepts for blind children (based on Hall 1982)

Aesthetic terms[4]	Spatial terms	Quantity	Time	Size	Qualities
handsome	in front	more	today	big	old
beautiful	behind	less	morning	small	young
ugly		half	evening	little	similar
		quarter	night	medium	
		enough	before	fat	
		pair	after	thin	
		kilo		long	
				short	
				deep	
				shallow	
				longer	
				smaller	

The list is definitely not finite and can be extended by other problematic concepts and categories. Warren (1994:62), for instance, explains:

> "In adapting to everyday life, it is not vital to understand these characteristics at the level of physical laws or theories, but it is important to understand that basic concepts of physical regularity. For example, when released objects fall down rather than up, and other things being equal, this is a perfectly reliable property of the physical world".

Similarly, Hall (1982:16) explains that while for sighted people spatial concepts may be obvious, for blind children they may be less so. Elaborating on this, she says:

---

[4] For the study investigating the understanding of aesthetic terms on a group of blind adolescents (aged 11-12) see Piskorska (2008).

"Imagine yourself facing a table with a chair in between your body and the table. The chair is pushed under the table. You are facing the 'back' of the chair but you are facing the 'front' of the table. This is so because the chair has a front and a back which are inherent in the definition of chair. Your position in relation to the chair does not determine its front or back, which never change. On the other hand, the front or back of the table is determined by the position of an observer in relation to the table. The front or back of the table changes as the observer changes position".

These and other spatial relations may pose additional difficulties for blind children's comprehension.

It is generally assumed that the differences mentioned above, along with potential difficulties and gaps in knowledge, are the main impediments in the linguistic and pragmatic development of blind children. However, despite a serious deprivation of visual experience, many blind children develop language relatively normally and similarly to sighted children. It should be also underlined that, unless visual impairment is accompanied by concomitant disorders, it does not affect the intellectual abilities of a person. This has been well written about in literature (see e.g. Begum 2003).

Even before children learn to use language efficiently and communicate verbally, they readily engage in interactions with other people. Adults' words, gestures and facial expressions trigger various types of behaviour, providing evidence that even young children are eager to take part in the communication process. However, the lack of direct access to visual information experienced by visually impaired children has its consequences in interpersonal communication, which rests on the ability to recognise and interpret ostensive behaviour and to express one's own intentions ostensively. We can expect that blind children, who cannot observe other people's body language, will be unable to imitate different types of behaviour, which impairs and considerably limits the repertoire of gestures and facial expressions which are generally utilised in communication. It is also possible that these children will be reluctant to engage in social interactions and that they will be less successful in expressing their intentions. What is more, many blind children may be unaware of the role they play as participants in communication, and as a result they remain passive and irresponsive, especially if they have already got accustomed to being rarely prompted or encouraged to interact (Rogow 1982).

The assumptions mentioned above have been supported in numerous studies investigating the non-verbal communication of blind children. Rogers and Puchalski (1984), for instance, observed that blind infants produced fewer gestures aimed at engaging parents to interact as compared to sighted children. Troster and Brambring (1992) reported a limited amount of facial expressions and Pérez-Pereira and Castro (1995), Preisler (1991) and Rowland (1983), also found an absence of conventional gestures in blind children. Parke et al. (1980), in the analysis of sighted and non-sighted children's frequency and appropriateness of using non-verbal cues (i.e. smiling, nodding and raising eyebrows), showed that blind children smiled more and nodded less than sighted children, but that these instances happened at the appropriate moments. Surprisingly enough, they raised their eyebrows as often as sighted children, but often when it was not expected or appropriate.

Research also revealed that blind children use different patterns of gestural language. Urwin (1984) described the behaviour of a blind boy who dropped his head when he was listening, which to many of us signals just the opposite. Seminal work by Fraiberg (1977), who in her longitudal study observed blind children from the age of 12 months old, indicated that blind children also used spontaneous vocalisations less frequently than sighted children. Also, they rarely initiated communication. As argued by the researcher, establishing joint attention with the blind children was difficult, and this affected their ability to socialise. However, the same study demonstrated that blind children could respond to verbal requests and express intentions verbally at approximately the same age as sighted children, which suggested that many pragmatic abilities developed normatively and were unaffected by vision loss.

Although blind children are said to be able to recognise other people's intentions, numerous studies testing blind children on 'theory of mind' (hereafter we will refer to 'theory of mind' as ToM) abilities demonstrate that attributing thoughts and feelings to other people poses serious problems. Landau and Gleitman (1985) for instance, discuss the case of a blind three-year-old girl who had to come very close to a person to demonstrate her new clothes. As argued by the researchers, the girl could not take the perspective of the sighted person and considered exclusively her own point of reference. Evidently, the problem with the understanding of the concept of seeing contributed to the problems with the ToM. Without fully understanding this concept, the girl was unaware that a sighted person can see from a distance and that seeing is different from touching in this matter.

In another study, McAlpine and Moore (1995) gave a group of visually impaired children (aged 4 to 12) an interesting task: they asked them to explore a food container and milk carton in which there were not, as one might have expected, food and milk, but a sock and some water. Next, they asked the children what somebody who had not explored the contents of the two objects, would think were inside. They observed that the youngest totally blind children in the group failed the false-belief task. These findings were confirmed by Minter et al. (1998) in a similar experiment performed on blind and sighted children (5 to 9 years old). In the first part of the experiment, the children, instead of a food container and milk carton, were given a warm teapot to touch, inside which instead of warm liquid there was sand. Then, the children were asked what they had at first thought was inside, and what their friend would have thought there was in the teapot. Generally, the sighted children gave incorrect answers much less frequently than the blind children (10 per cent). The latter made fewer mistakes in the theory of mind task if asked about their own initial thoughts (42 per cent of wrong answers), rather than somebody else's (52 per cent of wrong answers).

In the second part, bearing similarity to Happé's 'Sally-Ann' experiment, one experimenter put a pencil in a box. When he left the room, another person moved it to another box. The children's task was to answer where the first person would look for the pencil when he returned. The test was passed by 80 per cent of blind and 100 per cent of sighted children. Taking into consideration all of the studies examining blind children's theory of mind, in the last experiment we can observe a definite progress in their performance. In light of the previous studies, the findings suggest that mind-reading abilities progress with age, even if blind children may be a little slower in acquiring them. They also indicate that due to lack of vision children may not always be able to control or follow changing circumstances, therefore wrongly interpreting what other people think. Contrary to sighted children, who observing different situations and people's reactions in these situations, are better able to imagine other people's feelings and thoughts, blind children have limited access to what is actually happening. Problems with second-order interpretations may also be a result of the fact that blind children are more focused on the 'here and now'. For instance, the moment they knew what was actually in the container or teacup, they were very careful not to make a mistake and adapted their knowledge appropriately. A study by Pring et al. (1998), in which blind and sighted children were asked to attribute mental states to characters in two stories involving sarcasm, pretence, persuasion or lying, showed that blind children had a more limited knowledge of social interactions and hence were less successful in judging the mental states of other people.

Despite these impediments in blind children's development, in many areas sighted and blind children are reported to develop on a par with each other. Bigelow (1990) and Lueck et al. (1997), argue that the emergence of speech in both sighted and non-sighted children occurs at approximately the same time, and that the sequence of developmental milestones is similar in both groups (Sacks 2006). This is thought to be even if certain differences in language acquisition and use can be found. Since the lack of vision limits the understanding, interpreting and acquisition of various concepts, many blind children use words (being phonetic, syntactic or semantic realisations of the concepts) in the contexts in which they first heard them (Dunlea 1989). They do this without extending them to other situations or meanings (Andersen et al. 1984). Consequently, they tend to use formulaic speech more frequently than sighted children. To illustrate this, Peters (1994) gives an example of a two-year-old blind child who used *Didja* ('Did you') to indicate that something had just happened, as illustrated in (66) and (67):

(66)   *Didja find it.* (I found it).
(67)   *Didja dump it out.* (I dumped it out.)

It is also a frequent occurrence that the achievement of pragmatic abilities signals the development of linguistic and pragmatic competence, and at the same time obscures the identification of serious problems in language use. Rogow (1982) gave an example of a ten-year-old congenitally blind boy, who despite speaking in full sentences and imitating the speech of other people with precision (considering tone, pitch and other prosodic features), could not ask questions, express his needs verbally or initiate a conversation. As described by Rogow, the boy's speech "seem[ed] to lack purpose or relation to the context in which it occur[ed]" (1982:21), which indicated serious problems in language acquisition and use.

The extensive production of echolalia (i.e. repetitive use of words or phrases outside a meaningful context) is frequently used by blind children as a compensatory strategy (Prizant 1985). Although it is said to be typical and very frequent in autistic children, it is also observed in normally developing sighted children for a short period of time. In many children it is a normal stage of language development in which they learn how to use language and communicate, even if they do not understand everything which is said by adults. Yet if the stage lasts too long or is particularly pervasive, it means that a child has got lost somewhere between what words really mean and how to use them in contexts. Some children, like the boy mentioned above, may produce long and complex utterances that they have heard, but they disregard the context and this contributes to other people's confusion.

As we have already mentioned, many studies comparing the performances of blind and sighted children, point to differences in the use of speech acts and linguistic development in both groups. For instance, as reported by Dunlea (1989), they use more imperatives than sighted children, which is typical at a very early stage of language development. The children are also observed to use more attention-seeking expressions and refusals, but fewer assertions and expressions to denote offering or showing something than sighted children. Besides, more frequently than sighted children do blind children use speech acts with the intention to gather information (Burlingham 1961, Kekelis & Andersen 1984), and produce more questions, as revealed in a study by Erin (1986).

Testing blind, visually impaired and sighted children (aged 4 to 10) on their frequency of question-asking, the investigator asked the children to explore various household items which were collected in one box. The study demonstrated a significant correlation between the degrees of vision and age in children's performance. The youngest and totally blind children were the most frequent askers of questions, most of the time using wh-questions. Yes/no questions were the second most frequent, particularly used when the children produced guesses. The sighted children asked questions much less frequently. Among those they produced, one could hear a preference for rhetorical questions, these were used to perform a social, rather than knowledge-seeking function.

Due to the fact that blind children are said to lack creativity in their use of language (Fraiberg 1977, Urwin 1984, Dunlea 1989, Dunlea & Andersen 1992), the general belief is that they have problems with understanding figurative language. The ability to understand simple metaphors, irony and other figures of speech is observable in sighted children during preschool years. What is known about when blind children begin to understand figurative language is close to nothing. Although many researchers hold that "children with visual impairments are particularly vulnerable to missing out on this type of development" (Pagliano et al. 2007:267), there is a serious lack of experimental data to support this claim.

One of the very few existing studies examining the comprehension of verbal humour in blind and sighted children (aged between 7 and 15) was performed by Tait and Ward (1982). In the experiment, the children were asked to label short texts as jokes or normal texts. The findings revealed that success in the task depended on the age and IQ of the participants, not on the degree of vision loss. Blind children proved to be no different from sighted children in this task, and this conflicts with the general assumption that blind people have problems with understanding humour.

A study by Kennedy (1993), examined the drawings of blind children (aged 6 to 14) who were asked to illustrate a spinning wheel and a running man. The study revealed that the children were certainly able to employ metaphor in their drawings. The children's 'non-literal' pictures showing the spiral movement of a wheel and a man with his knees up, bent arms, and extra leg indicating his motion (see Fig.2-5), were observed in all blind participants regardless of age. This might suggest that they are not so different from sighted children when it comes to understanding metaphor.

Fig.2-5 Metaphorical depictions of a spinning wheel and a running man made by blind children (source: Kennedy 1993:231, 233)

Many researchers also report that blind children have difficulties with understanding and using deictic terms. Among others, Mulford (1981), examining blind and sighted children on the acquisition of spatial terms (*this, that, here, there*), observed some discrepancies between the groups. As the researcher underlined, blind children demonstrated a delayed acquisition of these terms and certain errors in their use of these terms could be observed, even in children aged 6. The study indicated that blind children were able to use proximal terms (*this, here*), before they learnt to use distal terms (*that, there*). No such order could be distinguished in the cases of the sighted children.

In a similar study, Bigelow and Bryan (1982) attempted to examine blind children on their acquisition of locational terms (*in, on, under*). They discovered that the children found it much easier to place an object in relation to themselves than in relation to some other object. Other studies have also revealed that blind children have a tendency to refer to themselves as '*you*' instead of '*I*' (see e.g. Mulfort 1981, Dunlea 1989,

Pérez-Pereira & Conti-Ramsden 1999). Fraiberg (1977) offers an interesting explanation of this phenomenon, saying that children deprived of vision demonstrate a delayed acquisition of 'self-concept', and this contributes to the problem. Andersen et al. (1984) provide another explanation, claiming that deictic terms are strongly related to the role that the speaker plays in a communicative situation, something which blind children may not have grasped yet. Perfect (2001) predicts that the problem with the usage of '*you*' instead of '*I*' may also be the effect of delayed echolalia. The lack of vision may also affect the understanding and use of other words, especially the words which refer to objects insufficiently, or those never explored by the children, thus leading to the emergence of so-called 'verbalisms'. It seems well-justified to assume that in the contexts where vision provides the major cues to meaning, blind children may have major difficulties in comprehension (Landau & Gleitman 1985).

To conclude, the impact of visual impairment on the development of pragmatic abilities and early communication is still an under-discussed issue, one which raises many doubts and questions. The available empirical data are in most cases either outdated or selective to the extent that drawing conclusions on their basis is either difficult or impossible. Many findings involve the observations of a few individual children, this may raise controversy and may lead people to question the validity of the results. Little is known about what blind children find unproblematic, and there is still a tendency to downplay their mental growth, describing it as delayed or seriously affected, therefore disregarding successes and the progress they make in other areas.

From the available body of literature, it is safe to say that greater flexibility in the comprehension of (explicit and implicit) utterances in both sighted and blind children, progresses with age and experience. Logical reasoning, deduction mechanisms and the application of inferential processes greatly depend on children's maturity, competence and background conceptual knowledge. No matter if blind or sighted, children utilise the same cognitive processes in order to retrieve sensible interpretations consistent with their expectations of relevance. Due to perceptual differences between sighted and visually impaired children (some of which have been mentioned in this chapter), the comprehension and formation of concepts in general knowledge are not the same between the two groups. Consequently, these differences may have an influence on the way utterances are interpreted, this is following the principle of relevance in which the first accessible assumption based on contextual knowledge is chosen. The question is if the differences between blind and sighted children are also present in adults who were born blind or lost vision in childhood. Also, the question is whether the blind people can overcome comprehension problems related to their lack of visual experience and direct access to contextual cues.

The cognition and comprehension of blind adults

Despite the general interest of researchers in some aspects of blind children's development (including discussions on the cognitive, linguistic and communicative differences and difficulties they demonstrate), little attention has been paid to blind adults' psycholinguistic abilities and communicative performance. Consequently, there are hardly any studies embracing the transition from childhood to adulthood, or comparing the performance of blind children to that of adolescents and adults. If there were, they could provide evidence for the progress in the developmental areas presented in the previous sections. Some interest in blind adults' abilities and difficulties can be observed in the realm of neuroscience (covering neuroanatomy, neuropsychology and neurolinguistics), which investigates "the nature of human mental processes in relation to brain anatomy, its physiology and functions" (Puppel 2001:144).

A great majority of the available studies concerning blind adults concentrate on perceptual differences, orientation and mobility training, as well as various aspects of blind people's social life. However, it seems to be ignored or totally overlooked in literature if a blind adult, similarly to a blind child, has problems with certain cognitive tasks. It is not known how their language comprehension differs from that of sighted adults, which in consequence gives rise to many misconceptions about blind people. These definitely affect their social lives, career opportunities, interpersonal relations and self-esteem. For instance, as reported by Smith and Kandath (2000), many sighted people tend to patronise blind people, treating them as immature and their condition as not so much limitation but rather retardation. Some sighted people when turning to blind adults speak loudly and slowly, while hearing is not a problem at all. Sighted people are also embarrassed to use common phrases with 'see', 'look' or 'watch' in the presence of the blind, because having no or little knowledge of blind people's cognition they think it may offend the visually handicapped.

A handful of studies examining blind adults in most cases involve young adults (usually academic students), but studies investigating older people (from working age to retirement) of different educational attainments are entirely missing. There are scarcely any studies dealing with cognitive differences between congenitally and adventitiously blind adults. All things considered, it is unknown what effect visual impairment really has on comprehension and the interpersonal communication of adults, a lot can (and should) be researched in this area.

As reported by the World Health Organization (WHO), approximately 314 million people worldwide are visually impaired, among whom 45 million are blind. The number of blind adults is increasing due to health conditions connected with longer life expectancies. There are as many as 1.4 million children (under 15 years old) who remain blind until adulthood[5]. It is estimated that there are 100 thousand blind people in Poland, of whom 73 per cent are members of the Polish Association of the Blind (hereafter we will refer to the Polish Association of the Blind as PAB). It is reported that only 8 per cent of the totally blind members are employed, usually in local branches of the PAB, public institutions or sheltered employment establishments. A large number of blind people at working age are eager to work but cannot find a job. The PAB also discloses that as many as 95 per cent of all visually impaired adults are unemployed, on unemployment benefit or receive a disability/retirement pension.

Among the available scientific literature can be observed two leading approaches to blind people's abilities, in which they are described as performing worse or so dissimilar to sighted adults that comparison does not seem possible. There are hardly any reports of the superiority of the blind over the sighted in comprehension tasks, and blind people are generally assumed to be less competent participants of the communication process than sighted adults. However, a lot of experimental data are inconsistent or contradictory, and this makes it extremely difficult to draw any valid conclusions. Additionally, most researchers working with blind people observe considerable variations between individuals in all manners of tasks. As a result, no general behavioural, cognitive or emotional patterns typical for visually impaired people, can be found and there are "no known consequences of congenital blindness or visual impairment that can be seen consistently in all adults with congenital visual impairments" (Welsh & Tuttle 1997:78).

The lack of homogeneity in this representative group stems from the complex nature of visual impairment and the manifold effects it may have on individuals. The etiology of the impairment, visual acuity, past visual experience (or lack of it), additional disabilities (diagnosed or latent) as well as access to (mainstream or special) education and assistive technology, the support of relatives, and finally personal traits have an enormous impact on blind people's "sensory abilities, cognitive abilities,

---

[5] http://www.who.int/mediacentre/factsheets/fs282/en/

motor abilities, psychosocial abilities, travel skills, and independent living and vocational skills" (Welsh & Tuttle ibid.). For the sake of systematisation of what has been said about blind people's cognition and comprehension, and in order to detect the effects blindness may have on adults, we will follow the same order in the analysis of adults as we presented in the previous sections about blind children. We will start from perceptual and conceptual knowledge and end with linguistic and pragmatic abilities.

As we discussed above, children deprived of vision have limited access to certain concepts. The lack of prior visual experience and the necessity to rely on senses other than vision (providing insufficient perceptual input), result in the incomplete and impoverished conceptual knowledge of abstract terms, elements of the surroundings and laws of nature. It is not fully known which of the problematic concepts are successfully surmounted by blind children and ameliorated through appropriate education, nor is it known which of them disappear over the course of development and which are never fully understood. As observed by Welsh and Tuttle (ibid.62), "[a]s a consequence of growing up without vision, many adults may not fully develop certain abstract concepts, which in turn can sometimes result in functional difficulties". It is also possible that the lack of needed intervention reinforces faulty concepts formed in childhood, adolescence or adulthood.

While young children very often reveal certain cognitive difficulties in the utterances they formulate, it is much more difficult to detect and eliminate the problems in blind adults. This is because their utterances may not expose any gaps in knowledge until certain issues show themselves unexpectedly during natural conversation. A good illustration of this is reported by Smith (1987), who described a congenitally blind woman convinced that a plane flaps its wings when it flies. Since she had not had any opportunity to verify this assumption, until late adulthood she had believed that planes fly in the same way as birds. It seems evident that the woman, probably in childhood, must have had the concept of flying described to her by a sighted person who confusingly compared a plane to a bird which moves its wings when flying. From the perspective of a person who has never seen either a plane or a bird, the assumption is well-grounded, but nonetheless faulty. The example clearly indicates that sighted people's knowledge of blind people's mental representations of the world is very limited.

An interesting method of learning about how blind people perceive and understand certain concepts is to analyse their drawings. From pictures made by blind people who have little or no previous drawing experience, we can infer that they use different drawing techniques (some considering vantage points) in presenting the detailed and accurate pictorial representations of various objects and their functions (see Kennedy 1980, 1993; Axel 2003 for review). One of the earliest studies using this method was performed by Katz (1946), who asked blind adolescents to draw some random objects and after a few weeks he asked them to recognise what they had drawn. The participants successfully recognised the drawings in over 75 per cent of cases, which proves that what they had drawn was in no way accidental. Afterwards, Katz swapped the drawings to find out if the participants could recognise the drawings made by their companions, he obtained similar results. He also observed that many of the drawings were very similar to the ones produced by sighted children, which means that a large amount of conceptual information can be obtained through tactual exploration, so long as the integrated and elaborate images of objects are provided.

Although one may think that drawings as a research method are more appropriate for children or adolescents rather than adults, a number of experiments performed by Kennedy and his colleagues show that these drawings can tell us a lot about the conceptual knowledge of blind adults and the progress they have made in conceptualisation since childhood. For instance, in one of his studies, Kennedy (1980) asked blind adults to draw a dining table. In most of the cases it was drawn as a rectangle with four appendages. Some participants also used other vantage points to produce the drawing (see Fig.2-6 (a)) and offered thorough explanation of how different perspectives change the depiction of a table.

For instance, as reported by Kennedy (1993:108), they said:

"If you're looking straight down, you'd draw a rectangle without legs, because you won't see them (…) If you drew it directly from the side, you'd only see two legs (…) but to see it this way [as a rectangle with four legs] you'd have to be under the table."

This explanation seems to demonstrate a full understanding of the concept of a table, just taken from different perspectives. However, when Kennedy asked the participants to complete the picture of a table by adding legs to a rhomboid (oblique projection) or trapezoid (convergent perspective) as a tabletop, only one person considered the rhomboid shape as a typical rectangular tabletop, just taken from a different perspective (see Fig.2-6 (b)). The others assumed that the shapes indicate unusual tabletops. None of the participants (congenitally, early or late blind students) completed the pictures appropriately.

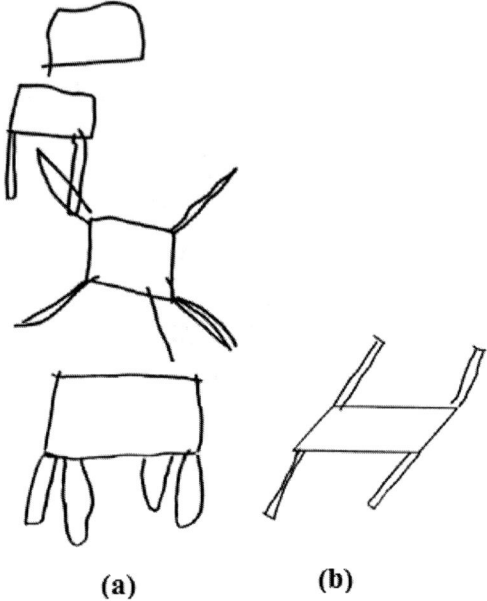

(a)   **(b)**

Fig.2-6 (a) Four drawings of a table made by blind adults using drawing conventions and vantage points of their choice. (b) The drawing of a blind person depicting a table in oblique projection (source: Kennedy (1993:109-111))

In the same experiment, blind students were asked to draw a hand with one finger on top of the other. The depiction turned out to be problematic for almost all participants, who either gave up or thoughtfully engaged the experimenter in discussion so as to get some cues. The difficulty arose from participants' problems with understanding spatial concepts which, as we argued above, are also to be observed in blind children. Having been told that the finger on top is the one that we can see and the one underneath is not seen, they correctly omitted the overlapping lines as shown in Fig.2-7 below.

Fig.2-7 Drawings of hands with crossed fingers by blind adults (Kennedy (1993:98))

Kennedy also asked blind adults to draw a glass so as to show its roundness. Many of the participants commented that there are many ways in which a glass might be drawn and they used different techniques (e.g. an 'open' glass vs. a 'closed' glass with the upper rim), the presentation of the 'pictorial pun' (Kennedy 1993:106) representing the roundness of a glass turned out to be difficult (see Fig.2-8).

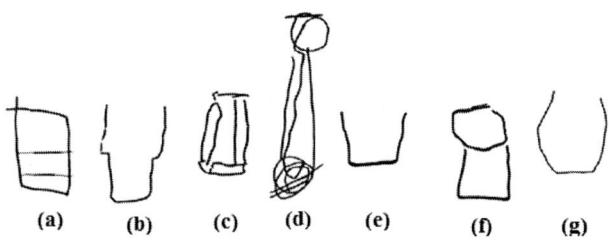

(a)   (b)   (c)   (d)   (e)   (f)   (g)

Fig.2-8 Different attempts at presenting the roundness of a glass by blind adults (Kennedy (ibid.100-105))

Some participants presented a glass with thinner or thicker lines (e.g. (a) and (b) above), an indicated upper rim and bottom (e.g. (c) and (f)), and curved walls (e.g. (b), (e) and (g)). Out of many attempts, no one showed an eclipsed bottom or top of a glass except one participant who showed them as circles (presented in (d)).

Analysing all the findings, Kennedy argued that "blind people draw using the same outline system that governs their recognition of haptic pictures" (ibid.95). It is also easily observed that the utilitarian value of the representations (in which each line stands for some element or feature), dominates the aesthetic merits, these seem to be less important. These representations bear similarity to the ones produced by the sighted children and adults, those with little practice in drawing.

The same method employed to investigate blind and sighted children, has revealed some discrepancies in the understanding of visual and spatial concepts between the two groups (see e.g. Bendych 1994, Millar 1994, Więckowska 2006, Jaworska-Biskup 2009 for review). Comparing the studies of blind children and adults, we can say that although more complex concepts and their representations (e.g. oblique projection, convergent perspective, overlapping of objects/elements, depiction of features such as roundness, rotating or manipulating objects mentally) may still pose a problem for blind adults, they present a better understanding of concepts than young children deprived of vision. What is more, the studies give evidence that blind adults can obtain relevant information about objects and concepts through tactual exploration, which (if accompanied by detailed explanation) does not necessarily put them at any disadvantage in terms of perception or cognition.

In two earlier studies: Kennedy et al. (1972) and Kennedy and Fox (1977), decided to examine blind people on their ability to read and understand pictures. They presented 34 sighted adults (blindfolded) and 8 blind adults (students of Harvard University) with pictures which were either imprints or projections of hand-sized objects (hand, fork, mug, face), or larger objects (flag, table, man with crossed and raised hand). Fig.2-9 illustrates the pictures.

Fig.2-9 Pictures used in the studies by Kennedy et al. (1972, 1977) (source: Kennedy (1993:57))

The sighted participants managed to identify 2.4 drawings per person, while the blind were less successful and only identified 1.25 drawings. However, as reported by Kennedy and his colleagues, their guesses were very close to the correct answers. For instance, some blind participants thought that the picture of a fork represented a claw, while a hand was frequently identified as a leaf or flame. It was observed that the errors were not random but made perfect visual sense. Over the course of the whole study the picture which both blind and blindfolded participants persistently failed to recognise, was a man with crossed arms in which the overlapping elements interfered with recognition. The remaining pictures were identified with a comparable success rate. Even if particular pictures were not recognised by individual participants, after a debriefing explanation they commented that it made sense and that they had not thought about it at that particular moment. This suggested that the poor performance of the participants in these particular cases did not stem from a lack of cognitive ability nor from any difficulties related to unfamiliarity with certain abstract terms or the insufficient exploration of objects. The vast repertoire of possible associations in the provided with additional contextual cues, the performance success would be higher.

To verify this assumption, in the next study Kennedy and his colleagues engaged 17 blind people (aged 17 to 47) to identify a set of pictures presented in short-story form. In order to encourage participants to comment and in this way to obtain greater responses from reluctant and shy people, they said they would like to know if these stories and pictures would be appropriate and comprehensible for blind children. In each story a few pictures gradually revealed different parts of one mysterious object allowing the participants to explore the objects step-by-step and at the same time introducing an element of anticipation and surprise. For instance, in a story about a tricycle the object was never explicitly named, but as the story proceeded the reader was presented with a frame, then a handlebar was added, finally wheels and a seat completed the picture. If the participants had problems with identifying the pictures, the experimenters helped them by naming the general category of the object (animal, food, furniture etc.). From all of the participants taking part in the experiment, only two asked for this kind of assistance and this allowed them to successfully recognise the pictures presented.

In general, the blind adults taking part in the study had no problems identifying the objects. Some minor difficulties with understanding the drawing conventions of the pictures (side view vs. top view) occurred at times, but did not prevent the subjects from successfully completing the task. In all cases the participants provided ample descriptions of where the different parts should be drawn in order to facilitate the recognition of the objects. This suggested that they had extensive knowledge of all of the objects. Finally this example, as well as other studies performed with the use of drawings, indicated that the success rate of the participants depended greatly on the contextual information they were provided with (a text, other pictures, categories or a list of possible objects) (see Kennedy 1993 for review).

The studies reveal that blind people at adult age make significant progress in understanding various concepts and bridge difficulties, some of which many blind children struggle with. They are perfectly aware of visual concepts like objects in motion (Kennedy ibid.), perspective (see also Juricevic & Kennedy 2006), inaccessible or unexplored objects, and they demonstrate great accuracy and logical reasoning in identification tasks. For example, as shown in a study by Heller (1989), the deliberate omission of certain elements intended to make pictures easier to read, in fact hindered recognition. The researcher presented an interesting comment made by a blind person, who said that the picture she was shown had to present something other than a telephone, since there was no cord. It may also suggest that blind people's representations are more stable and less flexible than in the case of sighted people. This is because the sighted can observe many objects of the same category different from one another in design, size or shape, but retaining the same elements and functions.

In the same study, Heller examined the importance of past visual experience in congenitally blind, late-blind and blindfolded (sighted) adults. It turned out that there were no significant differences between the groups in the recognition of geometric relief shapes, but the late-blind subjects (whose past visual experience and tactual experience gave them an advantage), were found to be superior in the identification of drawings of familiar objects. These findings were confirmed in a similar study by Dulin (2008), who investigated the effect of prior experience on length estimations of congenitally blind, early-blind and late-blind adults. It should be noted that in many respects, congenitally and adventitiously blind adults and children do not differ considerably, but for instance, "(…) the performance of later-blinded people on a range of spatial tasks is more similar to that of sighted people than of early-blind people" (Ungar 2000:224). This observation calls for extensive research in an area which has the potential to reveal interesting details about blind people's conceptual knowledge, limitations and the differences between early- and late-blind individuals.

The experiments investigating the comprehension of utterances involving visual concepts, support the observations obtained from the studies performed on the basis of drawings. They also provide evidence that blind adults' conceptual knowledge is sufficient for effective reasoning and comprehension processes. For instance, in three experiments performed on sighted, blindfolded and blind adults, Knauff and May (2004) show that blind adults' reasoning is not delayed by the retrieval of mental images. This is because they derive information from tactual exploration and auditory perception. The experimenters presented the groups with recorded sentences containing three types of relations, all categorised by Knauff and Johnson-Laird (2000, 2002) as visual-spatial, visual or control. They expected the participants to solve problems by deciding if the conclusion in each case was valid or not. The visual-spatial relations involved visual and spatial components (e.g. below, above). The visual relations involved only visual components (e.g. cleaner, dirtier), but the control relations did not involve any of these components (e.g. smarter, dumber). An example of a task with visual relation is given in (68).

(68)   *The dog is cleaner than the cat.*
         The ape is dirtier than the cat.
         Conclusion: *The dog is cleaner than the ape.*

By measuring the latency of responses in all three groups they discovered that the type of relation used in sentences did not have a positively or negatively influence on the answers in the group of blind adults. This was a contrast to the remaining groups who performed less successfully in solving the visual problem, they performed slightly better in the control problems and were the quickest at solving the visual-spatial problems. However, the study also showed that the blind subjects made fewer correct inferences (76 per cent) and needed slightly more time than the rest of the groups to give answers to the tasks, this was regardless of the relations used.

Elsewhere, Röder et al. (2000) in another study, presented congenitally blind and sighted adults with sentences containing expected and congruous, or unexpected and incongruous words, placed either in the middle or at the end of sentences. The participants' task was to decide if the sentences had meaning or not. The words in the middle of the sentences were strongly semantically and syntactically primed, hence the reason that they were processed faster than the words in natural or incongruent contexts. The groups did not differ in error rates (<2%), but the blind participants identified incongruence earlier than the sighted. The researchers explained that the advantage of the blind in this task, was probably due to the enhanced processing in which their expectation (based on a syntactic structure) propels the comprehension of words. The dependence of congenitally blind children on syntactic analysis (particularly when visual context was the major cue to meaning and the sentence contained unfamiliar words), was also observed by Landau and Gleitman (1985).

The hypothesis that blind adults can deduce meaning on the basis of syntactic/semantic knowledge, was tested in a subsequent experiment by Röder et al. (2002). In this experiment blind and sighted adults were asked to listen to sets of words (consisting of adjectives and legitimate nouns or pronounceable pseudonouns), and decide if the target nouns were legitimate or not. The legitimate nouns were (a) syntactically and semantically, (b) only syntactically, (c) only semantically or (d) neither syntactically nor semantically associated with the adjacent adjectives. The intention was to discover the influence of priming in the comprehension of the subjects. Both of the groups needed less time to deal with sets containing semantic and syntactic priming effects (a). The results revealed no difference in error rates between sighted and visually impaired participants, but again the advantage of the latter in decision time, in particular for 'pseudo-words', was observed. According to the researchers, the findings did not support the hypothesis that blind adults' semantic concepts are impoverished or less extended, since they did not demonstrate a lack of semantic priming. The enhanced syntactic processing myth was also refuted as the participants did not show an increased syntactic priming effect. In fact, the study lends support to the assumption that blind people are superior at perceptual processing, as shown by their shorter reaction times.

Since blind people derive the greatest amount of information through touch and hearing, and these senses play a crucial role in cognitive processes, their tactual and auditory abilities are said to be better developed and more sensitive than in the case of the sighted. A large number of studies concerning auditory and speech perception have been performed to verify these assumptions, some of which have produced contradictory data. For instance, Zwiers et al. (2001) argued that blind people are not as confident with auditory localization, while Ashmed et al. (1998) claimed that they perform on a par with the sighted. Still more views are held by Lessard et al. (1998), and Muchnik et al. (1991), who maintain that it is actually the blind who are superior in this task. Generally, it is accepted that blind people demonstrate faster and superior auditory and speech perception (Niemeyer & Starlinger 1981, Röder et al. 1999, see Boroojerdi & Cohen 2003 for review), which may be the result of their more effective comprehension (Foulke & Sticht 1974). In explicitly communicated utterances blind people may indeed perform faster and more accurately than the sighted. This is considering not only linguistic input but also accompanying extra-linguistic features, such as audible sounds and noises. However, Perkins (2010) argues that due to 'the quality of input data,' blind people may fail to appropriately understand ironic utterances, such as a word in (69) said with a grimace:

(69)   *Wonderful!*

The lack of direct access to contextually relevant visual cues may also affect reference assignment, effective disambiguation and incoherence resolution. It may also prevent an understanding of various forms of humour, indirect replies or requests. Until now however, these assumptions have not been supported by a sufficient amount of experimental data.

As claimed by Pérez-Pereira and Conti-Ramsden (1999), the problems with abstract and figurative language use and reasoning experienced by blind children, are overcome in late adolescence. This appears to be confirmed by a study performed by Minervino et al. (2009) on a group of 15 sighted and 15 congenitally blind undergraduates (Spanish native speakers). In the experiment the participants listened to metaphorical expressions of 'seeing' or 'grasping' (see an example of a pair presented in (70)), and were asked to explain the intended meaning of the utterance.

(70)   SEEING METAPHOR: *Juan tiene mucho ojo [eye] para los negocios.*
        [Eng. Juan has a good eye for business deals.]

        GRASPING METAPHOR: *Juan tiene mucha mano [hand] para los negocios.*
        [Eng. Juan is very handy when it comes to making business deals.]

Their task was also to evaluate on a Likert scale how well they thought they had understood the utterances (from 1 meaning 'poor comprehension' to 5 meaning 'very good comprehension'). In both of the groups 'seeing' metaphors were better understood than 'grasping' metaphors, and there were no significant differences in performance, or in the evaluation of comprehension (above 4.5 in both groups) between the sighted and blind participants. These results suggest that blind people can understand metaphors just as well as the sighted, and the lack of previous visual experience does not prevent them from understanding figurative language whilst utilising visual concepts.

Very little is known about blind people's comprehension when it comes to different forms of humour. Taking into consideration the fact that vision plays a significant role in the interpretations of cartoons, comic strips, caricatures, practical jokes, mimes etc., and bearing in mind that blind people's mental representations of the world might be qualitatively and quantitatively different (assumed on the basis of information obtained from different channels), they are expected to be less competent in the comprehension of humour than sighted people. Additionally, the lack of vision may hinder the understanding of certain cultural and social references used in various jokes or other humorous utterances. This is also yet to be examined. Although many sighted people claim that blind people are persistently sad, depressed and have no sense of humour (Sak-Wernicka 2010), some visually impaired adults are observed to tell jokes and appear very witty in social situations. Roberts (1998:x-xi) reports in the following account:

> "Those who become blind bring to this unchosen condition the full array of personality characteristics, including a sense of humor. In fact, some of the funniest people I have known were blind. Take Bob Ingersol, a blind man from my hometown, for instance. Many people who knew him and loved him were often the recipients of Bob's practical jokes. As a high school student, far from home at Illinois School for the Blind in Jacksonville, I looked forward to Bob's encouraging and news-filled letter, which usually ended with such bits of earthy humor as, "Some final advice from your friendly stock broker: Sit on your American Can and hold your Water". Lloyd, a blind piano tuner, would slip a few pieces of the family silver in the coat pockets of friends who were visiting for the first time in order to enjoy their reactions when he "accidentally" discovered these items while helping them on with their wraps. Then there was Floyd, a lifelong friend, who would respond to the inquiries of waitresses as to how much cream he liked in his coffee with "just enough to see if there is a fly floating in it. (…) I have observed that an active sense of humor is a definite asset to those who are required to adjust to a life without vision."

Landau and Gleitman (1985) also show that blind people demonstrate a thorough understanding of visual concepts, and even if they themselves do not perceive visually, they can learn from sighted people's explanations of what visual perception entails. Hence when the researchers asked blind adults to define the verb 'to notice', here is one of the responses they came across:

> "[It is] to see something that comes into your view. But not only to see it but to perceive it and understand it. You could sit on this rocking chair and not notice the colour of it at all. Might have to be looking at something specifically to notice it". (p.65)

The precision with which this blind person explains the concept, relating it to other concepts (e.g. colour) implies that blind people's mind-reading abilities are unaffected by visual impairment and they allow them to understand what vision is for those who see, and what kind of information sight provides. Despite blind children's difficulties with attributing thoughts to other people (which has been revealed in many experiments discussed above), as observed by Baron-Cohen (2001:84) "(…) the language of individuals born blind is beautifully laced with the full range of mental-state terms". This allows them to appropriately mentalise and imagine other people's states of mind. These same assumptions were also confirmed by Bedny et al. (2009) who conducted two experiments on sighted and early-blind adults with the intention of investigating the role visual experience plays in the development of the theory of mind network.

In the first experiment they asked the participants to listen to stories (mental or physical representations of reality) and to answer true/false questions about them. The second experiment involved listening to stories (concerning people's beliefs based on seeing or hearing, people's bodily sensations and control stories without people), and judging the positive or negative valance of the stories. In the two studies, blind and sighted participants obtained similar results. There were no significant differences in accuracy or reaction time. In the first experiment both of the groups responded faster when they were expected to answer the questions on the basis of physical representations, this was rather than in the belief condition. In the second experiment, no significant differences between hearing or seeing conditions were observed in either groups. The results showed that despite different developmental experience, the blind and sighted adults did not differ in reasoning when it came to mental states, even if the activity involved mentalising about seeing.

Additionally, in order to find out if the participants' performance was based on theory of mind abilities, they performed a follow-up memory experiment in which the blind and sighted subjects read a part of the original story and were asked to recall if the source of the protagonist's belief had been visual or aural. Although in this task all of the participants performed equally well, in literature it is possible to find many studies revealing that blind adults demonstrate an enhanced short-term memory capacity which may result in superior processing skills (see Röder et al. 1999, 2000, Amedi et al. 2003).

Considering all of the findings presented above, we can observe a serious inadequacy of research examining blind adults' cognitive abilities. As we pointed out at the very beginning of this section, the certain impediments in blind children's development caused by limited (or no) access to various concepts, may contribute to the occurrence of gaps in the children's knowledge. These may remain undetected for a blind person's entire life, the result of which is that in various communicative situations the person may arrive at different interpretations than sighted people or they may understand differently or totally misunderstand the utterances of sighted people. It is also possible that a poorer knowledge of different concepts will result in impaired deduction, inference and/or association abilities, these in turn will result in less successful interpretations.

As it was mentioned at the beginning of this section, we know very little about gaps in blind adults' knowledge and for years researchers have failed to devise an effective method of detecting them. Recently, a method has been developed by Bogusław Marek, who observing that gaps in blind people's knowledge are best exposed during long and informal conversations, has suggested that the best way to find out what blind people cannot understand is to start solving crossword puzzles with them. This provides an opportunity to not only test their general knowledge, but also to ask them questions and let them elaborate on various concepts or, in case of failure, to find out whether or not they make connections between clues and answers. Following this idea, a pilot study was performed examining congenitally blind adults during which the subjects were asked to solve a crossword prepared for this purpose consisting of various clues chosen from different crosswords for sighted people. The participants of the study were Polish native speakers (two female students and two male graduates of the John Paul II Catholic University of Lublin, Poland) aged 19 to 25.

During the preparation stage it turned out that the participants were aware that words could cross in a crossword puzzle but were unaware of the whole structure of a crossword grid. During a training session, the subjects were presented with a Braille version of a crossword (Appendix A). Although they knew that the name 'crossword' is derived from the fact that in a crossword, words run across one another, the layout of squares corresponding to different numbers running down or across were very difficult for the participants to coordinate. They also found it problematic to understand in which direction a word runs (left or right, up or down), which again corroborates with the difficulties of blind people in the understanding of spatial relations.

The same version of the crossword, but appropriately adapted to the needs of blind people was prepared as a computer application (see Appendix A for a screen print-out) compatible with Braille displayer Super Vario and screen reader Window-Eyes. In comparison to a traditional crossword, the application enabled a blind person to read clues and fill in squares. Once a guessed word had been typed (for instance, down), the letters which were shared by another word or other words (across) were automatically filled. This significantly reduced a plethora of possible answers and, in effect facilitated the solving of the puzzle.

Although the clues of the crossword referred to various aspects of general knowledge, they were sorted into three main categories according to related concepts such as visual, tactual or abstract. Aside from general knowledge, extensive linguistic and pragmatic knowledge was necessary for the participants to be able to complete the crossword. In accordance, they were not only tested on their world knowledge, but also, among other things, on their ability to extend concepts, resolve lexical ambiguities, form humorous associations, and understand metaphors. The context provided by the clues was relatively broad and open to numerous ideas, associations and thoughts, which may have posed an additional difficulty and made the recovery of intended answers more challenging. However, this also allowed the experimenters to analyse the assumptions made by the participants when arriving at their final interpretations, and detect potential gaps and impediments in their process of interpretation.

Also for this purpose, the participants were encouraged to share their ideas and freely express their thoughts during a general session in which all participants contributed and helped each other. It should be noted that the primary aim of the study was not to discover how many clues individual subjects managed to guess, because even among sighted people there are those who are good at solving crosswords and those who find them too difficult. The main idea was to better understand (by means of the crossword) how the conceptual knowledge of blind people differed from that of the sighted. The sighted participants were also asked to solve the same crossword in a traditional format, this was during a similar session organised on another day. Both of the sessions were recorded.

The crossword consisted of 20 clues in all (11 across and 9 down), which did not represent a sufficient number to be able to draw conclusions on its basis. Therefore, a follow-up study was carried out (and recorded), during which the blind participants were further challenged by more than 90 additional clues. The follow-up session involved solving the clues which were read aloud to them. The study revealed very similar tendencies. The only exception was that the blind subjects presented many more ideas before they decided on the correct response, especially when they did not know the number of letters in the intended answers, and also when they were not given any letters. It was also sometimes difficult to change their way of thinking and encourage them to think of alternative associations to particular concepts. Consequently, in the follow-up study they needed more time to recover the intended answers, which seems understandable considering the wide choice of possible answers. Apart from these, we did not observe any additional differences in the way that they responded in the two studies. It is due to the fact that the results obtained from the pilot study (performed on blind and sighted participants) and follow-up study (conducted exclusively on a group of the blind participants) will be presented and discussed together.

The analysis of the recordings showed that blind people were better at solving the clues which involved tactual concepts, which indicates their reliance on this source of information. Very often their first associations referred to tactual concepts, this was contrary to sighted people who did not show any preference for tactual concepts and were equally willing to offer answers referring to other concepts, as illustrated in (71) below.

(71)   Clue: *coś do trzymania* 'something to keep up with/to hold'
        Intended answer [abstract]: *fason* 'appearances'
        Blind subjects' ideas [tactual]: *uszko* 'handle', *klucz* 'key'
        Sighted subjects' ideas [abstract, tactual]: *forma* 'shape', *pion* 'line', *wieszak* 'hanger', *ręka* 'hand', *uchwyt* 'handle', *klamka* 'door-knob'

In the case presented above the blind participants offered the correct answer much faster than the sighted people, who seemed to be overwhelmed by the large number of possible options. The same tendency was observed in response to other clues. Even if two (or more) meanings of words required a resolution of lexical ambiguity, and even if these meanings referred to entirely different categories, the blind participants were still able to demonstrate their extensive general and linguistic knowledge. For instance, in (72) presented below, they were expected to overextend the concept of 'kozak', taking into consideration that it may refer to (a) a boot (tactual), or (b) an adventurer, Cossack (abstract). The clue turned out to be equally simple for both blind and sighted participants.

(72)   Clue: *but z temperamentem* 'an adventurous shoe'
        Intended answer: *kozak* 'boot; adventurer/Cossack'

Some clues however, turned out to be more difficult for the blind participants. Even in the confusing situations when visual and unknown concepts presented themselves, their associations were logical and well-justified. A good illustration is a clue taken from the follow-up study in (73), which the blind participants were challenged to, in response to which only one individual knew that the intended answer was 'wypoczynek'. This Polish word can be used to refer to (a) a rest (abstract) or (b) a sofa or a lounger (tactual), both of which are quite ambiguous. Additionally, meaning (a) is generally used much more frequently. Probably because of that other participants did not come up with the answer and even having learnt what the intended answer was, they thought about the first meaning (a). Interestingly, the answers offered by the blind participants (i.e. 'sale' and 'stocktaking') also referred to abstract rather than just tactual concepts.

(73)   Clue: *podczas przerwy w sklepie meblowym* 'during a lunch break
         in a furniture shop'
         Intended answer [abstract, tactual]: *wypoczynek* 'lounger'
         Blind subjects' answers [abstract]: *wyprzedaż* 'sale', *remament*
         'stocktaking'

We also observed that the sighted participants had some problems with answering the clues. A good illustration of this happening is presented in (74) below, in which the first option offered by the blind subject was correct, this was not however the case in the group of the sighted.

(74)   Clue: *tam zobaczysz różne numerki* 'you will see many numbers
         there'
         Intended answer: *szatnia* 'cloak-room'
         Blind subjects' ideas: *szatnia* 'cloak-room'
         Sighted subjects' ideas: *portfel* 'wallet', *autobus* 'bus', *loteria*
         'lottery', *szkoła* 'school', *raport* 'report'

Despite falling into the same category as those involving visual concepts, some clues were solved more quickly and easily than others. While, for instance, the clue presented in (75) did not pose any problem to any of the groups, the one in (76) turned out to be problematic for blind participants.

(75)   Clue: *na przeciw szóstej* 'opposite six'
         Intended answer: *północ* 'midnight'

(76)   Clue: *wąż z piórami* 'a snake with feathers'
         Intended answer: *boa*

Although they managed to provide the correct answer, perhaps because they knew the name of only one snake which was spelt with only three letters, they clearly thought exclusively about the species of reptiles. Only two people seemed to have known that the word might also refer to some kind of shawl, but they did not know if it could be worn in winter, who usually wears it and for what reason.

This example as well as the one presented in (77) shows that the blind participants found it much more difficult to arrive at an intended answer if visual metaphors were involved. In these cases the clues turned out to be insufficient, and the participants asked the experimenter for some hints. If still unable to offer the correct answer, the blind subjects were given the answer that was expected, and were asked to explain why it was correct.

(77)   Clue: *zawstydzony chrzan* 'an embarrassed horseradish'
         Intended answer: *ćwikła* 'beetroot'
         Blind subjects' answers: *?*
         Sighted subjects' answers: *marchewka* 'carrot', *burak* 'beetroot'

The blind participants had problems with explaining how the answer in (77) was related to the clue, and why it was correct. They could not associate it with the expression 'as red as a beetroot' meaning 'very embarrassed'. The difficulty with metaphors containing visual concepts in the group of blind participants was confirmed in the follow-up study, as presented in (78).

(78)   Clue [+visual]: *żółty egoista* 'a yellow egoist'
         Intended answer: *narcyz* 'narcissus; narcissist'
         Blind subjects' answers: *Chińczyk* 'Chinese'

In this case the participants were expected to associate this clue with the word 'narcyz' which refers to both (a) a flower (a narcissus) and (b) a self-centred man (a narcissist). Not one of blind participants came up with this answer even though they were able to provide a detailed explanation of what the words meant. Additionally, some admitted that they had not previously known that a narcissus has any colour. This might suggest that the concept of colour (problematic for blind children) remains difficult for blind adults, even if their knowledge of this concept is more extensive and they have already learnt what colour particular objects have. The only answer which we obtained in response to this clue was 'a Chinese', in which we can observe not only an amusing association with the yellow colour but also the heavy reliance of the blind participant on stereotypic knowledge. Other blind participants found this answer hilarious and laughed wholeheartedly at it.

    Contrary to the general assumption that blind people have no sense of humour, during the study they demonstrated intelligence and an appreciation of humour, especially in response to the clues in (79a)-(79d).

(79a)   Clue: *ostatnia impreza* 'the last party'
Intended answer: *pogrzeb* 'funeral'
Blind subjects' answers: *stypa* 'wake', *pogrzeb* 'funeral'

(79b)   Clue: *owłosiony szprzęt* 'hairy equipment/tool'
Intended answer: *szczotka* 'brush'
Blind subjects' answers: *nos* 'nose', *genitalia* 'sexual organs'

(79c)   Clue: *z igłą w rączce* 'with a needle in an arm/handle'
Intended answer: *adapter* 'gramphone'
Blind subjects' answers: *pielęganiarka* 'nurse', *agrafka* 'safety-pin'

(79d)   Clue: *ostry pies* 'a sharp dog'
Intended answer: *szpic* (note that 'szpic' in Polish may mean (a) a spike and (b) a spitz–type dog)
Blind subjects' answers: *hot dog*

They found these clues not only amusing, but also relatively easy. Many times they laughed at other participants' ideas, or referred to funny situations or sketches that they had heard and came in to their minds. In (79a) all of the participants appreciated the black humour used in the clue, and in (79b) the sexual humour was easily indicated. The clues in (79c) and (79d) were slightly more challenging and ambiguous. The word 'rączka' in (79c) might mean (a) a small hand (diminutive) or (b) a handle, and as a result may refer to thousands of different things. Although the blind participants failed to recognise that the intended answer was 'a gramophone', they had a good laugh when they heard the ideas that two blind participants offered (presented in (79c)). The same reaction was triggered by a response of one of the participants to a clue in (79d). In this situation one participant wisely responded that 'a sharp dog' is 'a hot dog'. It should be noted that the Polish word 'ostry' can mean both 'hot' and 'sharp'.

Both of the groups (blind and sighted subjects) had no significant problems with clues containing abstract concepts, and even if they did not offer the correct answer immediately, their ideas were very close to the intended answers, like the ones presented in (80) below.

(80)   Clue: *wołanie w żyłach* 'screaming through your veins'
Intended answer: *zew* 'call'
Blind and sighted subjects' answers: *krew* 'blood', *ból* 'pain', *tętno* 'heartbeat',
puls 'pulse', *cholesterol*, *życie* 'life', *nadzieja* 'hope', *zator* 'embolism',
obieg 'circulation', *gen* 'gene', *białaczka* 'leukaemia', *krzyk* 'a cry'

The groups, already knowing the answer, had no problem with associating it with the expression 'call of blood' and explaining that it refers to a primitive instinct.

However, metaphors containing abstract terms gave rise to some dubious and erroneous collocations in the group of blind people some of whom mistakenly claimed that the expressions existed and were in use in the Polish language. As illustrated in (81), one of the blind participants used the expression 'wiatr z głowy' (*wind off one's mind) and explained that it meant exactly the same as 'problem z głowy' (problem solved).

(81)   Clue: *z głowy* 'off one's mind; off/from one's head'
        Intended answer: *skalp* ' scalp'
        Blind subject's answer: *problem*, **wiatr* 'wind'

In the case of (82), the first association offered by blind people derived from the expression 'zrobić kogoś na szaro' (be cheated/taken for a ride) made perfect sense and was indeed in use (even if it was not the intended answer). When asked what the expression actually meant, one blind person claimed of its equivalence to (a) 'zrobiony na średnio' and (b) 'zrobiony na czysto', these as a matter of fact are not normally used in the Polish language.

(82)   Clue: *zrobiony na szaro* (lit.) 'made grey'; (idiom.)
        'cheated/taken for a ride'
        Intended answer: *karp* 'carp' (served with grey sauce)
        Blind subjects' answers: *ktoś* 'someone' = **zrobiony na średnio*
        '*medium done', **zrobiony na czysto* '*well done'

Despite certain problems with individual clues (which were also observed in the group of sighted participants), the study shows that blind adults generally possess an extensive knowledge of not only tactual, but also abstract and visual concepts. This is what allows blind adults to perform a multitude of complex mental operations. The study shows that they can also be equally successful in doing crosswords if provided with the same amount of information as sighted people. Their general and linguistic knowledge (which for some is expected to be affected by their visual impairments) does not put them at any disadvantage either. What is more, many problematic concepts seem to be either reduced or eliminated. The enthusiasm of the blind participants (who were excited to have a chance to solve a crossword themselves, and to check their knowledge), along with the interesting findings obtained from the pilot study, suggests that there is a rationale behind carrying out large-scale quantitive research in this area. We also claim that just as in the case of sighted people, crosswords may provide effective memory training and broaden general knowledge, these learning tools may have an equally beneficial effect on blind adults. Hence they should be given the chance to enjoy them.

Summary

Considering the empirical data presented in this chapter, it seems that visual impairment does not affect the linguistic abilities of blind adults to the extent that one might expect and "is not a significant deterrent in a communicative situation" (Smith & Kandath 2000:396). Although these assumptions have not been confirmed by a satisfactory amount of research studies, and there are still more questions than answers which cannot be settled on the basis of single cases and selective findings, blind people (despite certain perceptual and cognitive differences) are likely to be equally competent reasoners and just as effective participants of communication as the sighted. It also appears that:

> "(…) the different routes that blind children must take to master language ultimately lead to the development of full linguistic competence comparable to that of the sighted." (Barry 2002:201)

However, it is still not known to what extent blind adults can understand utterances (explicit and implicit), how much they are aware of the role of gestures in communication, and if the sensory information available to blind adults can compensate for their lack of vision. Due to compensatory strategies which are developed during the course of their lives, it is not entirely clear how visual concepts are formed and if what they know actually corresponds to reality. Finally, we still do not know the degree to which prior visual experience has an effect on visually impaired adults and if their performance is more similar to that of the blind, or of the sighted.

In this chapter we have attempted to show the complexity and vastness of visual impairment as it affects children and adults, and also to show how it embraces numerous conditions which decide how serious an effect this has on mental processing and linguistic performance. We aimed to present basic terminology, methodology and the findings of the studies while demonstrating the potential differences between blind and sighted children and adults. This was with the intention of stressing the problems and insufficiencies of empirical data in this area. Outlining the developmental aspects of blind people's pragmatic abilities and predicting the consequences blindness may have on comprehension, we attempted to lay the foundations for the presentation of our empirical study. This will examine congenitally and early-blind adults on the appreciation of contextual cues in their understanding of explicit and implicit utterances. Since hardly any studies concerning blind people have been performed within the realm of pragmatics, in particular the investigations of its application to Relevance Theory and to the analysis of blind people's pragmatic abilities, in the present chapter we were forced to refer to other disciplines to shed some light on the problem. In the next chapter we hope to show that the relevance-theoretic assumptions presented in chapter one have 'testable consequences' (Wilson 2005:625) and potential to describe, explain and make contributions to our better understanding of visual impairment and its influence on a person.

CHAPTER THREE

CONTEXT AND COMPREHENSION:
A COMPARATIVE STUDY OF BLIND
AND SIGHTED ADULTS

Introduction

Considering the body of literature presented in the previous chapter, visual impairment and its effect on pragmatic abilities still appear to be highly unexplored issues which require in-depth research and elucidation. Due to various methodological problems (see Norgate 1997 for detailed discussion), there is little interest in this area of linguistics and studies are rarely carried out systematically, which effectively means that many aspects of blind people's comprehension and pragmatic abilities have yet to be examined. A handful of empirical studies performed on visually impaired adults show that the individuals, despite certain impediments in language and concept acquisition experienced in childhood, may be able to effectively utilise acquired knowledge and interpret information provided through different senses to understand communicated utterances.

However, these findings mainly concern the understanding of individual sentences rather than longer stretches of texts or even entire dialogues, and this may have a significant effect on the results. It goes without saying that the understanding of separate utterances is much easier from the perspectives of both participants and experimenters analysing the data. However, in real life we are expected to understand underdetermined and ordinary utterances which are parts of longer verbal exchanges set in particular situations. We are required to refer to other events (previous or future) and we need to constantly update available information.

What is more, many studies compare visually impaired people with sighted individuals. There are however, few studies which investigate the potential differences between congenitally blind and sighted adults, as well as congenitally blind and late-blind individuals. While the differences between blind and sighted children are more frequently discussed in literature and concern different aspects of their development, we still do not know if totally blind adults deprived of vision since birth or early childhood interpret utterances and situations in a similar way, or as effectively as the sighted. This in turn has led to many misconceptions about blindness and blind people's cognitive abilities.

In the following chapter we aim to present a study which was conducted on a group of blind and sighted adults with the intention of examining the importance of contextual cues in the comprehension of utterances, all in various real-life situations. The participants were tested on their ability to understand explicit and implicit utterances (provided as text, recording or film) on the basis of verbal and non-verbal cues, the linguistic and extra-linguistic features of language, and different aspects of general knowledge. The methodology of the study is based on Relevance Theory and its assumptions which were discussed in the previous theoretical chapters, provide a background for the analysis of the results. The findings may have important implications, not only for the analysis of Relevance Theory, but also for the functioning of blind people in social contexts. We hope that this study will shed some light on the unexplored aspects of blind people's comprehension and cognition, and will make sighted people more aware of the difficulties and obstacles blind people have to face in day-to-day communication. Finally, we hope the study will help sighted people to improve everyday contact with the blind, to eliminate causes of miscommunication and to inspire the design of educational aids and materials, so as to cater for blind people's needs.

The study

As we have stated many times in this work, very little is known about blind people's pragmatic and cognitive abilities. Despite some attempts at exploring this area, there are still too few experimental studies examining blind people to confidently be able to state whether a person without vision may function normally, competently interpret utterances, and successfully communicate in everyday life. It is also not entirely clear the extent to which a congenitally blind person's knowledge is different from that which a sighted person perceives, knows and understands. As a result, we are unable to help a blind person if what he or she knows turns out to be insufficient or incorrect. While the relation between vision and cognition is readily discussed in literature, the effect that blindness has on comprehension still remains a mystery.

Being aware of that fact, the main purpose of the study is to contribute to the general discussion about blind people and their performance, as well as to promote interdisciplinary interest in this area. Our aim is also to complement or verify the few existing studies performed on blind people, with the intention of investigating the individuals' pragmatic potential, and to dispel certain misconceptions about their comprehension and cognition. Many a time during this study we heard the views that blind people are less intelligent, deprived of a sense of humour and are generally slower in thinking than the sighted. While the sighted people taking part in the study were at first a little apprehensive and ashamed of being assessed, having discovered that the study would compare them to a group of blind people, they became more bold and self-confident, as if taking for granted that they would perform better than the other group.

As we mentioned before, the study is aimed at investigating the roles of different contextual cues in the comprehension of ordinary language, in as natural circumstances as possible. For this purpose, it is imperative to examine the interpretations of various utterances set in different situations in the two groups, and analyse if they differ due to different conceptual knowledge, the channels through which contextual information is acquired, or to the presence of incoherence, ambiguity, irony or other pragmatically challenging tasks. We predict that, following the relevance-theoretic assumptions, due to the differences in the amount, variety and quality of the contextual material, certain discrepancies in the comprehension of the two groups should occur. If that is true, it is necessary to identify the particular pragmatic mechanisms or sub-tasks which turned out to be particularly problematic and hindered the process of interpretation. Our purpose then will be to create a universal tool which will enable these differences to be exposed and potential problems to be detected in blind and sighted people's comprehension. This should also make it possible to examine the comprehension of utterances among other groups of adults suffering from other disabilities or disorders, regardless of their age, gender or native language.

Hypotheses

In the study we put forward the hypothesis that due to differences in contextual information, there are certain discrepancies in the understanding of natural and ordinary utterances between blind and sighted adults. These stem from the quality and quantity of contextual material derived from different sensory channels. Since communication is not exclusively dependent on a linguistic input, but also entails visual information in the form of, for example, gestures, mimes, and observable phenomena (which are inaccessible to blind people), we expect that in many cases their understanding will be partial, less effective or inferior to that of the sighted. In situations when communication is greatly dependent on paralanguage and little is communicated verbally, blind people may be confused or even unable to recover any interpretation, this is contrary to sighted people who have access to visual cues.

Secondly, it is us who assume that the satisfactory amount of relevant contextual information (derived from different sources) is of prime importance for comprehension and decide whether a speaker's intentions are appropriately recovered or not. As a result, it seems straightforward that limited or no access to certain contextual information (not always compensated by other cues) will have a significant effect on the comprehension of blind and sighted people's reading of utterances, rather than listening to them. In the first case, the comprehension of utterances will also be much more effort-consuming for both the blind and sighted adults. However, a few studies concentrated on the differences in mental imagery between blind and sighted people (DeBeni & Cornoldi 1988, Knauff & May 2004, see Hatwell 1993 for review), suggest that sighted people perform better in recalling images, in particular when it comes to visual or spatial representations, and when a task is particularly complex. Consequently, we can expect that when reading a text, sighted participants may perform more successfully than blind individuals.

We also claim that previous visual experience and the differences in conceptual knowledge caused by the lack of it, have an effect on the comprehension of utterances, and this will result in problems with understanding in the cases of congenitally blind or early-blind adults. As predicted by Relevance Theory, in these and previously mentioned situations the participants are expected to either maximise the relevance of the obtained material and conclude on the basis of the contextual assumptions accessible to them (even if not always correctly), or abandon the inferential process completely if the information proves insufficient, ambiguous or too incoherent. The same inferential procedure may well apply to sighted people who are not provided with the necessary contextual information.

On the other hand, blind people are known to have well-developed compensatory abilities which allow them to make up for the information they cannot visually access. This helps them to be more attentive to contextual cues, for example, through hearing. Blind people's auditory and speech perception, as shown in many empirical studies (some of which have been discussed in chapter two), is more sensitive to additional contextual information such as noises, suggestive sighs, and emphatic pauses. As a result, it is very likely that the comprehension of blind people in these situations may not only be appropriate and comparable to that which the sighted people in the same situations would understand, but also we expect that sighted people deprived of visual cues in real-life circumstances (e.g. during a phone call rather than a face-to-face conversation), will be less successful in interpreting utterances than blind people who can take full advantage of the accessible information more effectively. Therefore, our final hypothesis is that sighted people if deprived of vision, which provides the majority of contextual cues, will find utterances less comprehensible and more ambiguous than blind people.

Participants

To be able to verify the hypotheses presented above, we invited two groups of blind (B) and sighted (S) people to our project with the intention of analysing and contrasting their performance. All of the participants were Polish native speakers living in villages, small towns and big cities in different parts of Poland (for the analysis of participants' residences see Table 3-1).

Table 3-1 Participant characteristics

	Sighted (n=60)	*Blind* (n=55)
Gender		
Male	27	24
Female	33	31
Age range		
19-25 yrs	19	17
26-35 yrs	17	13
36-45 yrs	6	11
46-67 yrs	18	14
Mean (SD)	35.36 (18.00)	36.54 (19.30)
Education		
primary	0	8
secondary	31	30
higher (BA degree)	9	8
higher (MA degree)	20	9

The subjects varied in age, gender, and educational record. The age range of participants (19 to 67 years old) was relatively wide, hence, the study embraced participants with different work experience and social status.

Among them, there were students, blue, pink and white-collar workers, the retired and the unemployed. In total, 60 sighted and 55 blind people agreed to take part in the experiment, all of whom met preliminary selection criteria.

At first we excluded under-age people (children, adolescents). We assumed that it would be very difficult to determine their comprehension abilities at the same time as taking into consideration the age at which they can be assessed as adults or categorised as children. Additionally, it was thought that the participants would not perform as well as the adults due to the fact that their world knowledge, conceptual knowledge, logical reasoning or linguistic abilities were still developing. In this situation, it would have been very difficult to state which factors affected their performance to the greatest extent: age or visual impairment.

The same as young age, very advanced age disqualified people from taking part in the study. Although we believe that many elderly people retain mental dexterity, as studies have revealed (Salthouse 1991, Horn & Hofer 1992), late in their lives people are known to have problems with memory, association, imagination and logical thinking. These were all involved and required in the study. As a result, the people who took part in the study were between the ages of 19 and 67. The mean age in the two groups of participants was 32;0 for the sighted and 35;6 for the blind.

Secondly, we took efforts to eliminate from the study subjects with diagnosed mental disabilities, as this could falsify results. Finally, for the group of blind subjects we selected only congenitally blind or early-blind participants. Adults who were partially sighted or who lost vision in later periods of life (i.e. in late childhood, adolescence or adulthood) did not take part in the study. In the previous chapter we presented arguments that people born blind and those who lost vision early in their lives differ in some respects from late-blind people. Since potential differences between the groups have yet to be explored, a comparative study examining the performances of the congenitally or early-blind people with the late-blind people (while utilising the research tool and procedure presented in this book), would definitely produce interesting results for the future. The selection of congenitally or early-blind participants for the study was aimed at forming a homogenous group of blind people who had no access to (or no recollection of) visual concepts or contextual information provided by vision, and also those whose conceptual knowledge and linguistic abilities (which rapidly developed in school years) may have been affected by the lack of vision. Table 3-2 presents the percentage of congenitally blind and early-blind participants (divided into three groups B1, B2 and B3) who took part in the study.

Table 3-2 The contribution of congenitally and early blind participants in the study

Participants	Sub-groups	Frequency	Percentage
Congenitally blind	B1	13	38.2
	B2	12	35.3
	B3	9	26.5
Early-blind	B1	7	33.3
	B2	7	33.3
	B3	7	33.3

As observed in previous empirical studies performed on blind people, it is extremely difficult to find subjects to meet all of the exact criteria that many researchers require. Blind people generally differ from each other in many ways such as by visual experience and acuity, age, educational record and many others. Each blind person is an individual who has unique life experiences, all of which evade formal categorisation but which have a significant influence on his or her performance. For instance, in the group of blind adults we find not only those who are congenitally (totally or partially) blind, were blinded in early infancy or late childhood, but also those who were partially sighted in early childhood and whose vision decreased until it was totally lost in adulthood. Some visually impaired people have residual vision, some can see light and recognise shapes, and still others have no vision at all. As a result, it is not straightforward what effect visual impairment and its course may have on a person's functioning, as well as to which group the person should be assigned.

A large percentage of blind people are the elderly who lost vision at adult age, usually in the aftermath of accidents or various diseases (such as diabetic retinopathy or glaucoma), but it is quite a challenge to find a representative group of congenitally totally blind adults. That is why in the study we decided not to disqualify adventitiously blind people (who lost vision in infancy or early childhood), and there were a few reasons behind this decision. Firstly, a large number of adventitiously blind people were born with a partial visual impairment which may have affected their cognitive, linguistic, motor and social development since the earliest years of childhood, just as in the case of congenitally blind people. Secondly, as we argued in the previous chapter, many pragmatic abilities such as irony, sarcasm or metaphor comprehension began to develop in late school years i.e. at a time when the people had already lost their vision totally. Consequently, we assume that even if there are some differences between congenitally blind and early-blind people, they are minimal and should not have any influence on the reliability of the study or results obtained in it.

Another methodological problem is that blindness may occur with concomitant handicaps, which unfortunately are not always diagnosed, but which may have an impact on the participants' comprehension and/or functioning. Although we made great efforts to eliminate people who lacked the competence to take part in the study (consulting the specialists who worked with the prospective participants and knew them very well in the institutions in which the tests were performed), we are aware that undiagnosed disabilities may still have some effect on the responses offered by certain individuals.

Finally, many blind people are not associated with any institutions, do not work and do not keep contact with other blind people. As a result, contacting them and engaging them into the study was sometimes not possible. Keeping in mind all of these methodological problems, it seems understandable that many studies are based on a small number of participants (sometimes involving just a handful of people) who can hardly be called a representative group. The second solution is to perform a study on a large group of blind people but accept the lack of homogeneity and disregard such strict selections. Many of the difficulties mentioned above also came up in our study. Although we managed to engage a large number of visually impaired people (n=115) instead of just a few individuals, and we kept the strict selection criteria, the consequence was that we did not manage to perform the study on two equal groups of the blind and sighted.

Some of the visually impaired people who met the preliminary requirements of the study were members of the Polish Association of the Blind, Blind Co-operative Society or Occupational Therapy Workshops. Other participants were recruited from the John Paul II Catholic University of Lublin or other Polish schools and universities. The permission for conducting this study was first obtained from the president, director and psychologist of the institutions mentioned. The participation in the study was voluntary and all of the participants were individually asked if they were willing to contribute.

Material

Our primary concern in the study was to test blind and sighted participants on their interpretations of utterances, which contained implicatures, ambiguities (structural, pragmatic or lexical), incoherences, metaphors, irony or other figures of speech. They were also tested on their abilities to recognise a speaker's attitude and state of mind. In order to achieve the desired effect comparable to a real life situation, it was necessary to prepare materials based on such situations. Since inevitably any scenarios invented for the purpose of this study would be unnatural to some extent, we decided to choose scenarios from overheard conversations, a myriad of which we listen to on a daily basis. Since some utterances might be appropriately interpreted only in the presence of a sufficient amount of contextual cues, and following the relevance-theoretic assumptions, these are also provided by a previous text or utterance, we decided not to use individual sentences taken out of context, but entire (if relatively short) dialogues.

In order to prepare the material, we started from listening to people's (formal and informal) conversations at bus stops, in shops and supermarkets, on television, in offices etc. As a result, we managed to collect a considerable amount of material which we then analysed according to its appropriateness, complexity and usefulness to the study. After the analysis period we chose twelve dialogues. Unpredictable and non-trivial as they were, these natural verbal exchanges required developed pragmatic abilities when searching for the intended interpretations. So as not to excessively complicate the task, among other things we rejected the dialogues which involved context-switching and referred to information which was not present in the dialogue, and therefore could not be derived by participants. In this way, we attempted to eliminate situations in which the dialogues could not be appropriately analysed, especially as the participants had no prior access to the crucial information of what had been said or what had happened.

Following the relevance-theoretic assumptions, linguistic input on its own is an insufficient source of contextual information. As we argued in chapter one, in order to be able to interpret a given utterance or communicative situation, it is necessary to be provided with additional cues and to derive contextual information from other sources. Our general knowledge and perceptual abilities are indispensable in this process, supplying information which cannot be obtained from semantic representations or syntactic relations alone. To examine these assumptions we prepared a script of the dialogues, devoid of any commentaries, and giving participants a free choice as to their interpretation of the dialogues.

In the study, our aims were twofold. Firstly, we wanted to discover if auditory perception could provide a greater amount of contextual information than text and, as a result, improve comprehension. Secondly, we aimed to investigate how a lack of visual information affected interpretations and if visual information was absolutely necessary in some, if not all of the situations. In order to find answers to these questions, we decided to divide the blind and sighted participants of the study into three equal groups, and ask them to interpret dialogues presented to them in the forms of text, recording or film. So as to prepare the recording and film for the study, we asked for the help of an amateur theatrical group (students of the John Paul II Catholic University of Lublin). The actors performed the dialogues as short scenes which were recorded by a professional cameraman. Next, using a computer program, the soundtrack was separately recorded.

While all blind and sighted participants who were asked to read and listen to the dialogues were provided with the same amount of contextual information, it was different for the groups watching the films. This was because in our opinion the film supplied the sighted with a greater amount of contextual information, and put the blind at a disadvantage. It seemed obvious that the blind participants would perform less successfully in the listening task compared to the sighted participants watching the film. The results would be much less predictable if blind participants were provided with the pieces of information they could not obtain from the recording. A more and more popular way of supplying blind people with visual information is by audio description, this is an additional narrational track providing necessary comments for blind viewers (especially during performances in theatres, cinemas or exhibitions in museums). In order to make up for the missing information, in the study we decided to utilise this method and presented blind participants with a recording of the audio description. In this way, the blind participants obtained additional information which they would not have been aware of and would not have been provided with otherwise (e.g. where the dialogues took place, what the speakers were doing, how they were behaving etc.). These commentaries however, were not intended to hint at any interpretation, and could not present the experimenter's preferences or interpretations of the situations. For this reason, the comments provided by the audio description (hereafter AD) were presented to a specialist beforehand, carefully prepared in advance and recorded as a separate soundtrack with the Audacity computer program.

Finally, in order to analyse the participants' interpretations of the dialogues, we designed a questionnaire in which we asked three questions about each of the presented dialogues, each focused on a different pragmatic aspect (see Appendix B). In total the questionnaire included thirty six questions, the completion of which took from twenty five to forty minutes. This depended on the way the dialogues were presented (as a text, recording or film), and the abilities of each of the participants, and of course to which group (of the blind or sighted) they belonged. Since each person is known to understand situations or utterances on the basis of his/her own cognitive environment, we can assume that no two people when asked about their interpretations of a situation, would give the same answers. Even if what they understand basically comes down to the same conclusion, their interpretations will differ somewhat. This assumption was confirmed by a pilot study in which eight participants were asked to answer open-ended questions after reading, watching or listening to dialogues prepared for the study. We observed that the subjects focused on different pieces of information in the dialogues, in the quest for their own interpretations. This sometimes led to the production of loose and far-fetched interpretations. Very often they disregarded ambiguous and incoherent cues, and avoided providing explicit answers to any question. In these situations, it was not always possible to analyse the answers and decide whether they were correct or not.

Many of the participants also found it extremely difficult to formulate their own interpretations in a clear or logical way. They tended to parrot sentences from the dialogues (sometimes after making small changes), or recapitulate the main points of the conversations, but they still failed to offer sufficient answers. In order to facilitate the analysis of the participants' responses as well as to help them verbalise their interpretations, we designed a questionnaire with closed questions. The participants were given a few possible options of interpretation to choose from, including strong, weak and faulty assumptions, idiosyncratic interpretations, or no interpretation (due to the lack or shortage of contextual information). The participants were allowed to mark only one of them, one which they thought was the most similar to their own interpretation.

Although we took great efforts to include all of the possible answers that might be given in response to each of these questions, we knew that some individuals might still analyse the dialogues in their own individual ways and find none of these answers appropriate. Due to this fact, one of the options that participants could choose from was to provide their own individual response. We also realised that some subjects might find the dialogues difficult to comprehend, or the information involved in them confusing or insufficient for any interpretation. In this case, none of the answers offered seemed appropriate for them. These subjects were asked to choose the option 'I don't know'. The questionnaire also contained a few questions in which participants were asked to evaluate the attitudes or feelings of the speakers in the dialogues on a scale from 1 to 5.

As we have already mentioned, the questions were designed to test the understanding of utterances involving various pragmatic sub-tasks (such as the comprehension of implicature, reference assignment, ambiguity and incoherence resolution, humour and irony detection, the comprehension of metaphor etc.). In all of the dialogues the participants had to perform various sub-tasks which were interrelated, so one sub-task involved another sub-task and the completion of one sub-task had an effect on performing the other. Analogically, a failure in performing these tasks could trigger a chain reaction and result in misinterpretation. This is also in line with relevance theoretic assumptions, since as explained in the theory, comprehension involves the simultaneous performance of many pragmatic sub-tasks (Wilson & Sperber 2005:615).

Procedure

Blind and sighted participants of the study were divided into three relatively equal sub-groups. All of them were asked to analyse the same material (discussed in the previous section), presented as a text, recording or film. In this way, the participants were provided with different amounts of contextual information. Accordingly, the participants of the study were readers, listeners (or over-hearers), and/or observers who were not directly involved in the communicative situations and hence were able to analyse them objectively.

The first group of sighted participants (S1) were asked to read a text (the scripts of twelve dialogues). After each dialogue they were asked to answer three questions related to the dialogue in the questionnaire. The second group (S2) listened to the recorded dialogues (without reading the scripts) and completed the same questions from the questionnaire. The third group (S3) watched the film with the dialogues performed as short scenes and the participants were also asked to fill in the questionnaire. As in the case of S2, the group S3 was not given the script of the dialogues. The same procedure was used in the group of blind participants who were also divided in three sub-groups (B1, B2 and B3). The only exception was that the third group (B3) instead of watching the film listened to the recording with AD.

The participants, regardless of their group or sub-group, were tested either in an isolated and quiet room in the institutions in which the study was carried out, or in individuals' homes. This depended on the participants' preferences. The main intention was to ensure a comfortable, relaxed and friendly atmosphere. No participant was assigned to more than one sub-group and could participate in the experiment only once. The participants were tested during individual sessions, and any comments, problems or queries concerning their interpretations of the dialogues were appreciated and noted down. At the same time, the experimenter refrained from commenting, explaining or helping the participants in performing the tasks, even if they tried to provoke discussion.

Both of the groups reading the dialogues (S1, B1), were allowed to read the text only once. Likewise, the groups listening to the recording (S2 and B2) and the recording with AD (B3), and also the group watching the film (S3), were only allowed to listen to the dialogues or watch the scenes once. Before the experiment started, all of the participants had had the purpose of the study explained to them. They had also been instructed not to give more than one answer to any of the questions, and each time to choose the option which was the most similar to their own interpretation, or alternatively to suggest their own response. They were also asked not to skip questions or to go back to previous ones and correct given answers, even if in the meantime they changed their mind. The time for the completion of the task was not controlled so as not to make the experiment stressful or discouraging for the participants. The questionnaire had been prepared in four versions: in black print for the sighted participants reading the text and listening to the recording or watching the film and appropriately adapted in Braille for the blind participants also reading and listening.

Analysis

As in everyday life situations, the comprehension of utterances in the study required activating various pragmatic (inferential) mechanisms. Some of these, such as free enrichment or the formation of ad hoc concepts, were indirectly examined in the experiment (although they undoubtedly had an impact on participants' ultimate performance). This was contrary to the participants' abilities to understand implicatures, detect humour and figurative language, assign reference, resolve ambiguity and incoherence, and recover other people's states of mind, which were our main concerns in the study. The dialogues presented to the participants differed in their configurations when these pragmatic mechanisms (or sub-tasks) were involved. Also involved was the role of visual and auditory stimuli, as well as the general knowledge necessary for successful interpretation. Analogically to real-life conversations, all of the dialogues were unique, even though their speakers used the same linguistic tools.

Owing to the fact that the participants, instead of interpreting individual sentences, were expected to understand utterances in particular situations (or even whole dialogues), presenting quantitative results alone would not provide satisfactory answers to all of the questions addressed in this book. The analysis of results based on rough figures and statistics might have indicated which pragmatic sub-tasks were particularly difficult for the (sub-)groups of participants, and in which of them one (sub-)group performed better than the other. They will not however, tell us why certain problems in interpretation occurred, how interpretations in the groups differed, what made the participants choose these answers (not the other), and, finally how blindness affected the understanding of the dialogues. This is why we analysed the participants' responses not only statistically (which generally allows certain tendencies to be observed), we also found it necessary to look at the participants' individual answers and the comments they made during the experiment. This was in order to better understand their interpretations and the problems they may have faced in the study.

As we have already mentioned, the dialogues examined in the study involved different configurations of pragmatic sub-tasks. Since they were tested in various dialogues by using different questions, for the sake of convenience and clarity we classified the questions according to the tasks which they examined, as indicated in Table 3-3. The performances of the participants are discussed following the order presented in the table i.e. starting from the understanding of implicatures and finishing with the participants' mind-reading abilities. As a result, our discussion will not be based on the order of the scenes or questions in the questionnaire, but on the presence of the pragmatic sub-tasks listed in the table. Inevitably, it will require switching from one dialogue to another when analysing these sub-tasks, the result of this is that one dialogue is discussed a few times, but each time taking into consideration the different aspects involved in it.

Table 3-3 The classification of the dialogues and questions in accordance with the sub-tasks they examined

Dialogue	Question	Implicature	Reference assignment	Ambiguity resolution	Incoherence resolution	Humour detection	Figurative language comprehensi	ToM
					Pragmatic sub-tasks			
1	1	•						
	2							•
	3				•			
2	1		•					
	2				•			
	3							•
3	1	•						
	2	•						
	3			•				
4	1							•
	2						•	
	3				•			
5	1							•
	2	•						
	3					•		
6	1			•				
	2							•
	3		•					
7	1							•
	2				•			
	3					•		
8	1		•					
	2						•	
	3					•		
9	1	•						
	2				•			
	3						•	
10	1			•				
	2			•				
	3							•

11	1			•
	2	•		
	3			•
12	1			•
	2		•	
	3			•

The correct interpretations of utterances in the dialogues presented in the study were possible only if the pragmatic tasks involved in them were successfully completed. The questions referring to particular dialogues were designed to examine participants' pragmatic abilities of performing the pragmatic sub-tasks indicated in the table, and analysing their consideration of contextual cues in the process. Depending on if a participant managed to successfully perform the tasks or not, he or she chose a different interpretation. We asked the participants to answer questions which showed their abilities to recover implicatures, assign reference, detect humour, irony or sarcasm; resolve ambiguity and/or incoherence, interpret figurative language and recognise speakers' attitudes. In each of the questions only one answer was regarded as correct, while the rest demonstrated additional or faulty assumptions involving elements which had not been mentioned or implied in the dialogues. Apart from the correct choices, participants' incorrect selections had important implications in the analysis of the participants' comprehension, and will be discussed separately.

Participants who performed the sub-tasks successfully were expected to choose the correct interpretation, while those who had problems with them marked other answers which were consistent with their incorrect interpretations. Participants could also choose to provide a personal interpretation which was then analysed by the experimenter. They fell into the same categories as the suggested options (correct or incorrect), but were expressed subjectively. If an individual's interpretation could not be found similar to any of the options provided, an additional category was created (this will be further discussed and demonstrated with appropriate examples when presenting the results of the study). Failure to answer a question and choosing 'I don't know' was analysed in the same way, i.e. as an insufficiency of contextual material, or a participant's inability to arrive at any interpretation. In all of the groups, a few subjects provided uncooperative responses. Such answers were not taken into account when analysing the results of the study.

It should also be remembered that some of the other suggested options could have appeared appropriate or even probable when a limited amount of contextual cues (e.g. reading the text) were given. However, these should have been eliminated by participants as more and more contextual cues were introduced to the recording or film, or when contextually relevant visual and auditory information supported the interpretation processes. These would have ultimately provided evidence for the participants' assumptions. As well as drawing necessary information from linguistic input and perception, all of the dialogues involved references to general knowledge. Due to certain differences in blind people's conceptual knowledge resulting from (impoverished, inadequate, or a lack of past experience), we expected that in some cases this factor may have contributed to an inadequacy in the performance of some blind participants.

Results and discussion

In the analysis of the results, the total scores for each sub-task in all groups of the blind and the sighted participants were calculated. For each answer the participants could receive 1 or 0 points. The participants' answers were entered into the SPSS program and statistically analysed. In order to ascertain if any statistically significant differences between the groups and sub-groups of the participants occurred, ANOVA and 'post hoc' tests were performed. For the sake of clarity, we will present the analyses of the participants' performance in the pragmatic sub-tasks (indicated in Table 3-2 above) separately. In order to avoid confusion, we will first present the results obtained within the groups of sighted and blind participants, and later we will compare them and discuss the findings. In our analysis we used a notification system which was aimed at facilitating the identification of scenes and questions under discussion. The first number in the notification stood for a particular scene (from 1 to 12) presented to the participants, and the second number represented one of three questions referring to the same scene. For instance, task 10.2 corresponded to scene 10 and also to the second question in the questionnaire, 7.3 referred to scene 7 and the third question in the questionnaire and so on. The same principle applied to the rest of the scenes and questions. This system will be in use throughout this chapter.

Implicature

One of the primary abilities which we wanted to examine in the study was the recognition and interpretation of implicitly communicated utterances. Tasks 1.1, 3.1, 3.2, 5.2, 9.1 and 11.2 were designed to test how effectively participants (in particular (sub-)groups) could utilise the available contextual cues, and to recover speakers' true intentions in the dialogues. The successful completion of the tasks, among other things, required going beyond a simple sentence meaning, it required activating deductive mechanisms and referring to general knowledge. Some scenes in the study (e.g. scene 1, 3 and 5) were typical situations involving reference to the available general knowledge scripts, and this reduced the cognitive effort necessary for their interpretation. The participants were expected to 'tune' them as new information appeared in the dialogues, and on their basis recover intended interpretations. Other dialogues (e.g. scenes 9 and 11) were more abstract and contained novel or unusual situations, in which case interpretations had to be based on making non-trivial assumptions. Due to these differences in the complexity of the dialogues, and the personal familiarity with the situations presented in them, we did not obtain exactly the same results in all of the tasks. Among these, some of the dialogues were processed by using general knowledge scripts by the participants and these turned out to be less difficult than others. However, some regularities and tendencies in the responses provided by participants within particular (sub-)groups were observed.

The majority of sighted participants reading the dialogues (group S1) correctly identified the implicatures and recovered speakers' intentions in all of the dialogues. In tasks 1.1, 3.1 and 5.2, in which they could choose among strong implicatures, weak implicatures, explicatures or provide their own answers, most correctly selected strong implicatures, thus producing an average of between 65 to 75% correct answers. Those who opted for the other answers, usually chose weak implicatures or explicatures and the answers were in roughly equal proportions (approx. 10-15%). The participants who selected explicatures understood the utterances literally and assumed that the speakers in the dialogues meant exactly what they said. For instance, in task 1.1 some participants believed that the woman in the dialogue wanted her husband to simply choose which type of tile he liked more; the dialogue could be interpreted in this way taking into consideration her question (83) only.

(83)   *Kochanie, które płytki do łazienki bardziej Ci się podobają: te zielone czy te z delikatną obwódką?*
          (Eng. *Honey, which bathroom tiles do you like more: the green ones or the ones with the subtle border?*)

In fact, her question in (84) implied that she had already made the choice herself and wanted her husband to choose the same.

(84)   *Nie sądzisz, że ta obwódka jest zbyt delikatna?*
         (Eng. *Don't you think that the border is too subtle?*

Similarly, in 3.1 some participants in this sub-group understood that when the girl said (85):

(85)   *Mam dwa bilety na "Don Giovanniego"!*
         (Eng. *I have two tickets for "Don Giovanni"!*)

she basically wanted to inform her interlocutor that she had these tickets, whereas her intention was to invite him to the opera, which failed to be recognised.

Weak implicatures, which the participants either chose from the suggested options or formulated as their own answers in response to the tasks, were frequently not even mentioned or implied in the scenes. This in certain cases put a question mark over their ability to recover the intended interpretations. The participants who chose the weak implicatures made additional assumptions based on their world knowledge and individual experience to a greater extent, rather than on the facts provided in the dialogues. For instance, some of them assumed that if the man in scene 5 did not want to buy new furniture for the house, the family must have financial problems (although no such thing was even mentioned by any of the speakers in the dialogue). In fact, the man gave other reasons for his reluctance. Some participants also inferred that the man did not want to buy new furniture because, as they commented, "(…) you need to be very careful not to stain or wear new things out, and when you have small children it is not easy". Considering this and other comments provided by the participants, we can conclude that most of them tried to link the key pieces of information in the dialogue to maximise the relevance. However, the information it seems was insufficient as they failed to establish global coherence and understand what the man in the dialogue intended to implicitly communicate.

The same pattern can be observed in task 1.1. In this case some participants also decided to provide individual answers (weak implicatures). They commented that the tiles were only a pretext and in fact the speaker (woman) wanted only to have a talk with the man. Some believed that she wanted to make clear in this way that she was in charge. Other participants claimed that the woman wanted to say that she would have to make the choice on her own and that she could not count on her husband. Still other participants in the same group (S1) claimed that the woman did not care what the man thought about which tiles he preferred. This bears similarity to the comments made by former participants. In these responses we can observe a strong influence of general knowledge on participants' interpretations, and this is how they drew these conclusions.

Hardly anyone in the group refrained from giving any answer at all to the questions. This suggested that, despite a great variety of possible interpretations which they offered, they were all able to understand the implicatures, even in ways that no other person did. Additionally, these responses implied that different participants focused on different aspects of the dialogues (e.g. in scene 1, on the woman's attitude to her husband, the choice of tiles or on their marriage and mutual relations). What all of the participants had in common was that in arriving at their interpretations they considered the perspectives of the speakers in the dialogues. For instance, when analysing the responses to task 1.1 in all the groups and sub-groups, we observed that the male participants were more inclined to criticise the woman and take the side of the husband, while the female respondents did just the opposite.

Contrary to the tasks previously discussed in 3.2, 9.1 and 11.2, the participants were presented with dialogues in which the utterances implicitly expressed agreement/acceptance or negation/refusal[1]. Instead of choosing among strong implicatures, weak implicatures and explicatures (as in the tasks discussed above), the participants were asked to choose yes or no answers (additionally graded with words 'rather' and 'definitely' in question 3.2). In these tasks, a comparable percentage of correct responses was obtained and the same number of participants chose answers other than the intended interpretations (approx. 10-15%).

Out of all of these tasks, the participants in group S1 found 3.2 the most problematic. A great majority (85%) of the respondents correctly deduced that in the dialogue (to which this task referred), the speaker (man) refused the offer of going to the opera when he said (86):

(86)   *Spotkamy się później!*
          (Eng. *Let us meet later!*)

Only 50% of the people in the group assumed that he was definitely not going there and 35% answered by choosing the weak implicature option. These subjects claimed that the man would probably not go to the opera, but that he was not certain yet. What is more, contrary to what had been implicitly communicated in this dialogue, 15% of the participants in S1

---

[1] Similar to Sperber and Wilson's famous example discussed in Chapter one and presented in (40)

answered that he would go anyway. As they commented (and the same comment appeared in other sub-groups of both blind and sighted individuals), it would be very rude if he did not go. As they explained, if a woman invites a man, it is very impolite to refuse. Therefore, even if unwillingly, the man should accept the woman's invitation. These interpretations were very much based on general knowledge schemata; which led them to choose this answer.

When compared with S1, the participants in group S2 (listening to the dialogues) gave very similar answers to those offered by the previous group in tasks 1.1, 3.2, 9.1 and 11.2. Similar proportions of explicatures and weak implicatures (approx.10-15%) were also observed. In task 3.1 however, we can observe greater discrepancies. Group S2 in this task revealed a stronger tendency to choose the weak implicature option (50% of participants) and interpreted the intentions of the speaker in the dialogue as boasting, showing off or attempting to impress her interlocutor, rather than inviting him to the opera. As they explained, they arrived at this interpretation due to the auditory cues (the woman's tone of voice) provided to them, and these turned out to be misleading and insufficient for proper interpretation.

In response to task 5.2, more participants than in the previous group (30%) understood implicature as explicature. They understood that the speaker in the dialogue did not wish to buy new furniture because the children would not like the change, while strictly speaking it was not true. The children were mentioned in this utterance, as the speaker later explained, they would hate their parents if they divorced because of the never-ending quarrels about buying new things. The interpretation chosen by the participants was the result of the misunderstanding and ignoring of the speaker's explanation. Some participants also provided their own answers to this question (also weak implicatures) in which they claimed that the man did not want to buy new furniture because "it would not improve the relations between him and his wife, who were going through a crisis". Only 45% of the participants gave correct answers in this task. Considering all of the responses given by all of the participants in this group, fewer people listening to the recording than reading the text could not give any answer and consequently chose the 'I don't know' option (in questions 5.2, 9.1 and 11.2 the percentage ranged from 10 to 15% total answers).

Contrasting the results obtained in all of the groups of sighted participants (see Fig. 3-1), group S3 (watching the film) provided with both visual and auditory contextual information performed comparably to the other groups in most cases.

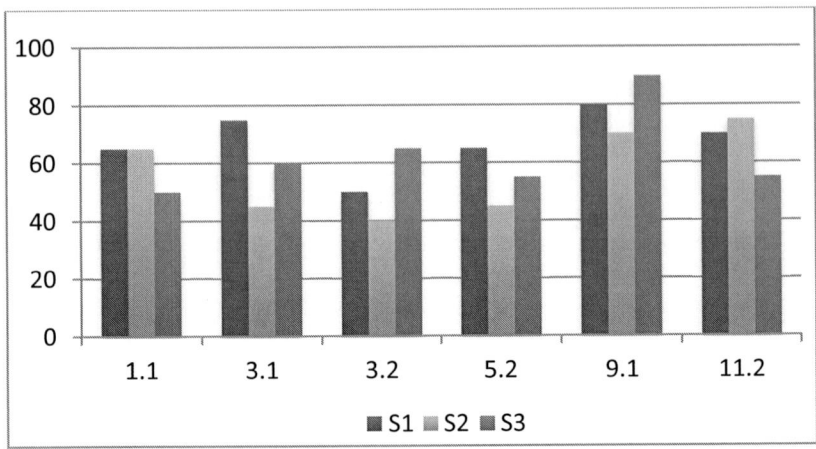

Fig. 3-1 The percentages of correct interpretations of implicatures in the groups of sighted participants

The only exceptions to this were tasks 1.1 and 11.2 in which there were fewer correct responses from this group. In 1.1 only half of the participants chose the strong implicature option, while 30% of the S3 participants chose weak implicatures. These subjects claimed that the wife's intention in dialogue 1 was to make sure that she and her husband were a well-matched couple. Apparently the participants came to this conclusion by taking into consideration the woman's last comment presented in (87), coupled with her body language.

(87)   *Widzisz jak doskonale się rozumiemy.*
         (Eng. *You see how well we understand each other.*)

The participants commented that she looked "as if she desperately sought a man's love" and was "endearing to her husband". Others claimed that the wife attempted to show that she was always right and that the man was not involved in choosing the tiles. This seems to be in conflict with the comments of other participants mentioned, and this shows the different interpretations that the sighted participants arrived at when observing the same situation.

Only half of the participants in S3 responded correctly to task 11.2. They assumed that the speaker in the dialogue used to buy clothes for her husband in a shop for the overweight, but seeing that the man (who learnt of this fact) felt offended, did not want to overtly admit it. As many as

30% of these participants were unable to give any answer at all. Many of them assumed that hardly anybody always buys clothes in the same shop, which again reveals their dependence on general knowledge. Still others could not see any reason why the speaker should want to buy clothes for her husband in this kind of shop. Some participants also concluded that the wife bought the sweater just that once, and perhaps that she was not planning to do it again in the future.

A great majority of the blind participants in group B1 (reading the dialogues) correctly interpreted the implicatures in the dialogues and chose the intended (strong) assumptions. They gave very similar answers to sighted participants in S1, also in the proportions of weak implicatures and explicatures chosen by them in tasks 1.1, 3.1 and 5.2, which ranged from between 5% to 15%. The participants in most cases chose the suggested options instead of providing idiosyncratic interpretations. A few comments that they made during the study concerned task 3.1. In their responses, some participants claimed that the woman "seemed to be hoping for intimacy". Providing responses to 5.2, they commented that the husband did not want to buy new furniture because he had promised to buy new things for the children, and that he would have to break the promise if he and his wife decided to spend money on buying new furniture. Very few people in this group were unable to interpret the dialogues and failed to provide any answers.

In the case of tasks 3.2, 9.1 and 11.2 (involving recognition of implicitly communicated refusal or agreement), this group performed equally well as when challenged with the questions previously discussed. No statistically significant differences between the blind and sighted groups (B1 and S1) were observed either. Similar to S1 in task 3.2, most of the blind participants correctly understood the man's intentions (80%), but only 45% were convinced that he would not go to the opera. There were 35% of participants in B1 who answered that he probably would not go there, 15% of them (relying on general knowledge), answered that he would not turn down the woman's invitation and would eventually go. As many as 90% of the blind participants in B1 correctly claimed that when the man in 9.1 asked if he had called the neighbour to apologise to her, said (88) he implicitly communicated that he had.

(88)   *Tak jak mi kazałaś!*
         (Eng. *Just like you told me!*)

Only 10% misinterpreted this utterance and thought that he had not done it.

In task 11.2, 75% of the participants chose the correct answer saying that the wife's utterance suggested that she would always buy clothes for her husband in the shop for the overweight. There were 10% of the participants who claimed that she did not always buy the clothes in the shop, while 15% of them did not know what to choose. Most interestingly, one blind person observed that "there was nothing about 'a shop for the overweight' in the dialogue". This may shed some light on the blind people's choice of incorrect answers in this case. As illustrated in (89), the speaker in this dialogue wanted to make clear his indignation and hence used the pejorative expression 'dla grubasów' (Eng. 'for fat people').

(89)   *Kupiłaś [ten sweter] w sklepie dla grubasów?*
        (Eng. *Did you buy [this sweater] in the shop for fat people?*)

In the questionnaire however, a more neutral and politically correct wording 'dla puszystych' (Eng. 'for the overweight') was used. These phrases trigger distinct associations. The word 'puszysty'[2] has strong associations with the word 'puch' (Eng. fluff) and has different meanings referring to e.g. sponge cake (meaning 'light and well-made'), cream ('light and frothy'), a toy ('fluffy'), or a person ('overweight'). The multiple readings of this word perhaps resulted in ambiguity and thus the participant's inability to assign reference to the situation. In other words, the person was confused and could not interpret the implicature in this dialogue. Having been told that 'the shop for the fat' and 'the shop for the overweight' is the same thing, he chose the correct answer. Yet it seems interesting that while a sighted person can easily associate the two words as describing the same feature (but with different emotional colouring), blind people may not necessarily be completely aware of the concepts and what it means to be fat, or why we use the word 'overweight' to talk about fat people.

The blind participants in group B2 (listening to the dialogues) gave similar responses in tasks 3.1, 3.2 and 9.1 as group B1. Their responses did not differ to those offered by sighted participants in tasks 5.2 and 3.2. In fact this group gave more correct answers than the sighted participants in S2 to tasks 3.1 and 9.1, as many as 84.2% of the blind participants in group B2 correctly recognised and interpreted the implicatures. However, in task 5.2 the participants performed less successfully than group B1, and in 1.1 and 11.2 they performed less successfully than both B1 and S2. In response to task 1.1, less than half of these participants (36.8%) chose the

---

[2] nominative case

strong implicature, while 42.1% chose the weak implicature and 10.5% opted for the explicature. In turn, in task 11.2 57.9% of the participants selected the correct answer, but over 26% did not know the answer to the question and nearly 16% chose the incorrect answer.

As in the previous group (B1), the blind participants in B2 rarely offered their own answers and preferred to choose the given options. The only exception was task 5.2 in which more participants than in B1 chose the weak implicature and to which a few people decided to provide their own interpretations. Analysing the comments, it can be observed that more frequently than in the previous groups of blind (B1) and sighted (S1, S2, S3) participants, did the individuals in the group consider that the man in this dialogue was serious about divorcing his wife, and that he had been recently considering it. What is more, they claimed that the purchase of the new furniture would lead to the divorce. They also commented that maybe the man did not want to buy anything new because they would divorce anyway. Additionally, some individuals commented that perhaps the man did not like making changes, and that was why he was reluctant to buy anything new. Summing up, it appears that for the blind participants deprived of visual cues, it was much more difficult to recover that the man was joking and that it was not his true intention to divorce his wife. Assuming that he was serious and that the choice of new furniture might be the main reason behind the divorce, they were evidently more likely to understand the speaker's utterance as an explicature rather than an implicature.

The answers provided by group B3 (listening to the recording with AD), in most cases were comparable to the answers given by group B2 (in tasks 1.1, 3.2, 5.2 and 9.1) and to B1 (in 3.2, 9.1 and 11.2). We did not observe any statistically significant differences between groups B3 and S3 in questions 1.1, 9.1 or 5.2, as illustrated in Fig. 3-2.

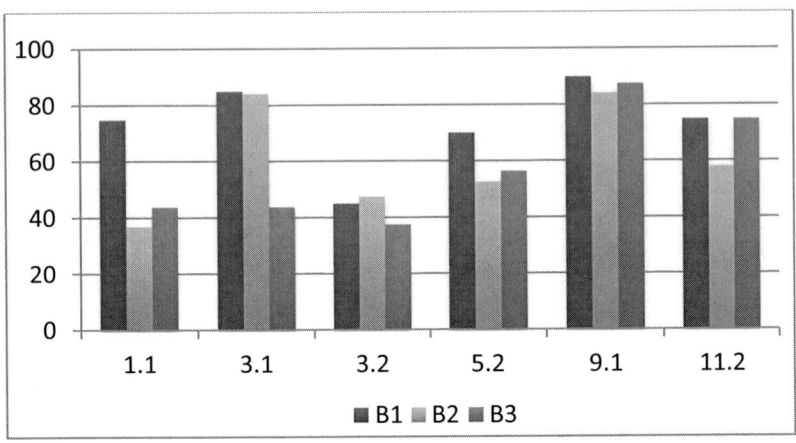

Fig. 3-2 The percentages of correct interpretations of implicatures in the groups of blind participants

In question 1.1, similar to B2, less than 50% of the participants in B3 correctly chose strong implicatures, while over 30% selected the weak implicature and over 10% the explicature option. Similar results were also obtained in group S3, in which the percentage of abandoned interpretations (i.e. amount of chosen 'I don't know' answers) came to approximately 10%. Comparing the results with the percentage of correct answers in groups S1 and B1, it seems that the auditory and visual information (provided by AD) triggered a wide range of additional assumptions which turned out to be more attractive to the participants in this group. The blind participants deprived of visual information but provided with auditory cues, tried to set the scene in a familiar situation by making necessary associations and drawing extra assumptions. Accordingly, they for instance commented that the speaker's (wife's) intention in scene 1 was to redecorate the flat, which was not an incorrect answer and demonstrated their pragmatic and deductive abilities. Some participants also commented that her intention was to arouse her husband's interest and that she would agree on anything he said. Still others commented that the wife knew which tiles she liked and probably that she had already been in the shop with the tiles thousands of times; she only wanted her husband to approve of her choice, so as to avoid any disagreement later.

In spite of the fact that in 3.2 as many as 75% of the participants in B3 correctly understood that the man's utterance represented a refusal to the woman's invitation, only a small number of the participants (37.5% in total) were certain that he intended to turn down the invitation, and the same percentage of the participants answered that he would not go. There were 25% of the participants who gave the incorrect (positive) answer to the question. This suggests that the participants hesitated, and found the auditory cues provided by the recording with AD insufficient and equivocal, this forced them to resort to their general knowledge much more. In this case the participants performed less successfully than the sighted group S3 who gave 65% of correct and fully asserted answers. Also, in the case of task 3.1 they found it equally possible that the woman in the dialogue was boasting and trying to invite the man to the opera. Consequently, an equal number of participants (43.8%) in this group interpreted her utterance as boasting and as an invitation to the man. Evidently, the information provided in the dialogue turned out to be too ambiguous for them.

In the case of task 9.1, group B3 provided as many as 87.5% of the correct answers, these were very similar to the answers provided by the remaining blind and sighted sub-groups. Also in question 5.2, only 56.3% of the participants provided the correct answer, the remaining groups responded in a similar way. The participants in B3 offered the highest percentage of correct answers in task 11.2, in which they performed more successfully than groups B2 and S3. In this case, apparently audio description provided them with the contextual information necessary to appropriately interpret the utterances in the dialogue. Yet the comment of one individual, who said that the husband had to have been short if the wife bought him clothes in a shop for the overweight, suggests that certain problems with the concepts concerning body appearance may still occur in blind adults. The person seems to have wrongly assumed that all overweight people are short, which of course applies only to some people, as equally well an overweight person may be tall. The faulty assumption may have stemmed from a misunderstanding of the three concepts: fat, short and tall. This comment appears to be particularly important in the analysis of the dialogue, taking into consideration the fact that the man in the dialogue was not short but tall. This means that the blind subject's idea was totally different to what a sighted person saw in the same situation.

Despite the minor differences presented above, the blind and the sighted groups did not differ significantly in the interpretation of implicatures ($F(5,114)=1.69$, $p=.143$; see Table 3-4 for detailed descriptive statistics).

Chapter Three

Table 3-4 Mean scores for blind and sighted groups in interpreting implicatures

		Mean	SD
Sighted	S1	4.05	1.23
	S2	3.30	1.41
	S3	3.70	1.59
Blind	B1	4.40	1.27
	B2	3.63	1.34
	B3	3.46	1.40

The answers and comments of the participants show that the interpretation of an utterance (even a simple one), is not based exclusively on decoding logical forms. This observation lends support to the ostensive-inferential model of communication put forward in Relevance Theory and presented in chapter one. Evidently this process is performed on the basis of various contextual cues. When some of the clues prove insufficient or ambiguous, general knowledge (containing ready-made scenarios of various stereotypical situations), plays a prominent role in arriving at an interpretation. This problem-solving strategy was frequently employed by participants in all of the (sub-)groups. The findings also show that a lack of contextual information (visual or auditory cues) does not prevent blind or sighted people from searching for interpretations consistent with their expectations of relevance. Even if the information they were provided with turned out to be insufficient, they rarely abandoned the process. Before they gave up, they referred to their general knowledge in search of assistance. Only if they could not deal with the incoherence, or the maximisation of relevance did not bring any better results, were they unable to provide any interpretation.

Additionally, we observed that although vision gives access to essential contextual cues and plays a critical role in comprehension, it does not always guarantee the successful recovery of implicatures. The same can be said about auditory information and other sources of contextual assumptions, which if helpful, are hardly ever fully communicative in their own right. Clearly this observation supports the claim made by Dan Sperber and Deirdre Wilson (as presented in chapter one), that the outcome and success of the interpretation process can never be warranted. Therefore, it cannot be predicted in advance or taken for granted if one is able to understand implicitly communicated utterances. Effort-consuming as it is, the recognition and interpretation of implicatures is dependent on pragmatic, logical and deductive processes, as well as the accessibility of complementary contextual information derived from different sources. Despite the unpredictability of the interpretation process, in most cases the accessibility of varied extra-linguistic cues appeared to facilitate the blind and sighted people's understanding of implicature, especially if those pieces of information provided strong evidence for one interpretation over another.

Considering the results obtained between the six groups, despite minor differences in understanding particular dialogues, we did not observe any statistically significant differences between the blind and sighted participants in the recovery of implicatures. Very few participants in these groups understood the utterances explicitly or failed to provide any answer at all, this shows that blind people are no less successful in understanding implicitly communicated utterances than sighted people. It also appears that blind people can compensate for missing visual cues and can exploit other sources of contextual information to arrive at the successful interpretation of a situation.

We also observed that the sighted participants in the study offered more varied and idiosyncratic interpretations which stemmed from their visual experience and extensive conceptual knowledge. In some cases however, as we demonstrated, these two factors sometimes deterred them from arriving at the intended interpretation. In this respect, the blind participants' interpretations were more based on facts which they scrupulously analysed. In effect, they performed more successfully in certain situations than the sighted participants. However, we did notice certain gaps in the blind participants' conceptual knowledge, which might have influenced how they interpreted the utterances, also in non-experimental situations. Surprisingly enough, the interpretations which they offered in the study were correct and consistent with the communicated utterances, but their comments and explanations sometimes revealed some misunderstandings and misconceptions.

Reference assignment

In order to understand the utterances that we used in the study, the participants had to understand what or who the speaker was referring to using imprecise referents. Determining this was a prerequisite for the successful completion of other pragmatic sub-tasks, among these were the resolution of ambiguity and incoherence (discussed in the next sections of this chapter). In most cases reference assignment was performed automatically and involved determining what was meant by expressions such as *I, you, her, it, one* etc. Yet in the study our attention was particularly focused on the cases where this was more effort-consuming (such as the assignment of 'bridging reference' discussed in chapter one). In this study we decided to concentrate on the cases where reference assignment was dependent on immediate access to visual and/or auditory cues. In order to examine how well the participants of the study would perform with and without these kinds of information, in tasks 2.1, 6.3 and 8.1 we asked the participants to specify what the speakers in the dialogues were referring to. In tasks 2.1 and 8.1 they could either choose from the suggested options or offer their own ideas. In 6.3 no suggestions were offered and the participants were asked to formulate their own responses.

A great majority of the sighted participants in all of the sub-groups correctly responded to the reference assignment tasks (see Fig. 3-3), and the percentage of correct responses in most cases ranged from 80 to 100%.

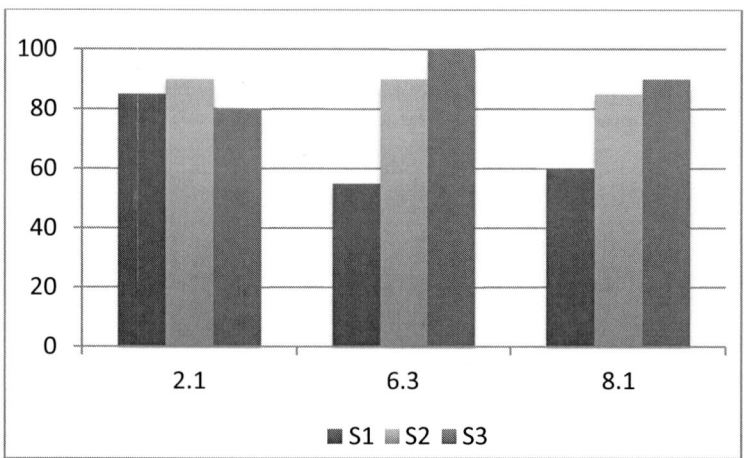

Fig.3-3 The percentages of correct responses in the groups of sighted participants in reference assignment tasks

There were no significant differences in the answers provided by the sub-groups to task 2.1, in which most of the participants correctly deduced that the woman in the dialogue by using 'it', was referring to spilling the wine, as illustrated in (90).

(90)   *Kiedy to się stało?*
         (Eng. *When did it happen?*)

Out of the three groups (S1, S2 and S3), those provided with auditory or both auditory and visual cues, did better than the group reading the text. In particular, tasks 6.3 and 8.1, in which the access to visual and auditory information turned out to be particularly important; a drop in the percentage of correct answers was visible.

In 6.3 the participants were asked what 'tab' the speaker in the dialogue was referring to by saying (91):

(91)   *Pociągnij za paseczek!*
         (Eng. *Pull the tab!*)

The understanding of this utterance involves the assignment of bridging reference. This is providing that no access to visual and auditory information is granted, and it is only possible if this word is associated with what had been previously communicated (as discussed in chapter one). In this case, it was that the other speaker had bought a new CD. Only 55% of the participants in S1 (comparing with the 90 and 100% of correct responses provided by S2 and S3 respectively) correctly understood that it was referring to the plastic tab facilitating the opening of the CD wrapping. There were 40% of the participants in the group who could not provide an answer, and 5% associated it with a garment of clothing. When analysing the answers in this group and the profiles of the participants who belonged to it, we discovered that there was a strong correlation between age and the answers of these participants. The younger participants in this group (19-25 years old) offered a greater number of correct responses than the rest of the age groups. The age effect was not observed in groups S2 and S3 in which 90 and 100% of participants, regardless of age, provided correct answers.

In task 8.1 only 60% of the participants in S1 correctly inferred that the speaker (the mother) in the dialogue, was referring to the behaviour of children by saying (92):

(92)   *To się nadaje do 'Animal Planet'!*
         (Eng. *This would be good for 'Animal Planet'!*)

There were 35% of the subjects who thought she was talking about something that she saw but which was not specified in the dialogue, while 5% did not offer any answer. The percentage of correct answers improved significantly in groups S2 and S3, who responded correctly between 85 and 90% of the time. The noises of children dashing into the room and misbehaving at the table, additionally supported by the observation of the situation, allowed the participants in S2 and S3 to eliminate other options and choose correct answers much more frequently.

Analysing the answers of participants in B1 and S1, we did not observe any statistically significant differences between the groups (see Fig. 3-4).

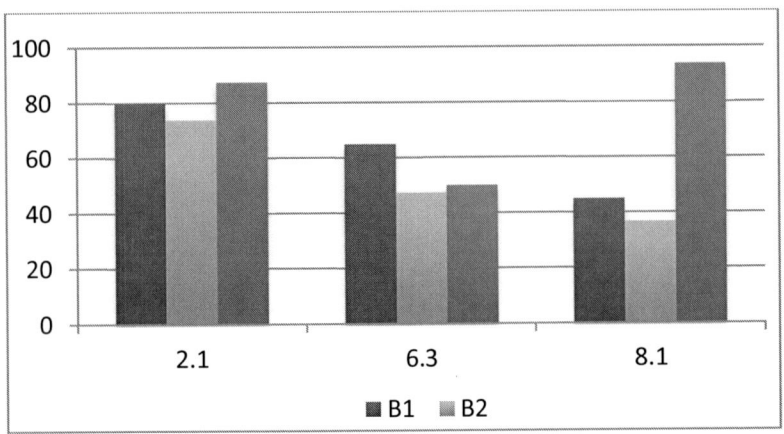

Fig.3-4 The percentages of correct responses of the blind participants in reference assignment tasks.

These two groups found tasks 6.3 and 8.1 particularly difficult. Similarly in 6.3, 65% of the participants in B1 correctly responded to this task, and 35% of them gave no answer at all. Even fewer participants in this group were able to correctly respond to task 8.1 (only 45%), and the rest of the participants claimed that the speaker was referring to something not specified in the dialogue (35%), to the dinner (15%), or pets playing (15%).

While in the case of sighted groups the percentage of correct responses increased significantly as they were provided with auditory and visual information, the results did not improve in task 6.3 in groups B2 and B3. This time only 47% of participants in B2 and 50% in B3 understood that the speaker was referring to the plastic tab on the CD wrapping. More participants in these groups than in the sighted groups believed that the tab referred to a garment or some other thing (e.g. a part of gramophone, a tape or recorder) (see Fig. 3-5 and 3-6).

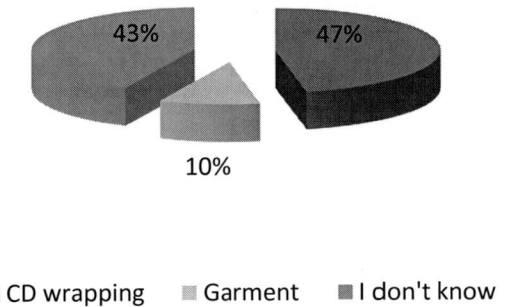

Fig.3-5 The responses offered by group B2 in reference assignment task 6.3.

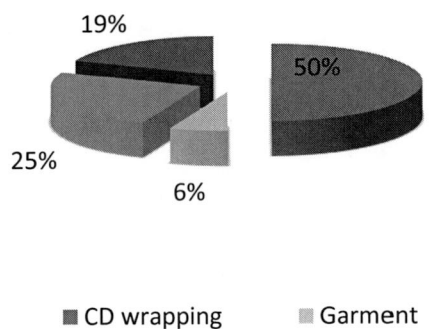

Fig.3-6 The responses offered by group B3 in reference assignment task 6.3.

As observed in group S1, the same correlation between the participants' age and the answers provided was identified, this was found in all sub-groups of blind participants. Young participants, as compared to older participants, gave a greater number of correct answers. Even if not precisely knowing what the 'tab' was, many of the young participants correctly deduced that the word used in this context had to have something to do with the CD mentioned before. This suggests that they maximised the relevance of the speaker's utterance in the scene and tried to resolve the problem. However, the lack of access to immediate visual cues and gaps in their world knowledge prevented them from the assigning reference in this case. Clearly, they were not aware that a tab is a part of a plastic wrapping because they had not seen it or explored it haptically (for the comparison of the performance of blind and sighted participants' age groups in the task see Table 3-5).

Table 3-5 The comparison of the performance of blind and sighted participants' age groups

	19-25 yrs	26-35 yrs	36-45 yrs	46 yrs >
Sighted participants	95,2%	77,6%	83,3%	66,6%
Blind participants	79,4%	51,1%	53,3%	34,4%

In task 8.1 the performance of blind participants in B1 and B2 was significantly improved upon by group B3, in which as many as 93.8% of the participants provided correct answers. For most of the blind participants who had no access to visual information, the dialogue in scene 8 was ambiguous and incoherent. This was because the recovery of the intended interpretation was largely dependent on the observation of the people involved in this scene. Although auditory cues may have helped the swift arrival at the intended interpretation (many participants in B2 commented that they could hear somebody coming to dinner), the visual cues provided stronger and more adequate evidence for the interpretation, as illustrated by the results in group S3. However these cues seem to be effectively compensated for by using AD. Group B3 appropriately inferred that the mother in the scene was referring to the children's behaviour rather than to the dinner served, the pets or something else. This was contrary to the beliefs of participants in groups B1 and B2. The recovery of to what the mother was referring also required making a connection between 'it' and of what 'Animal Planet' is (general knowledge). This also turned out to be problematic for some blind participants. Many of them (regardless of the sub-group they belonged to), did not know what 'Animal Planet' was and admitted that they had never heard of it before. Even some younger participants asked what was meant by it. Some individuals thought that it was not a TV channel, but rather a film (one person asked if the film "Planet of the Apes" was meant there). Still other participants, having heard the name, said that they 'watched' it regularly and were enthusiastic about telling us what they had heard in one of the programmes aired on the channel recently.

Similar to the sighted groups, a great majority of the blind participants correctly responded to task 2.1, and very few people chose wrong or no answers. Surprisingly enough, even in the absence of auditory and visual cues, 80% of the participants in group B1 could correctly establish reference. In the remaining groups of blind participants we obtained similar results. Unlike tasks 6.3 and 8.1, which could be seen as novel and non-stereotypical, in the case of 2.1 the participants had to deal with a more familiar situation using general knowledge schemata. This may explain why both blind and sighted participants performed better in this task than in the other reference assignment tasks. In 6.3 and 8.1 reference assignment was dependent on the access to visual images, these were not additionally described or mentioned in the dialogues. The existence of these both the blind and sighted participants in the groups reading the text and listening to the recording might be unaware. In task 2.1 visual information supported the interpretation process and thus reduced the cognitive effort by providing strong evidence for contextual assumptions. However, the findings show that even when blind and sighted participants had no access to the information, they could assign reference on the basis of other contextual cues, these included available linguistic input and general knowledge schemata.

The statistical analysis performed on the groups (see Table 3-6 for descriptive statistics) showed that the blind and the sighted participants differed in how successful they were in the reference assignment task ($F(5,114)=5.18$, $p=.000$).

Table 3-6 Mean scores for blind and sighted groups in the reference assignment task

		Mean	SD
Sighted	S1	2.00	.97
	S2	2.65	.67
	S3	2.70	.65
Blind	B1	1.90	.96
	B2	2.91	.79
	B3	2.19	.93

The post hoc tests revealed that the main differences occurred between groups S2 and B2 ($p=.002$), S3 and B1 ($p=.045$) and S3 and B2 ($p=.001$). The findings presented above show that reference assignment is a highly context-dependent task in which the effect of vision on the participants' performance can be easily noticed. The sighted participants were statistically more successful in the tasks discussed in this section than the blind participants. This shows that the lack of access to visual information may have been a hindrance to the blind. The performance of the sighted group S1 (who having no access to visual information performed similarly to blind participants and clearly had certain difficulties in assigning reference), demonstrates that the poorer performance in the groups of blind participants was not a matter of underdeveloped pragmatic abilities, but rather an insufficiency of contextual information. The study also reveals that visual information can be effectively provided by AD, which in the study improved the blind participants' reference assignment and their understanding of the utterances. We should also remember that the tasks used in this study mostly concerned cases where reference assignment was related to visual concepts. The performance of the blind participants in other tasks indicates that they can effectively determine referents in utterances, but this is much more challenging for them if visual information is involved.

Ambiguity resolution

The next pragmatic ability which we examined in the study was the ability to understand ambiguous utterances. As argued in Relevance Theory, ambiguity and indeterminacy are the inherent attributes of natural communication. This was why, we assumed that if we wanted to provide a satisfactory answer to the questions whether blind and sighted adults could understand the utterances in communicative situations equally well, and what role the context played in the process, it was critical that we analysed their interpretations from the perspective of resolving lexical, structural and pragmatic ambiguity in the dialogues presented in the study. Being successful in this task was particularly important for the completion of other pragmatic sub-tasks, with which ambiguity resolution proves to be highly related (as we argued in chapter one). For instance, effective disambiguation allows incoherence to be avoided (Asher & Lascarides 1995), and as we observed in the previous section, allows reference to be successfully assigned.

In this study we were particularly interested in the scenes in which different contextual information triggered different interpretations. Consequently, the speakers' intentions in these cases might be understood in two or more different ways. The participants' ability to understand ambiguous utterances was analysed in tasks 3.3, 6.1, 10.1, 10.2 and 12.2.

In these tasks they were expected to choose one answer from different options representing possible readings. Alternatively, they could suggest their own answers if none of the options appealed to them.

As we observed, a great majority of the sighted participants had no problems with understanding the ambiguous utterances in the dialogues. We did not notice any statistically significant differences between the sub-groups (S1, S2 and S3), who were all generally successful in performing the tasks (see Fig. 3-7).

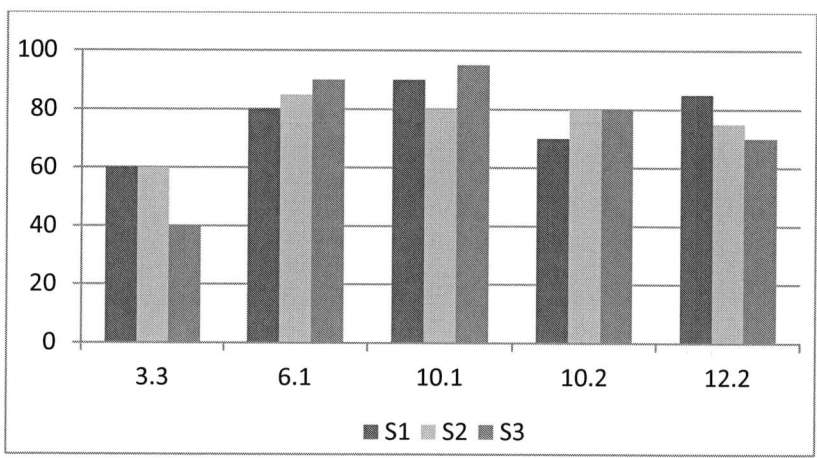

Fig. 3-7 The percentages of correct responses offered by sighted participants in ambiguity resolution tasks.

The participants in the groups offered a comparable percentage of correct responses, which in most cases ranged from 70 to 95%. The only exception to this was task 3.3, in response to which all of the sighted participants provided fewer correct answers than in the four remaining tasks. In this particular case, group S3 performed the least successfully, offering only 40% of correct responses. Despite the access to both visual and auditory contextual cues, this group performed less successfully than groups S1 (having no access to the cues) and S2 (provided with auditory cues only), which totalled at 60% of correct responses.

Analysing the participants' responses, we discovered that as many as 40% in S3 thought that the speaker in this dialogue wanted to communicate that he was planning to go to a boxing match. At the same time they maintained that he would not turn down the woman's invitation to the opera. Evidently, the misleading gestures and reaction of the man who thought that 'Don Giovanni' was the name of a boxing champion and assumed that the woman wanted to invite him to the match, triggered this interpretation. This would be perhaps justified if the two people were, for instance, talking in a gym or sports centre and the sound of punching into a punchbag could be identified. In which case, by saying (93),

(93)   *Spotkamy się później!*
         (Eng. *Let us meet later!*)

the man might have intended to communicate that he had to go to the boxing match and that he had no time to discuss the details of going to the opera.

When unable to resolve the pragmatic ambiguity demonstrated above, some participants in S3 (15% in total) also thought that the speaker by saying (93) wanted to make an appointment with the woman. This answer was chosen by an even greater number of participants in group S1 (30%) and S2 (20%). This suggests that in the absence of visual and audio-visual cues respectively, they understood the utterance differently than was the intention, which was that the man wanted to get rid of the woman.

In general, the sighted participants, regardless of the sub-group they belonged to, selected one of the options instead of choosing to give an idiosyncratic interpretation. However, a few individuals decided to offer their own answers to some questions, and this gave an interesting perspective to the interpretations offered by this group. Some of the responses were (at least partially) more complex versions of the suggested options in the questionnaire. For instance, in the case of task 10.2, 70 to 80% of the sighted participants in each of the sub-groups understood that the waiter in the dialogue, by saying (94),

(94)   *Rozumiem.*
         (Eng. *I see.*)

was accepting the woman's remark in (95) and seemed to be unaffected by it.

(95)   *Nie chcę robić afery, ale w karcie pod winami francuskimi mają Państwo 'Sodole'.*
         (Eng. *I don't want to make a fuss, but on the menu you've got 'Sodole' in the French wines' section.*)

One participant in group S1 commented that the waiter must have misunderstood the woman's intentions, and in fact "[had] no idea what the woman's point [was]". As this participant later explained, "(…) either he [was] not a wine connoisseur or [had] never seen the wine list offered in this restaurant". The same person also added that the man definitely ignored the woman's remark and decided to turn to her partner in hope that the man would simply make a decent order. Similar observations were made by a few participants in group S3, who claimed that "the waiter was trying to change the subject" and that he had not understood what the woman intended to say. The detailed accounts of the situation provided by these and the few other participants, indicated that the waiter's utterance in (94) was so ambiguous that it triggered many possible assumptions (strong and weak). Not only was it lexically ambiguous, as the word 'rozumiem' (Eng. 'I see') may refer to many different things, but instead of conveying information, this word may actually perform a phatic function in the conversation (e.g. aimed to reassure a speaker that the hearer is still listening and can follow). In this dialogue it also causes pragmatic ambiguity as it gives rise to many different assumptions.

Other comments of the sighted participants concerning task 10.1 referred to the same dialogue. This time however, the participants' attention was focused on the utterance of the woman (customer). The sighted participants generally had no problems with interpreting the woman's utterance as a complaint about a mistake in the menu, and provided from 80 to 95% correct responses. Some participants additionally noted that she was unpleasantly surprised that this restaurant could make such a mistake and include 'Sodole' in a French wines' section. Still others commented that her real intention was to show off and demonstrate that she was an expert in wines. Hardly anybody in any of the sub-groups (5 to 10% in total) found the expression 'robić aferę' (Eng. 'make a fuss') ambiguous, and wrongly understood that the woman was astonished that the restaurant served her favourite (and very rare) wine.

The successful interpretation of this utterance also required assuming that 'Sodole' is not French, but an Italian wine. Otherwise the inability to resolve incoherence could have stopped the participants from offering any interpretation. Although many participants complained that they had not heard about this wine and as a result they did not know which answer to choose, purposefully in this dialogue we did not exchange the name with the better-known 'Bordeaux'. This was because we claimed that the participants should have been able to deduce the meaning from other contextual cues available in the woman's utterance. The participants, searching for relevance, should try to eliminate incoherence, which is inevitable if one wrongly assumed that 'Sodole' is a French wine. In this situation, the woman's complaint turned out to be unjustified and hence incongruous. According to our expectations, between 80 to 95% of the sighted participants correctly identified the woman's intentions and resolved this pragmatic ambiguity, although not even one person during the study admitted that s/he knew that 'Sodole' is an Italian wine.

Interesting and amusing ideas came to the minds of participants in S1 when reading the dialogue in scene 6. In response to task 6.1, they were expected to resolve lexical ambiguity, and specify what the speaker could not cope with. In order to find a correct answer to this question, the participants had to consider not only Arthur's utterance (which said that he had bought a new CD), but also the utterances of the other speaker, saying (91):

(91)   *Pociągnij za paseczek!*
         (Eng. *Pull the tab!*)

Since the Polish word 'paseczek' is underspecified in this utterance and may refer to numerous things (e.g. a small belt, a strip of paper or material, a stripe, etc.), only by means of the available contextual cues could the participants disambiguate this word. Similarly, the word 'pociągnąć' (infinitive form), may mean 'to draw', 'to pull', 'to jerk', 'to pluck' etc., and hence it is lexically ambiguous.

A great majority of the S1 participants (80%) correctly understood that 'paseczek' (Eng. 'tab') referred to a plastic strip which facilitates the opening of a new CD, and logically the speaker had problems with using it to open the CD which he had bought. Few individuals either responded that the speaker did not know how to play the CD, or were totally unable to assign reference. The latter assumed that the tab mentioned in the dialogue stood for a part of a garment. They claimed that the speaker had problems with undoing a dress or bra. Similar associations also appeared in other (non-sighted) groups. This suggests that in the absence of visual information the participants had a wider choice of possible assumptions, and hence ambiguity resolution was much more difficult. It also demonstrates that the inability to resolve ambiguity results in the inability to account for incoherence in an utterance. In the case discussed above, participants who deduced that 'the tab' was some other thing than the plastic strip, would have found the dialogue incoherent and the speakers' utterances unconnected.

Analysing the responses provided by the blind participants, we observed that they were slightly less successful than the sighted groups, and provided fewer correct answers in ambiguity resolution tasks. In most cases, the percentage of correct responses was enough to be comparable in all three groups. More readily than in the sighted sub-groups, did the blind participants offer their idiosyncratic interpretations instead of choosing one of the options which were suggested. Very often they combined different elements chosen from a few options in the questionnaire. It seems that they could not decide on just one option as the dialogues were too ambiguous for them. Fig. 3-8 shows the percentage of correct responses in groups B1, B2 and B3.

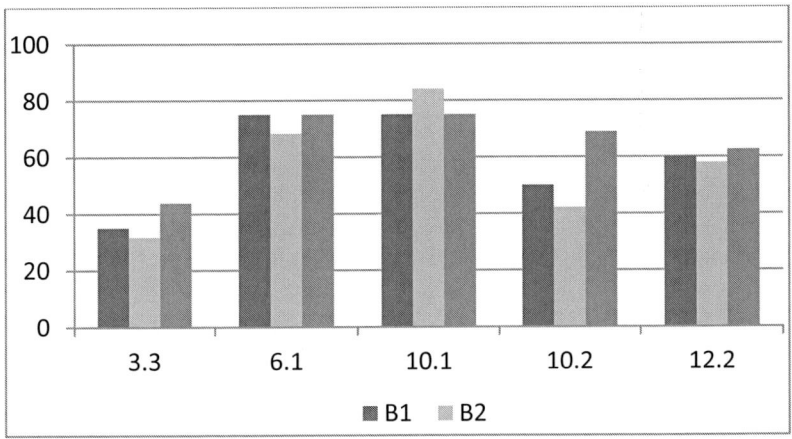

Fig. 3-8 The percentages of correct responses of blind participants in ambiguity resolution tasks.

When looking at the results, it appears that these groups did better in tasks 6.1 and 10.1, both of which rested on the resolution of lexical ambiguity. Tasks 3.3, 10.2 and 12.2 involved pragmatic ambiguity and were more difficult for the participants.

Similar to group S1, the blind participants in B1 found task 3.3 the most challenging. However, compared to the sighted group, B1 provided much fewer correct responses (35%). There was no statistically significant difference between the participants in B1 and B2, who were also less successful than the sighted participants in S2. The same tendency was observed in group B3, whose responses did not differ significantly from those in B1 and B2, but were statistically less successful than those of the sighted groups. A comparable number of people in all of the sub-groups of blind participants understood that the man in the dialogue did not have time to talk to the woman and suggested that they should meet later. Some people commented that the speaker would rather watch a boxing match than go to the opera, and that was why he made the excuse that he had no time. Actually, the speaker's behaviour was more ostensive than the participants understood. His intention was not to pretend that he was busy, but to overtly demonstrate that he was not interested in going to the opera. While most of the sighted participants were aware of this and noticed his ostensive behaviour, understanding the man's intention in this situation was much more difficult for the blind participants who did not have access to the information. Still other participants in B3 claimed that the man decided to meet with the woman to talk about the opera, this conflicts with the man's intention expressed in the dialogue.

In response to tasks 10.1 and 10.2 (which tested the ability to resolve lexical and pragmatic ambiguity present in the utterances of the woman and the waiter in scene 10), the blind participants were more successful in the first task. Even though they did not know if 'Sodole' was a French wine and tried to figure it out by asking the experimenter, as many as 75% in group B1, 84.2% in B2, and 75% in B3, correctly deduced without any help that the wine had to have been of some other origin and that the woman wanted to make a complaint about the mistake on the menu. A few participants added that although the woman said that she did not want to make a fuss, her true intention was actually to make the fuss in order to focus the attention on herself. Some participants in group B1 claimed that she wanted to gently draw the waiter's attention to the error in the wine list, this was not true to the recording in which the woman was evidently behaving maliciously. This comment shows that a text alone is insufficient for recognising the illocutionary force of an utterance and may provide inadequate information, perhaps as to the attitude of a speaker.

The second task (10.2), which referred to the response of the waiter, turned out to be much more complicated than the previous one. Only 50% of the participants in group B1, 42.1% in B2 and 68.8% in B3 understood that the waiter accepted the woman's complaint and that it did not affect him. There were 15% in B1, 10% in B2 and 12.5% in B3 who assumed that he accepted her order, this was even though she evidently had not ordered anything yet. A few individuals offered idiosyncratic interpretations in response to this task. For instance, some participants in B1 and B2 explained that the waiter did not understand the woman and did not notice her complaint. As they went on to explain, he just wanted to take an order, but he was not responsible for the menu and it was beyond his competence level and job description. A few other participants said that he ignored the woman and her complaint, or tried to change the subject. It should be noted that while all of the sighted participants inferred that the waiter who asked the question in (96), was referring to the woman's partner.

(96)   *A co dla Pana?*
         (Eng. *And for you sir?*)

Some blind participants (mostly in group B3) thought that the woman was alone in the restaurant and that the waiter was turning to some other customer. Some participants in group B3 also understood that "the waiter was asking the woman's husband about what he thought about her complaint". This comment demonstrates that the blind individual, despite being provided with some contextual information via AD, could not properly understand the waiter's utterance.

A few interesting responses were also provided to task 6.1. Some participants for instance, wondered if the speaker had bought an appropriate CD, and if his interlocutor would like it. In the case of the sighted participants performing the same task, a few thought that he had problems with undoing a dress or other garment rather than with opening the new CD. Despite certain difficulties, the majority of blind participants chose correct answers to the question, eventually providing from between 68.4 to 75% correct responses.

In the responses which blind participants provided to task 12.2 we can observe similar problems with disambiguation as in the tasks previously discussed. The utterance in the dialogue describing a cat as 'lying on the street and pretending to be asleep' involved not only ambiguity but also visual concepts. In other words, in order to properly understand this utterance, it was necessary to distinguish between the literal meaning of the utterance (that the cat was indeed lying on the street) and the figurative meaning (that he had been run over). There were 60% of the participants in B1, 57.9% in B2 and 62.5% in B3 who opted for the second meaning. A few participants claimed that the man was making fun of the animal because either he did not like cats, or he thought that the cat was ugly. Some individuals also believed that the man meant exactly what he said, which was that he had seen the cat actually lying there and pretending to be asleep. One participant in group B3 also offered the idiosyncratic interpretation that the man wanted to communicate the fact that he was indifferent to what had happened to the cat. However, the participant failed to explain what in his opinion had exactly happened. Despite certain difficulties in this task, hardly anybody (in any of the sub-groups) refused to provide any answer to this question, which meant that the available contextual information aided the participants in arriving at their interpretations.

The statistical analysis (detailed descriptive statistics in Table 3-7) revealed that there were significant differences between the blind and sighted participants ($F(5,114)=3.77$, $p=.003$). This mainly concerned groups S1 and B1 ($p=.033$), S1 and B3 ($p=.033$), and S2 and S3 ($p=.033$).

Table 3-7 Mean scores for blind and sighted groups in the disambiguation task

		Mean	SD
Sighted	S1	3.85	.87
	S2	1.03	.23
	S3	1.03	.23
Blind	B1	1.20	.27
	B2	0.97	.22
	B3	1.35	.33

The findings show that context plays a significant role in ambiguity resolution in both blind and sighted people. In particular, visual access to certain information and prior visual experience both appear to have an influence on disambiguation abilities. The sighted participants, even in the group which had no access to auditory and/or visual cues, could appropriately resolve the ambiguity in the utterances presented. Consequently, it seems that sighted people find it easier to understand ambiguous utterances than blind people, who are observed to be more prone to misinterpreting lexically or pragmatically ambiguous utterances. These difficulties may also have an influence on their abilities of resolving incoherence, which as we argued are specifically interconnected.

Incoherence resolution

Apart from the understanding of the speakers' utterances in the dialogues, the individuals taking part in the study were also examined on their ability to establish coherence in these dialogues at the levels of global and local structures, and in conjunction with other pragmatic tasks (these inherently linked with the incoherence resolution mechanism). In tasks 1.3, 2.2, 4.3, 7.2 and 9.2, we tested the blind and sighted participants on their ability to eliminate inconsistencies and incongruity in written and spoken texts.

In the majority of cases over half of the sighted participants (in each sub-group) were able to resolve incoherence when provided with contextual information in the form of written text, recording or film. The remaining answers were in more or less similar proportions (amounting to approximately 10%) and very few people did not mark any answer at all, which made up about 5% of all the responses. However, when compared to the other pragmatic tasks examined in this study and discussed so far, the sighted participants were less successful in performing the incoherence resolution tasks, which in fact were generally more challenging for all three sub-groups (see Fig. 3-9).

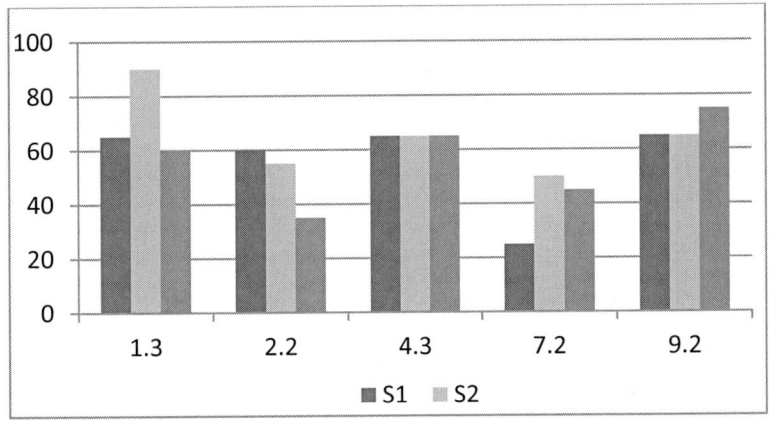

Fig. 3-9 The percentages of correct responses of sighted participants in incoherence resolution tasks.

As indicated in the diagram, in task 1.3, 65% of the participants in group S1 successfully established coherence in the dialogue and understood that the woman was trying to encourage her husband to choose the same (green) tiles that she had already chosen. The same interpretation was chosen by as many as 90% of the participants in S2, who in comparison to group S1 provided a greater number of correct responses. This may suggest that the contextual information they were provided with in the recording was qualitatively and quantitatively richer than the text. Surprisingly enough, the group (S3) watching the film were less successful than S2 (and comparable to S1) and the correct responses in this group amounted to 60%. The participants who provided answers other than those intended were unable to understand the woman's intentions properly and found the dialogue incoherent and incomprehensible. Many of them understood that in the dialogue, the woman by saying (97), wanted to express her surprise that she and her husband found the tiles which they both liked.

(97)   *Mnie też te bardziej się podobają. Widzisz, jak doskonale się rozumiemy ...*
        (Eng. *I like them more, too. You see how well we understand each other...*)

However, this interpretation has little correspondence to the previous parts of the discourse, especially since the man's first choice was different. It was because the woman knew which tiles she liked that she manipulated him into changing his mind, and she succeeded in it. In spite of this fact, some participants claimed that she gave her husband a choice, and that she was genuinely interested in what his preference was. Some participants (mostly in S3) also said that she probably wanted to come to a common conclusion with her husband, rather than to encourage him to choose the tiles which she liked.

In scene 2 the participants were presented with a dialogue in which the topic was not specified. The speakers in this dialogue seemed to be talking about different things (e.g. time, wine, something made of cotton and silk etc.) and their utterances might have appeared completely unrelated. The key to establishing coherence in this case was to assume (following the natural search for relevance) that there were certain relationships between the different parts of the discourse, and that the speakers were cooperating in this act of communication. It was crucial not only to understand this dialogue as an integrated whole, but also to observe these relations which connected the speakers' utterances. Task 2.1 provided some evidence of participants' general interpretations of what the speakers' were discussing in this dialogue. In task 2.2 we wanted to find out if they were able to understand one of the speakers' utterances in connection with what was being discussed throughout the whole conversation. For this reason, we chose the utterance presented in (98), which even when isolated from the rest of the conversation seemed incoherent. The two sentences look as if they were unconnected or might indicate that the speaker is switching contexts.

(98)   *Jakoś sobie poradzimy. To bawełna z domieszką jedwabiu?*
        (Eng. *We can deal with it. Is it cotton with silk?*)

Among the sighted groups who responded this task, 60% of the participants in S1 and a comparable number in S2 successfully established coherence. They correctly understood that the speaker expressing the utterance in (98) meant that it would be possible to remove the stain. In group S3, the percentage of correct responses offered by the participants made up only 35%, and this was much less than in both groups previously discussed. There were 65% of the participants in S3 (only 20% in S1 and 35% in S2) who understood that the speaker wanted to say that they could deal with problems, rather than with the wine stain. They commented that the speaker wanted to get the details of what had happened. It was possible that they were not certain if the whole text referred to one situation, or if perhaps something else had happened, about which the speaker was not talking.

These findings suggest that the participants who watched the film (S3) found this task more difficult than those who read the text (S1) or listened to the recording (S2). Additionally, 15% of the participants in S1 (who provided idiosyncratic responses to this task), correctly understood that the speakers were talking about a wine stain. While some participants explained that the speaker communicated that removing the stain would be easy for her, others claimed that she wanted to find out what had happened and in what circumstances the object (not specified in the dialogue) had been stained. However, they failed to explain why the speaker needed the information; hence it is hard to tell if the participants correctly understood that it would help her to find an effective way of removing the stain. The participants might have wrongly assumed that the person was just curious or angry with what had happened.

While in task 2.2 we tested participants on their ability to establish global coherence, in task 4.3 they were expected to account for coherence at more local level, that is, between particular segments of the utterance in (99):

(99)   *Bliźniaki miały w nosie zwierzęta i grały w kapsle. Ala chciała zobaczyć małego strusia, ale nie chciał wyjść z zagrody.*
        (Eng. *The twins didn't give a damn about animals and were playing caps. Ally wanted to see a baby ostrich, but it refused to come out of the enclosure.*)

On the basis of the information provided in this utterance, the participants were asked to specify how many children the speaker had taken to the zoo. In response to this task we obtained the same percentage of correct answers in all of the three groups of sighted participants, which made up 65%. The participants correctly inferred that the speaker in the dialogue must have been talking about three children (the twins and Ally). The rest of the participants either did not choose any answer (5-15%) or thought that the speaker had taken his two children (the twins) to the zoo, one of whom was Ally (20-30%). Following their way of thinking, the girl was uninterested in watching the animals (hence the reason why she was playing caps), and wanted to see the baby ostrich. Since no one can want and at the same time not want something, we can assume that these participants failed to establish coherence in this utterance and that their interpretations were inconsistent.

Similar results were obtained in task 9.2. In this task the participants were expected to relate the utterance in (100) to the fact that the man had had to call the neighbour to apologise to her (which was very difficult for him). Otherwise, it might be understood that something terrible (which was not mentioned in the dialogue) had happened and affected his life.

(100)   *Czy Twoje życie się zawaliło?*
         (Eng. *Did your world come crashing down?*)

A majority of the sighted participants successfully established coherence in this case, and in all three sub-groups a comparable number of correct responses was provided (65% in both S1 and S2, and 75% in S3). Providing their own answers, some individuals stated that the man had not talked to the neighbour yet and did not want to, in which case this conversation would have become incoherent and unrelated to the other parts of the dialogue. The speaker by saying (100) wanted to know if the apology had been so difficult for the man to make, which makes sense only if it was assumed that the apology had already been made.

Out of the five tasks examining the ability to make coherent interpretations of utterances, the sighted participants found task 7.2 particularly difficult. In the dialogue to which this task referred, one speaker complained that his parrot (which he had had for ten years) died. After hearing this utterance, one might think that the parrot must have been important to the speaker and he was sorry about what happened, especially if he underlined that he had had it for so long. However, when asked if he would buy a new parrot, the speaker answered (101):

(101)   *Jasne ... przecież to tylko worek piór.*
         (Eng. *Sure...after all it's only a bunch of feathers.*)

This seemed to contradict the previous assumption and implicated that he was not sorry at all, and what is more, he thought that his parrot was worthless. This is because of the irony present in the dialogue. Without recognising that the speaker who expressed (101) did not actually mean what he said and just ridiculed the other speaker's attitude in the conversation, coherence could not be successfully established. In group S1 only 25% of the participants were able to correctly understand this dialogue and resolve the incoherence. Sub-groups S2 and S3 performed comparably offering 50 and 45% of correct responses. These results show that failure in one task very often leads to the inability to perform another. The contextual cues taken from the recording and film evidently improved the number of correct responses and allowed at least some participants to detect irony and resolve incoherence. Still, 40% of the participants in group S1, 25% in S2 and 30% in S3 were unable to establish coherence in this dialogue and responded that the speaker would buy a new parrot, even though he considered the animals worthless. There were 20% in S1 and S2 and 5% in S3 who thought that he would not buy it because he thought parrots worthless. Some participants in group S1 who provided idiosyncratic answers, claimed that the man in the dialogue did not like pets and that he must have bought (or received) his parrot by mistake. A few individuals maintained that the speaker would in fact buy a new parrot because he was "accustomed to having a pet". Still others commented that he would buy the parrot "after some time", but did not explain why not soon. One participant said that the speaker talked nonsense, which implies that she could not resolve the incoherence in this dialogue. Some of the participants in groups S2 and S3 also decided to provide individual interpretations rather than choose one of the options suggested in the questionnaire. These were similar to the responses given by group S1. The only exceptions were the comments of a few individuals in group S3 who maintained that the speaker would buy a new parrot even though he knew that other people (other than himself) thought these animals worthless. Some of them also responded that he would buy a parrot, but it was not clear why. One person also recognised that by saying he would buy the parrot, the speaker was being ironic and in fact he was not intending to do so. This participant however, failed to recognise that the target of this irony was the other speaker and he claimed that this man was sneering at the dead parrot. This shows that this individual managed to detect some form of irony, but misinterpreted the speaker's intentions in the dialogue which echoed the indifferent attitude of the other speaker in the situation. As a result, the incoherence remained unresolved.

When analysing the responses of the blind participants to incoherence resolution tasks, we observed that they encountered similar problems to the sighted participants. In the majority of cases we did not notice any statistically significant differences between the blind and sighted groups, whose success in establishing coherence differed depending on the complexity of the dialogues. Generally the answers provided within particular sub-groups of blind participants did not differ remarkably (see Fig.3-10), but the individual comments which they provided gave us an insight into how utterances were understood and the different ways they attempted to establish coherence in them. They also allowed us to examine the influence that visual impairment could have had on their performance.

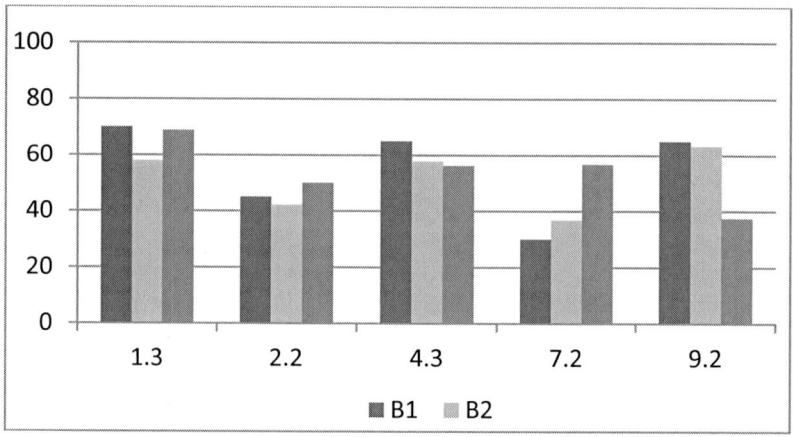

Fig. 3-10 The percentages of correct responses of blind participants in incoherence resolution tasks.

In task 1.3 the blind participants in all of the sub-groups provided a similar number of correct answers. The statistical analysis did not reveal any significant differences between the blind and sighted participants in the groups reading the text and watching the film or listening to the recording with AD. A comparable number of respondents chose to offer idiosyncratic interpretations which were very similar among these groups. Group B2 was slightly less successful than the sighted participants in S2 who provided 90% correct responses.

Despite the fact that in task 2.2 the blind participants in B1 provided statistically similar answers to those in sighted group S1, we observed that many more blind participants in group B1 (40% as compared to 20% in S1) understood that the speakers in the dialogue were talking about the woman's problems. A similar number of participants in B2 and B3 also chose this answer. Additionally, one participant when providing his individual answer, came up with the astonishing interpretation that the speaker and her interlocutor were waiting for someone who had unexpectedly called them. As he went on to explain, they knew the visit would be difficult because some delicate issues would be settled. This interpretation however, bears little correspondence to the speaker's question about a kind of fabric, which leaves this discourse incoherent. Although another participant wondered how a wine stain was related to this fabric and wanted to know if it would be easy to wash cotton with silk, he was still unable to provide a correct answer. Between 5 to 10% of the blind participants could not give any interpretation and failed to establish coherence in this dialogue.

The blind participants' performances were similar to those of the sighted participants in task 4.3. In this case 65% in group B1, 57.9% in B2 and 56.3% in B3 gave the correct responses. Approximately 30% of the respondents in each of the sub-groups wrongly understood that the speaker took two children to the zoo. About 5% of participants in B1 and B2 and over 18% in B3 did not know which answer to choose and failed to establish coherence in this dialogue. Some participants commented that it was not explicitly said how many children went to the zoo and that was why they were unable to give any answer. One blind individual observed that the speaker's utterance was self-contradictory. This person wanted to know if the word 'twins' always describes two people, or perhaps more (probably meaning triplets and quadruplets). He responded tentatively that the man took three children (two twins and a girl), but as he underlined, "only if there were two twins". This person's knowledge clearly had an effect on his interpretation and incoherence resolution ability. This might also apply to the other blind participants taking part in this study, those who did not give any answers or provided incorrect responses, but who also did not reveal the dilemmas they faced in this task.

Many of the blind participants found task 9.2 equally as problematic as the one previously discussed. Similar to groups S1 and S2, they offered approximately 65% correct answers. The rest of them were either unable to establish coherence and provide the interpretation which would be consistent with the accessible information, or failed to give any answer at all. When offering their individual responses, they commented that the speaker did not feel like talking to the neighbour and he did not like her. This suggests that they wrongly assumed that the speaker had not yet talked to the neighbour. Some participants claimed that he thought the neighbour was difficult. The participants in B3 performed less successfully than groups B1 and B2 in this task, offering only 37.5% of correct answers. They also performed less successfully than group S3, but interestingly enough more frequently than in those groups they understood the speaker's utterance in (100) literally.

(100)   *Czy Twoje życie się zawaliło?*
         (Eng. *Did your world come crashing down?*)

Task 7.2 was particularly difficult for the visually impaired respondents. Only 30% of the participants in B1 and 36.8% in B2 correctly interpreted the speaker's ironic utterance and were able to resolve the incoherence introduced by the seemingly conflicting utterances in this dialogue. The remaining participants failed to perform the task and provided either the wrong answer or no answer at all. Many of the subjects in these sub-groups (45% in B1, 36.8% in B2 and 31.3% in B3) understood the words of the speaker literally, and ignoring his previous utterance, inferred that he would buy a new parrot even though these animals are worthless. Much fewer participants (15% in B1 and B2 and only 6.3% in B3) chose the answer that he would not buy the parrot, because these animals are worthless. Some individuals decided to provide idiosyncratic answers which also revealed problems when it came to establishing coherence. For instance, they stated that the speaker would not buy a new parrot because he did not like the animals or as one person in group B2 put it when imitating the speaker's attitude, "because he couldn't use it to cook soup". Other participants explained that the speaker was considering buying another pet parrot, but not now because he had felt attached to the original parrot. Still others responded that the speaker was not attached but rather accustomed to this pet, and they observed that the speaker took the parrot's death calmly and without emotion. One subject in group B3 commented that she did not know in which sense the comment was made, and that was why she could not provide any answer. A large number of idiosyncratic answers provided by the blind participants illustrated problems with establishing coherence at the same time as attempting to maximise the relevance of utterances.

Despite the above mention cases, no statistically significant differences between the blind and sighted groups (see Table 3-8 for descriptive statistics) were found (F(5,114)=.802, p=.55).

Table 3-8 Mean scores for blind and sighted groups in the incoherence resolution task

		Mean	SD
Sighted	S1	2.80	1.32
	S2	3.25	0.96
	S3	2.80	1.43
Blind	B1	2.70	1.21
	B2	2.47	1.07
	B3	2.62	1.70

Taking into consideration the findings, it is evident that establishing coherence in spoken and written texts is equally challenging for both blind and sighted people. Access to visual and auditory cues does not always guarantee that an utterance will be interpreted as coherent, as demonstrated by the results achieved in groups S2, S3, B2 and B3. What is more, accessible visual or auditory cues, gaps in knowledge or even simple distractions, may result in the inability to resolve incoherence in discourses. However, as we observed, the lack of coherence in an utterance is not always synonymous with the inability to arrive at any interpretation. As we observed in this study, some participants, despite disregarding certain information at the expense of other pieces of information, managed to offer some kind of interpretation. Blind and sighted adults' abilities to resolve incoherence should be given further attention and requires further and more detailed analyses.

Humour and figurative language comprehension

One of the most challenging tasks which the blind and sighted participants were examined on in this study was their ability to detect and interpret humour and figurative language. In order to investigate the effect of contextual knowledge on the comprehension of different types of interpretative language use, we challenged the blind and sighted participants to tasks 5.3, 7.3 and 8.3 which examined the recognition and interpretation of a simple humorous utterance, sarcasm and irony. In tasks 4.2, 8.2, 9.3 and 12.3 they were tested on their understanding of metaphor, grotesque and hyperbole.

In general, the dialogues which contained different figures of speech were correctly interpreted by most of the sighted participants, not only in the groups watching the film or listening to the recording, but also those reading the text. All except for task 4.2, we obtained comparable results (see Fig. 3-11) in all cases and no statistically significant differences between the sub-groups presented themselves.

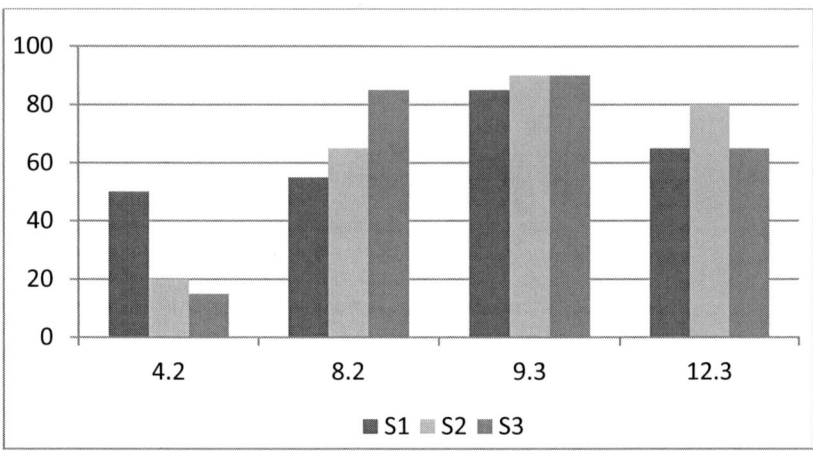

Fig. 3-11 Successful interpretation of figurative language by sighted groups (%).

In task 8.2 the participants were expected to interpret the speaker's utterance in (92):

(92)   *To się nadaje do 'Animal Planet'.*
         (Eng. *It would be good for 'Animal Planet'.*)

in relation to the family's behaviour. By juxtaposing 'it' with 'Animal Plantet' (a TV channel exploring wild and domestic animals' behaviour in different habitats), the speaker intended to compare the family's behaviour to the behaviour of the animals which might be seen on this TV channel. Around 55% of the participants in group S1 were able to arrive at this interpretation just by reading the text. We did not observe any significant improvement in the performance of group S2 who listened to the recording, but the percentage of correct answers rose to 85% in group S3 who both listened to the speaker's utterance, and who were able to watch the behaviour of the family along with the speaker's reaction. Visual and auditory cues definitely improved metaphor comprehension in participants, who drawing from their general knowledge, knew what 'Animal Planet' was and successfully assigned reference in the utterance. Still, the participants who did not know what 'it' and 'Animal Planet' referred to, could not establish coherence in the dialogue. Visual and/or auditory information neither compensated for this lack of knowledge nor eliminated these obstacles. As a result, some of the individuals in the sighted sub-groups thought that the woman was talking about pets or dinner, both which could have been shown on TV. A few respondents also understood that the speaker meant that the family could make a career on TV. These responses show that they failed to understand the presence of metaphor in this dialogue.

In task 9.3 the participants were asked to interpret the utterance of the speaker already presented in (100):

(100)   *Czy Twoje życie się zawaliło?*
         (Eng. *Did your world come crashing down?*)

Among other things, this utterance contains elements of metaphor, hyperbole, sarcasm and irony. A great majority of the participants in all of the groups (85-90%) correctly recognised the intentions of the speaker and understood that she was ridiculing her interlocutor's attitude. Very few participants in the groups interpreted the utterance literally and thought that it referred to something tragic that had happened in the man's life. This stemmed from the fact that they failed to establish coherence in this dialogue. Considering the correct answers obtained from all of the groups, we did not observe any significant effects of visual or auditory cues on the participants' performance.

Although in task 12.3 we obtained slightly fewer correct responses when compared to task 9.3, still a great majority of the sighted participants had no problems with understanding the speaker's utterance in (102) and that it referred to a cat.

(102)   *Leży na ulicy i udaje, że śpi.*
         (Eng. *Lying on the street and pretending to be asleep.*)

This utterance has some features of grotesque, combining comic associations with absurdity and unpleasant images. The speaker describing the living creature as 'lying on the street and pretending to be asleep' trivialises the fact that it is dead and talks about it in a sardonic way. At the same time this utterance may evoke the disturbing image of a cat run over by a car, which is something that sighted people have probably seen in their lives. In this utterance one can also find elements of personification, since the activity of pretending is usually associated with the rational thinking of humans rather than of animals. Hence, it is difficult to imagine an animal pretending to be asleep or doing other everyday activities (such as eating or playing) in real life. In fact it might be so misleading in this dialogue that some participants may assume that this utterance refers to a neighbour (not the cat) or someone else. Contrary to our expectations however, 65% of the participants in S1 and S3, and 80% in S2 correctly interpreted this utterance. All of these participants decided that the speaker wanted to say that the cat was dead. The rest of the sighted participants in these groups misunderstood the utterance and either provided no answer, or incorrectly claimed that the speaker wanted to say that the cat was sly, lazy or playful.

As we have already mentioned, task 4.2 turned out to be the most difficult for all of the sighted participants, in particular for groups S2 and S3 who provided only 20 and 15% correct answers. Contrary to what we observed in the tasks discussed above, the number of correct answers decreased in the groups provided with visual and auditory information, while the group reading the text performed the most successfully offering 50% correct responses. In response to the same task, a greater number of participants (regardless of the sub-group they belonged to) than in the previous tasks failed to resolve the problem and offered no answer at all (12% in S1 and S2, and 25% in S3). The participants were expected to refer to the speaker's metaphorical utterance in (103) and recognise that what the speaker had in mind in this situation was that the family stayed at the zoo until closing time.

(103)   *Doczekaliśmy się jedynie sprzątaczki.*
         (Eng. *In the end all we saw was a cleaning lady.*)

While a majority of the participants in S1 understood this utterance correctly, many participants in the remaining groups responded that the family did not stay long at the zoo because the children were bored (40% in S2) or uninterested (20% in S2 and 25% in S3). A few individuals responded that the family stayed at the zoo until the children finished playing caps. A possible explanation of this phenomenon might be the fact that while the participants in S1 treated all of the information in the text as equally important, those listening to the recording or watching the film treated the metaphorical utterance (the last in the dialogue) as marginal information or appositional, which in their opinion had little effect on the meaning of the whole dialogue. Analysing their answers, it seemed that they found the speaker's account of what had happened at the zoo much more relevant. Possibly if their attention had been drawn to this utterance, they would have appropriately analysed it. One should take into consideration however, that in everyday situations, hardly ever does someone specifically draw our attention to one particular sentence so as to make sure that we understand it correctly. We also tend to give prominence to some utterances and at the same time ignore others.

As mentioned before, tasks 5.3, 7.3 and 8.3 were aimed at examining the participants' comprehension of different forms of humour (see Fig. 3-12 for the results of sighted sub-groups).

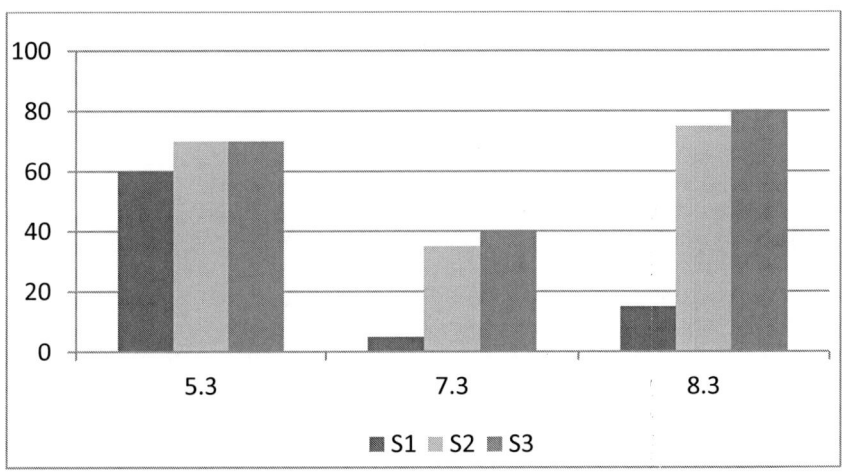

Fig. 3-12 The detection and comprehension of humour in the groups of sighted participants (%).

Task 5.3 tested the comprehension of a simple form of humour, while tasks 7.3 and 8.3 were aimed at examining the participants' interpretations of more complex and sophisticated, humorous utterances. In the first case, the participants were expected to decide if the speaker in (104) was serious about divorcing with his wife.

(104)   *Jak dywan to i krzesła, jak krzesła to i lustro, szafa, a na koniec nasze dzieci nas znienawidzą. (...) Bo się rozwiedziemy.*
         (Eng. *If a carpet, then chairs, if chairs, then a mirror, wardrobe, and then our kids will hate us. (...) Because we will get a divorce.*)

Although this utterance presented as a text may be seen as providing too little information to be certain what his attitude was in this situation, or to discover that he was only joking, 60% of the participants in group S1 assumed that the reason mentioned by the man (i.e. choosing new furniture for the house) would be too trivial a reason for divorce. The participants listening to the recording (S2) could hear the speaker and his wife talking calmly, and those watching the film (S3) (who additionally observed the couple hugging), performed comparably to group S1 and provided 70% of the correct interpretations. Between 20 to 30% of the participants in each sub-group were unable to detect the humour in this utterance with or without auditory and/or visual cues.

While in the case of the simple form of humour a majority of the sighted participants performed successfully and correctly interpreted the speaker's intentions, these same participants found task 7.3, much harder. It examined the participants' comprehension of irony in the following utterance:

(101)   *Jasne... przecież to [papuga] to tylko worek piór.*
         (Eng. *Sure...after all it [a parrot] is only a bunch of feathers.*)

In order to understand (101) correctly, it was necessary to recognise that this utterance was a reply and that it did not represent the speaker's attitude as demonstrated by his previous statement. In other words, the speaker in his utterance echoed his interlocutor's cruel and indifferent attitude when he asked the speaker if he would buy a new parrot in exchange of the dead one. If a participant failed to recognise this, it would not have been possible to resolve the conflicting information contained in this dialogue. As a result, an individual was likely to assume that the speaker had changed his attitude to parrots very rapidly, that he had never liked the animals, or they came up with other fancy interpretations. This prediction seems to be supported by the answers of the sighted participants in all of the sub-groups, most of whom could not solve this problem and failed to identify the irony in this dialogue. Very few people (approx. 5%) refused to give any answer.

The detection of irony in this dialogue was particularly difficult for the participants reading the text, and who provided only 5% of the correct responses. In the remaining groups (S2 and S3) this percentage increased to 35 and 40%. This shows that auditory cues (in particular the intonation of the speaker) and visual cues (e.g. the observation of his behaviour), helped the participants to arrive at the intended interpretation, but still many subjects found the information contradictory and confusing.

Many of the sighted participants in group S1 also had problems with task 8.3. Only 28, 55% of the participants in the group correctly understood that the speaker in the dialogue, by speaking metaphorically in (92), wanted to say that the children were behaving like animals.

(92)   *To się nadaje do 'Animal Planet'.*
          (Eng. *It would be good for 'Animal Planet'.*)

Only 15% of them recognised that the speaker was trying to be sarcastic. Evidently, the lack of additional contextual cues (auditory and visual cues in particular) hindered the recovery of this form of humour in this situation. As a result, an equal number of the participants in this group (15-25%) recognised negative feelings in the speaker's utterance, such as irritation, anger or indignation, and positive emotions such as surprise or amusement. In groups S2 and S3 a larger number of the participants recognised the sarcasm in this utterance and the percentage of correct answers improved significantly (75-80% correct responses).

The blind participants found the task examining the comprehension of figures of speech slightly more difficult than the sighted participants (see Fig. 3-13).

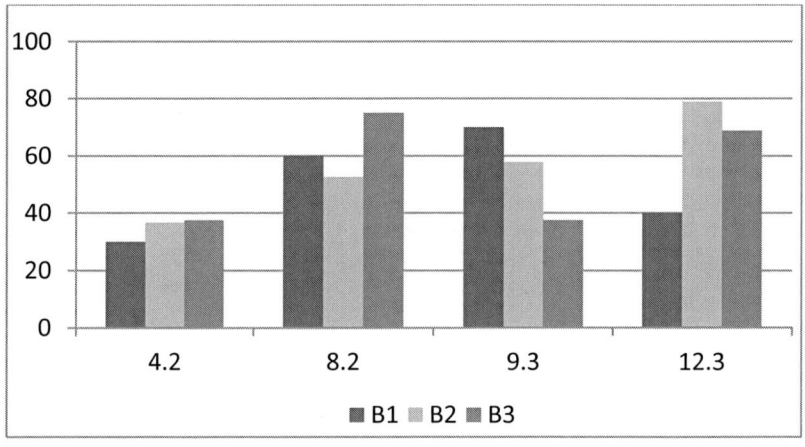

Fig. 3-13 The successful interpretation of figurative language in the groups of blind participants (%).

In task 4.2 (which investigated the understanding of the utterance containing metaphor), only 30-37.5% of the participants in each of the sub-groups responded correctly. Many people in these sub-groups failed to identify metaphor in the utterance in (103), and similar difficulties were observed in the groups of sighted participants (as we showed when discussing the results obtained in these groups).

(103)   *Doczekaliśmy się jedynie sprzątaczki.*
         (Eng. *In the end all we saw was a cleaning lady.*)

The participants belonging to groups B2 and B3 were provided with
auditory cues (with and without AD) and performed similarly in this task
to group B1 who were reading the text. From 15 to 25% of the participants
in each sub-group, claimed that the speaker meant that the family did not
stay too long at the zoo because the children were bored. From 5 to 18.8%
of them responded that the children were uninterested, and this was why
they did not spend a longer time there. A similar number of participants
stated that the family stayed at the zoo until the children had finished
playing caps. Additionally, the idiosyncratic answers provided by
individual participants, suggest that many of them were unable to resolve
the incoherence in this dialogue. For instance, they claimed that the
children stayed at the zoo for a shorter time because they were bored and
started to play caps. One participant also said that "if the family was
waiting for a cleaning lady, they would have had to stay at the zoo for the
whole day". Although this person marked the correct answer in the
questionnaire, he drew this conclusion by making the dubious assumption
that the family purposefully waited for the cleaning lady. As a matter of
fact, the father and the girl were waiting for a baby ostrich (not a cleaning
lady) which she wanted to see. Similarly, a few other participants
commented that the family waited until a cleaning lady appeared, but were
unable to associate this fact with the zoo closing time. Over 20% of the
participants in groups B1 and B2 were unable to provide any response.
Many asked how they were supposed to know how long the family was at
the zoo if it was not mentioned in the dialogue. However, very few
participants in B3 provided no answer to this task.

In task 8.2 the blind participants were more successful in
understanding figurative language. As in the previous task, the group
reading the text and those listening to the recording (with or without AD),
provided a comparable number of correct answers, but this time the
percentage of correct answers ranged from 52.6 to 75%. All of the sub-
groups of blind participants performed comparably to those of the sighted
participants. Although a majority of the blind participants managed to
identify metaphor in this dialogue, many of them incorrectly interpreted
the utterance due to the unsuccessful reference assignment of 'it' and gaps
in their knowledge. These difficulties were also observed in the sighted
participants and discussed when describing their performance in this task.
Having no access to visual information, some of the participants in group
B1 wrongly understood that the mother in this dialogue, by saying (92),

wanted to say that the cat which she was observing should be shown on TV.

(92)   *To się nadaje do 'Animal Planet'.*
         (Eng. *It would be good for 'Animal Planet'.*)

A few individuals in B1 and B3 thought that the mother meant the dinner could be shown on television. A small number of the participants in B2 also thought that she may have meant cockroaches or other insects in her house. There were 12% of the participants in B1 and approximately 25% in the two other groups who could not come up with any interpretation.

Unlike in the case of the sighted participants, the blind respondents provided fewer correct responses to task 9.3. Even though the group reading the text performed comparably to the sighted participants and offered 70% of the correct answers, groups B2 and B3 (listening to the recording with and without AD) performed less successfully than the sighted groups. Only 57.9% of the participants in group B2 understood the speaker's utterance correctly, while over 30% of the respondents in this group responded that the speaker, by saying (100), wanted to ask if the neighbour had offended her interlocutor, or the participant understood the utterance literally.

(100)   *Czy Twoje życie się zawaliło?*
         (Eng. *Did your world come crashing down?*)

Even fewer correct responses were provided by the participants in group B3 (who produced only 37.5% of the correct answers), and a majority of them (43.8%) showed a preference for the literal interpretation.

In the last task which examined the understanding of figures of speech, the performances of the blind participants improved with the amount of contextual cues they were provided with. Although only 40% of the participants in B1 provided correct answers to this task, the rest of them understood that the speaker, by saying (102), meant that the cat (to which the utterance referred) was sly (40%), or they offered other answers. Some claimed that it was not explicitly said what had happened to the cat.

(102)   *Leży na ulicy i udaje, że śpi.*
         (Eng. *Lying on the street and pretending to be asleep.*)

There were 78.9 and 68.8% of the respondents in B2 and B3 who correctly interpreted this utterance. These two groups gave very similar answers to sighted groups S2 and S3, which implies that the auditory information provided by the recording (and AD) allowed the participants to adequately understand this utterance, and thus their interpretations were not so different from those offered by the sighted participants listening to the recording or watching the film.

As we have already mentioned, besides their ability to interpret different figures of speech, the blind participants were examined on their understanding of humour (see Fig.3-14 for the results in this group).

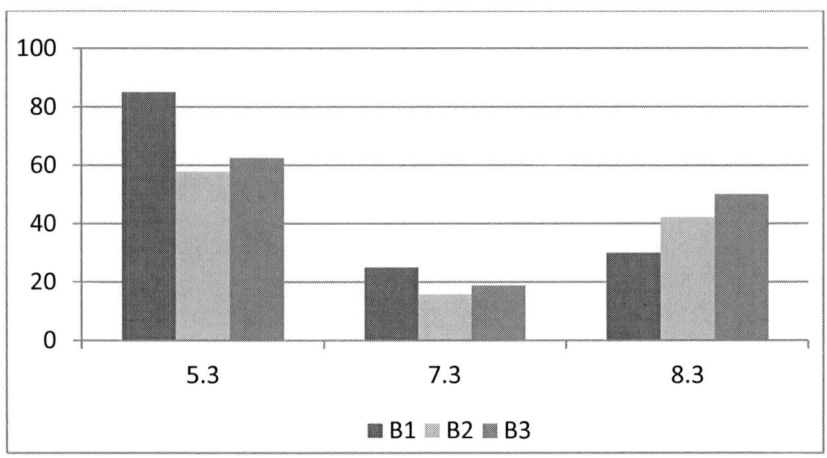

Fig.3-14 The detection and comprehension of humour in the groups of blind participants (%)

When presented with task 5.3 which involved the recognition of a simple form of humour (illustrated in (104) and repeated here for convenience), 85% of the blind participants in B1 provided correct responses.

(104)   *Jak dywan to i krzesła, jak krzesła to i lustro, szafa, a na koniec nasze dzieci nas znienawidzą. (...) Bo się rozwiedziemy.*
        (Eng. *If a carpet, then chairs, if chairs, then a mirror, wardrobe, and then our kids will hate us. (...) Because we will get a divorce.*)

As a result, they surpassed the sighted participants in S1 who offered only 60% of the correct answers. The participants in groups B2 and B3 performed similarly to the sighted participants, and offered 57.9 and 62.5% correct answers. Some individuals in B2 observed that it was not explicitly said that the man in the dialogue was intending to divorce his wife, and some of the participants in B3 commented that the speakers in this dialogue would probably not divorce if they were smiling at one another (as it was indicated in AD). However, most of the blind participants were confused and commented that "it was hard to say how the situation would end because evidently something wrong was happening between them" or that "the man did not know what he wanted". A few other participants commented that "how it was going to end would depend on if the wife bought the new furniture or not". This suggests that they thought the man was serious about the divorce but had not made the final decision. Still other participants said he was pretending that everything was fine, but deep down he was considering the divorce and had not told his wife about it yet. Due to the shortage of contextual information, many of the blind participants relied on their general knowledge and personal experience to interpret this situation. For instance, one participant described a similar situation with one of his friends who had had an argument with his wife about a flat which was too small and they divorced. On the basis of this event, he came to the conclusion that the couple in the dialogue would probably divorce.

When challenged with more sophisticated forms of humour, the blind participants generally performed with less success. In task 7.3 (which also aroused controversies in all of the three sighted groups), only 25% of the participants in B1, 15.8% in B2 and 18.8% in B3, correctly identified the irony in the speaker's utterance presented in (101).

(101)   *Jasne ... przecież to tylko worek piór.*
        (Eng. *Sure...after all it's only a bunch of feathers.*)

Many participants offered idiosyncratic answers which presented conflicting and paradoxical assumptions. For instance, a few individuals said that the speaker could not imagine his life without parrots, but at the same time he claimed that they were worthless and treated them like objects. Many of the blind participants (57.9% of S2 and 62.5% of S3) observed that the speaker might be sad, but he did not show it and mocked the situation. This suggests that they detected the humour in his utterance, but they failed to recover the speaker's intention. They seemed to ignore the role of the other speaker and the fact that the main speaker felt offended by his question. It was due to this fact that they were unable to understand the seemingly contradictory statements of the speaker. As a result, the irony remained undetected and the utterance misunderstood.

Task 8.3 involved the recognition of sarcasm in utterance (92), and also posed a problem for some of the blind participants.

(92)   *To się nadaje do 'Animal Planet'.*
         (Eng. *It would be good for 'Animal Planet'.*)

Compared to the sighted participants in S1, the blind respondents in B1 provided twice as many correct answers. Still, only 30% of the blind participants were able to appropriately recognise the sarcasm in this utterance, but the rest of them were unable to detect this form of humour just from looking at the text. Many of them claimed that the speaker was indignant rather than sarcastic (30%) or they did not provide any answer (20%). While the results in the sighted groups improved considerably as additional auditory and visual cues were introduced, the blind respondents in groups B2 and B3 performed comparably to B1 (42.1 and 50% correct answers). This indicates that they were less successful in the comprehension of this form of humour than the sighted participants. The blind participants who provided incorrect answers recognised other intentions in the speaker's utterance. As this type of humour is seemingly innocent but in fact represents a harsh remark, some blind individuals (similar to some sighted participants), indicated both positive feelings (e.g. amusement) and negative feelings (e.g. impatience or indignation) in this utterance. These negative feelings were mentioned more frequently by the blind participants.

The statistical analyses revealed no significant differences in the performances of the blind and the sighted participants in the dialogues with figurative language ($F(5,114)=.97$, $p=.43$). They differed however in the dialogues with humour ($f(5,114)=3.93$, $p=.003$). The post hoc tests showed that these differences were among the sighted groups (S1 and S2 $p=.017$, S1 and S3 $p=.003$). Detailed descriptive statistics are presented in Table 3-9 and 3-10 below.

Table 3-9 Mean scores for blind and sighted groups in the dialogues with figurative language

		Mean	SD
Sighted	S1	2.55	1.05
	S2	2.60	0.82
	S3	2.55	0.99
Blind	B1	2.00	1.02
	B2	2.26	1.32
	B3	2.25	1.12

Table 3-10 Mean scores for blind and sighted groups in the dialogues with humour

		Mean	SD
Sighted	S1	0.85	0.87
	S2	1.80	0.89
	S3	1.95	0.88
Blind	B1	1.40	0.75
	B2	1.15	1.01
	B3	1.31	1.07

Comparing the findings obtained in the two groups (blind and sighted) of participants, it appears that the comprehension of humour and figurative language can be difficult for both blind and sighted adults. As illustrated by the tasks described above, the success of the process can never be taken for granted. The findings also show that the availability of contextually relevant information as well as the successful completion of pragmatic sub-tasks such as reference assignment or ambiguity/incoherence resolution play an important role and may decide if the interpretation of these utterances is correctly recovered. Also, as predicted by Relevance Theory, the comprehension of figurative language and different forms of humour are effort-consuming tasks. Since a text enables a reader to analyse utterances at his/her own pace and a spoken text is more elusive, the channel through which these utterances are provided may in some cases have a significant influence on their comprehension. Accordingly, some of the blind and sighted participants reading the text were more successful in the interpretation of humour and figurative language than those listening to the recording or watching the film. Out of all of the tasks examining the detection and comprehension of humour and figurative language, all of the groups found irony the most problematic and effort-consuming. Very few participants could resolve the conflicts that many examples of irony contain and in which the speaker echoes the attitudes of another speaker, while at the same time dissociating from it.

Mind-reading

The final aspect of comprehension that we aimed to investigate in this study was the ability to take the perspectives of different speakers and understand their mental states, including their intentions, emotions, beliefs and desires. This ability (in literature called the 'theory of mind' or 'mind-reading') was examined via the use of tasks in which blind and sighted participants were asked to either rate or describe speakers' attitudes in a range of scenes.

In tasks 1.2, 2.3, 4.1, 5.1, 7.1, 10.3 and 11.1 these participants were to assess the intensity of certain emotions and mark them on five-point Likert scales. 'One' indicated the lack of any emotion or emotions which were hardly felt. 'Five' stood for the highest intensity of an emotion. In tasks 6.2, 11.3 and 12.1 the participants were asked to select (or suggest) an answer which in their option best demonstrated what the speakers in the dialogues were thinking in these situations. The percentage of the correct responses in the sub-groups was analysed. Due to the differences in measuring and analysing the results, the two types of tasks will be discussed separately. However, unlike the conventions adopted in the previous sections, this time we will discuss the results obtained by sub-groups altogether, without separating the blind and sighted participants. This will allow us to present the contrasts between these (sub-)groups and to indicate the differences between them.

In scaling tasks 1.2, 4.1, 10.3 and 11.1, the statistical analyses did not show any significant differences between the blind and sighted participants in any of the sub-groups. In these cases, all of the blind and sighted participants correctly recognised the speakers' attitudes on the basis of available contextual cues. In task 1.2 (as illustrated in Fig. 3-15), the groups negatively valued the speaker's (the husband's) attitude and correctly observed that he was minimally engaged in this situation. Interestingly, there were no significant differences between the groups reading the text, listening to the recordings or watching the film.

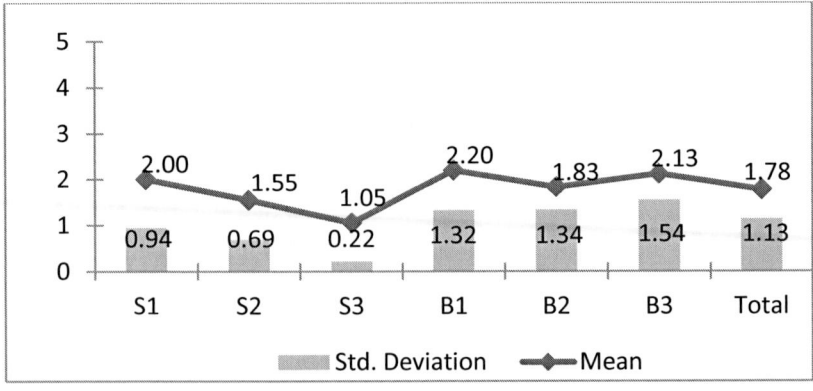

Fig. 3-15 The responses of blind and sighted participants to task 1.2.

No significant differences between the blind and sighted sub-groups, who correctly interpreted that the speaker was rather disappointed with the visit to the zoo were found in task 4.1. As in the previous case, the participants reading the text performed comparably to the participants listening to the recordings or watching the film, as indicated by Fig. 3-16.

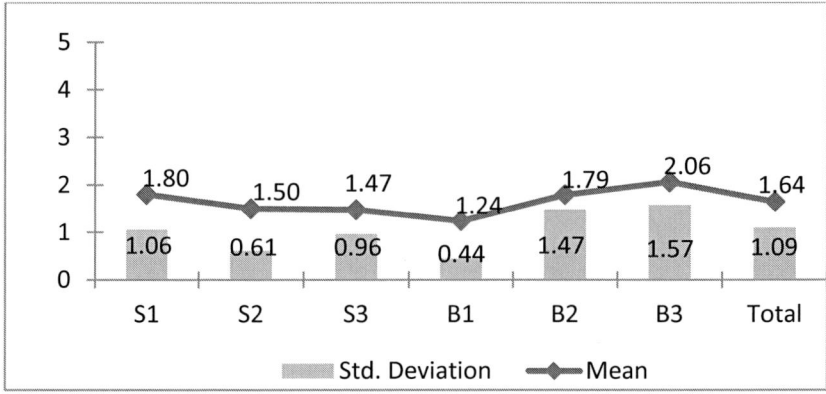

Fig. 3-16 The responses of blind and sighted participants to task 4.1

The blind and sighted participants also performed comparably in task 10.3. This time they were asked to evaluate three extreme emotions which the speaker might be demonstrating in scene 10 (i.e. surprise, satisfaction and indignation, see Fig. 3-17 for results). Not only did the participants have no problems with this task, but we also obtained very similar results in all of the sub-groups of blind and sighted participants, this was regardless if they read the text, listened to the recordings or watched the film. Among these emotions, the participants considered indignation and surprise to be the most salient in the speaker's utterance. While satisfaction was less evident and noticeable as an emotion, many of the blind and sighted participants rated it with high values, but commented that the person in the dialogue was satisfied with herself because she noticed the mistake in the wine list. This explanation demonstrates their in-depth understanding of the situation and their undisputable ability to attribute mental states to other people.

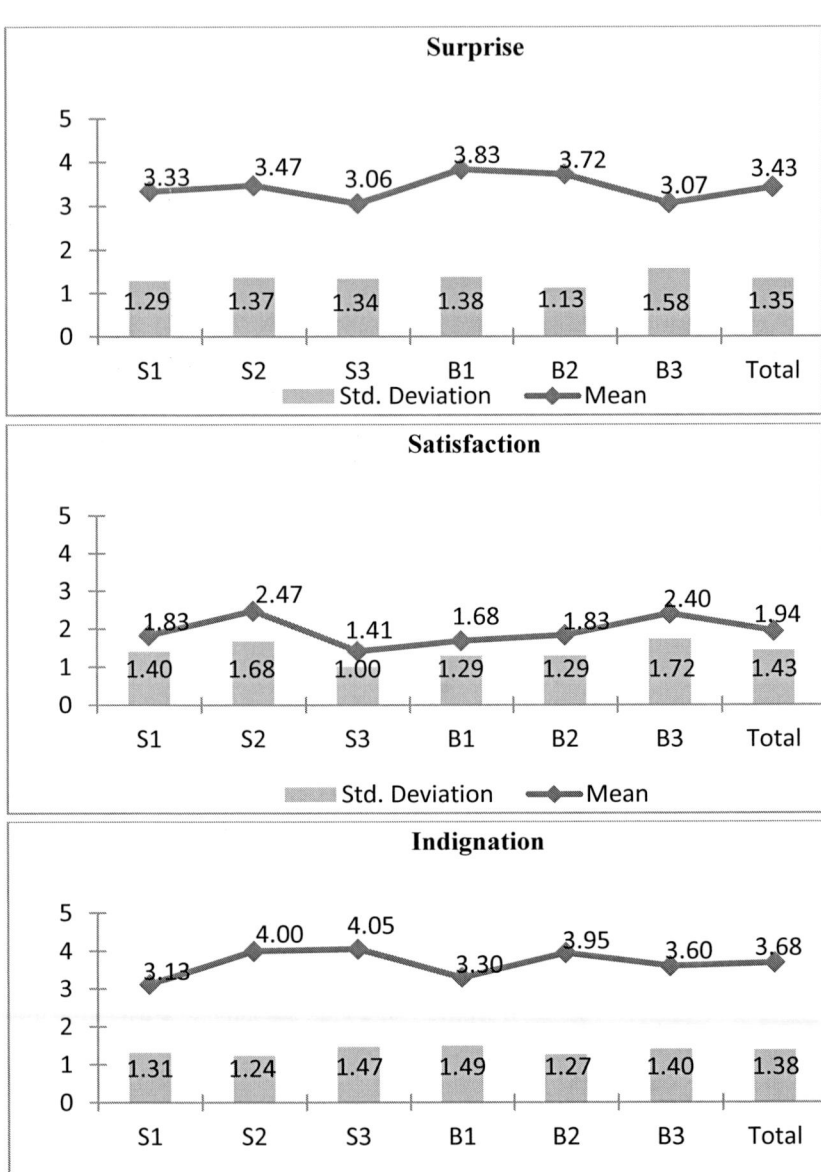

Fig. 3-17 The recognition of surprise, satisfaction and indignation in task 10.3 of blind and sighted participants.

No differences between the blind and sighted sub-groups were observed in task 11.1 either (see Fig. 3-18). The participants correctly understood that the speaker was not pleased with the gift his wife gave him. Although we had expected that the speaker's disappointment or even offence could have been more pronounced for the individuals having access to auditory and/or visual information, all of the groups (even those deprived of auditory or visual information) offered very similar answers to this task.

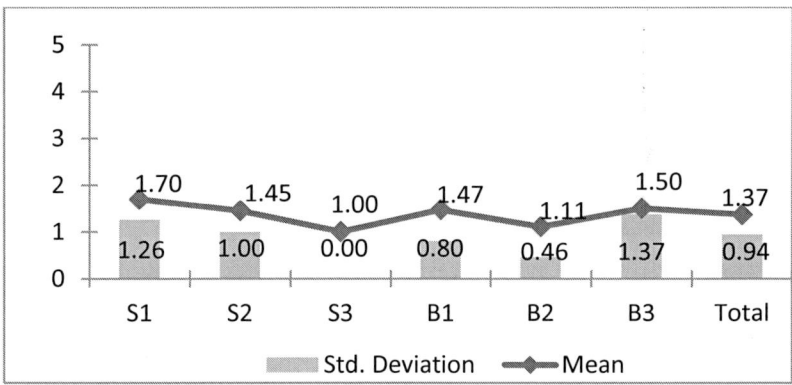

Fig. 3-18 The recognition of a speaker's attitude of blind and sighted participants in task 11.1.

The effect of the accessibility to certain contextual cues on the theory of mind, was however observable in the remaining tasks. As a result, the blind and sighted participants reading the text were at a disadvantage when compared with those listening to the recorded dialogues or watching the film. In task 2.3, the sighted participants in S3 rated the speaker as being more positive in this situation than the participants reading the text or listening to the recording. However, we did not observe this tendency in any of the sub-groups of blind participants (see Fig.3-19).

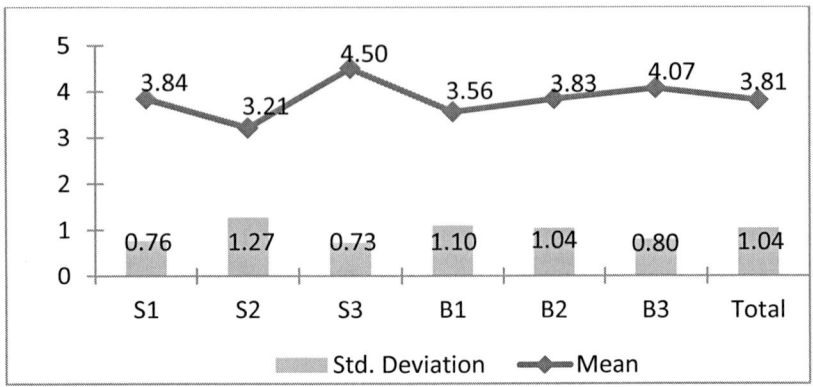

Fig. 3-19 The differences in the assessment of a speaker's attitude between blind and sighted sub-groups in task 2.3.

It is however possible to observe certain differences in task 5.1 between the blind participants in group B3 and the sighted participants in S3. Group B3 rated the speaker's willingness to buy new things for the house higher than S3, as illustrated in Fig. 3-20.

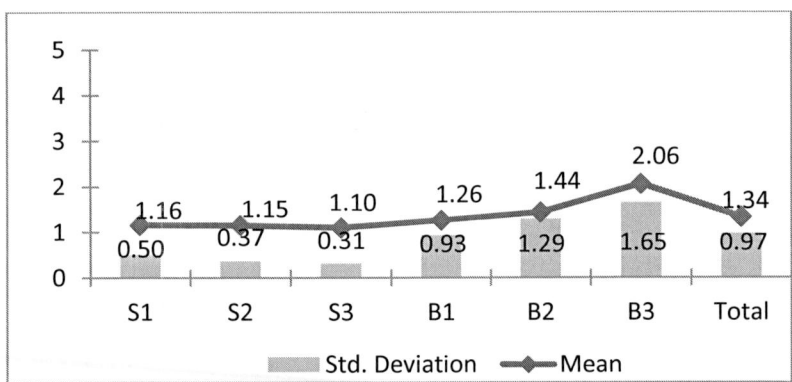

Fig. 3-20 The differences in the assessment of a speaker's attitude between blind and sighted groups in task 5.1.

In task 7.1 (which referred to the scene involving the recognition of irony), the analyses revealed even greater discrepancies between the blind and sighted groups. As indicated by Fig. 3-21, the blind participants in group B3 interpreted the speaker's attitude more appropriately, claiming that the man was more attached to the dead parrot than the sighted participants had thought he was. There was also a significant difference between the groups reading the text (S1 and B1) and the remaining groups listening to or watching the dialogue. The former groups were more likely to fail to detect irony and they recognised the speaker's negative attitude to his parrot.

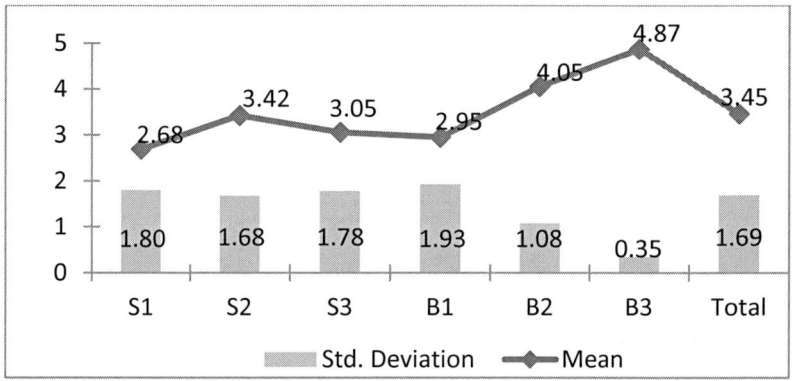

Fig. 3-21 The differences in the assessment of a speaker's attitude between blind and sighted groups in task 7.1

While the rating tasks discussed above turned out to be relatively easy for all of the blind and sighted participants (who performed very similarly), tasks 6.2, 11.3 and 12.1 were more difficult for all and we observed greater discrepancies between them. In task 6.2 for example, a majority of the sighted participants in all of the sub-groups, correctly recognised that the speaker in the dialogue was feeling impatient (see Fig. 3-22). Groups S2 and S3 provided a greater number of correct answers (90 and 75% respectively) than group S1 (50%). Out of all the sub-groups of sighted and blind participants, group B1 were the least successful in this task giving only 20% correct answers. Group B2 performed better than B1 and provided 57.9% of the correct responses. There were no statistically significant differences between groups B3 and S3. The groups which provided the greatest number of incorrect responses (i.e. S1, B1 and B2) worked using contextually insufficient material. They understood that the speaker offered help to the other speaker in the dialogue, rather than showing impatience.

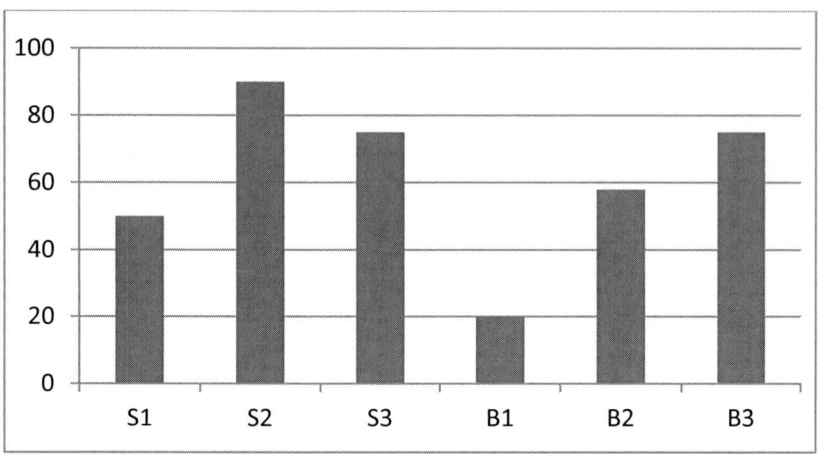

Fig. 3-22 Blind and sighted participants' theory of mind in task 6.2

A majority of the blind and sighted participants correctly responded to task 12.1 and understood that the speaker (the father) in scene 12 thought that his interlocutor (the daughter) felt sick because she had seen a dead cat (see Fig. 3-23 for the results).

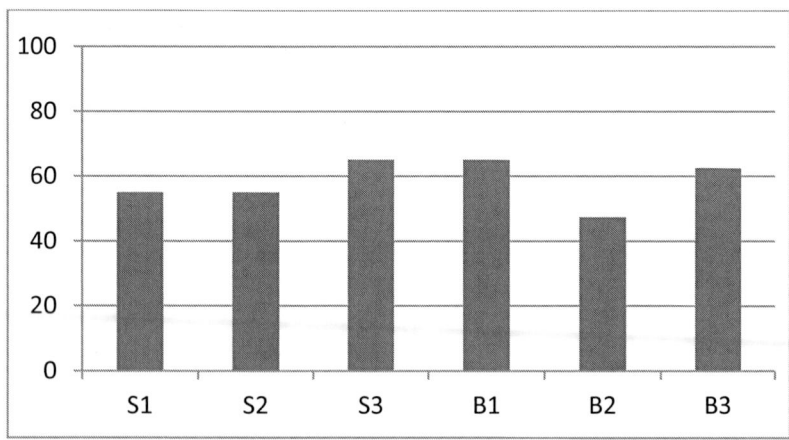

Fig. 3-23 Blind and sighted participants' theory of mind in task 12.1

All of the sub-groups' performances were very similar and no statistically significant differences were found between the blind and sighted groups, this was regardless if they read the text, listened to the recordings or watched the film. Quite a few participants, especially in groups S1 (30%), S2 (25%) and B3 (25%), understood that the father thought his daughter was ill. When offering their idiosyncratic answers, some individuals in group S3 claimed that the father thought that she was pregnant. A number of other subjects in B1 stated that the father thought she was constantly complaining, that was why he was not paying attention to her. A comparable number of the blind and sighted participants could not give any answer and found the task difficult and incomprehensible (5-12.5%). An interesting comment made by one blind participant in group B1, who when trying to resolve the problem said that "Marta said she did not see the cat, … or perhaps she saw it but did not want to admit it …" reveals further difficulties in attributing mental states to other people. It is evident that when searching for an interpretation this respondent did not actually take the perspective of the father but rather that of his daughter, and focused on what she thought in this situation.

Task 11.3 turned out to be the most problematic for all of the participants (see Fig. 3-24 for the results). In this case we can observe significant differences between the groups reading the text, listening to the recording and watching the film.

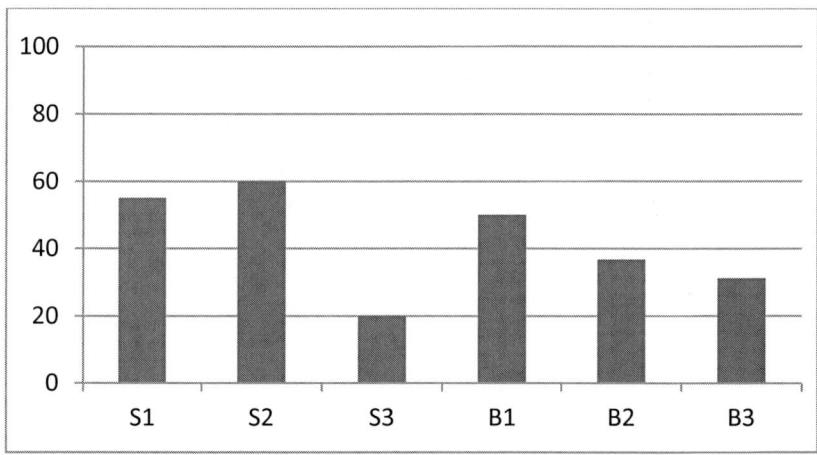

Fig. 3-24 Blind and sighted participants' theory of mind in task 11.3

The participants in this task were expected to go beyond what was communicated in this dialogue, and recognise the wife's rationale behind buying a sweater for her husband in a shop for overweight people. The blind and sighted participants reading the text performed comparably and offered 50 and 55% of the correct answers. They correctly understood that the woman had bought the sweater because clothes from this particular shop fitted him. The participants in group S2 performed comparably to those in S1. However, groups S3, B2 and B3 were the least successful in this task and provided 20 to 36% of the correct responses. A similar number of participants in each of these groups thought that the woman was of the opinion that these clothes were made of good fabrics, or that she wanted her husband to look tall and well-built (as she mentioned in the dialogue). However, they failed to recognise that these reasons were used as excuses by the wife when the husband got offended by her present. A few participants offered idiosyncratic interpretations. For instance, one individual in S3 claimed that she was tricky and "wanted him to look untidy, so that no other woman could have him", and another participant in B2 commented that "she does not know sizes and buys blindly". Finally, one participant offered an interpretation mixing all of the reasons presented as suggested options in the questionnaire, and said that "she thought the clothes were pretty, made of good fabrics and would make the husband look tall and well-built". Despite the different interpretations, hardly anyone in the groups refused to give any answer at all.

Two separate statistical analyses for the multiple choice task and the scaling task were performed. In the former the total scores for the groups were calculated and in the latter the mean intensities of the emotions recognised by the participants in the groups. In neither of the tasks statistically significant differences between the blind and the sighted participants were found ($F_{(5,114)}=1.88$, $p=10$ for the multiple choice ToM task and $F_{(5,114)}=2.27$, $p=0.52$ for the scaling task). The descriptive statistics are presented in Table 3-11 and 3-12 below.

Table 3-11 Mean scores for blind and sighted groups in the ToM task (multiple choice)

		Mean	SD
Sighted	S1	1.60	1.04
	S2	2.05	0.07
	S3	1.60	0.68
Blind	B1	1.35	0.74
	B2	1.31	1.00
	B3	1.68	0.87

Table 3-10 Mean scores for blind and sighted groups in the ToM task (scaling)

		Mean	SD
Sighted	S1	2.05	0.75
	S2	1.95	0.49
	S3	1.48	0.52
Blind	B1	1.98	0.64
	B2	2.17	0.70
	B3	2.14	1.15

Considering the results provided in response to the tasks examining 'theory of mind' abilities, the statistical analyses did not reveal any significant differences between the blind and sighted participants. The participants reading the text did not perform differently or any worse than those listening to the recording or watching the film. In the tasks where a text provided underdetermined or ambiguous information, auditory and visual cues helped the participants to appropriately interpret the dialogues and improved the amount of correct responses. Finally, we observed that the sub-groups of blind and sighted participants found the rating tasks much easier than choosing among different options. One possible explanation of this might be that all the participants regarded different aspects of the dialogues as important or consistent with their expectations. Although most of them came up with similar interpretations, their prior experiences and general knowledge triggered additional assumptions and they computed the information in entirely individual ways.

Concluding remarks and summary

It is difficult to say and specify in which areas significant differences between blind and sighted adults appear, and which of these differences had a critical impact on the mutual communication between these groups. In order to answer this question it would be advisable to examine each of the pragmatic sub-tasks discussed in this study separately, perhaps by using a similar procedure and research tool. Only then will we be able to discover if problems with any of the sub-tasks stem from visual impairment or other factors. The study presented in this book was aimed at examining the effect of differences in the accessibility of contextual information on the comprehension of blind and sighted adults. It should be regarded as a starting point for further and more detailed empirical work, exploring cognitive, linguistic and computational differences between blind and sighted people.

The findings show that the lack or insufficiency of contextual information may result in the misunderstanding or misinterpretation of utterances in both blind and sighted adults, and this confirms our first hypothesis. As we have underlined many times in this work, by contextual information we not only mean visual or auditory information (which in this study was of particular concern), but also general knowledge, linguistic input and other cues which trigger certain assumptions. The analysis of the answers provided by the participants of this study, also reveals that in the situations when visual cues provided strong evidence for an interpretation, the blind people were less successful than the sighted participants, which also supports our expectation. The study exposed certain gaps in blind people's general knowledge which were directly and indirectly related to misunderstanding certain visual concepts.

However, contrary to our expectations, the blind and sighted people reading the text (which provided limited and imprecise contextual cues), did not always perform less successfully than those listening to the recording or watching the film. Although the two other types of media offered a greater amount of contextual cues, at times some participants got distracted and found the information confusing and equivocal. The text allowed for greater control over the information provided, since it could be read and analysed at an individual's own pace. In general, when listening to other people communicating, some of the information escapes our attention or can be misheard. The lack of significant differences between the blind and sighted groups reading the dialogues, implies that both of the groups had well-developed imagery (and general knowledge) which helped them in the understanding of various situations, even in the absence of auditory and/or visual cues. However, these groups demonstrated a greater number of additional assumptions, thus showing that the linguistic context was more ambiguous.

We did not observe significant differences between the blind and sighted individuals who were listening to the recording. This provided no confirmation for our hypotheis that blind people are more sensitive and attentive to auditory cues, and that it is possible they might derive more contextual cues from listening to dialogues, and as a result, perform better than sighted participants. Although when the blind people analysed the utterances they frequently referred to noises they overheard in the background or a speaker's tone of voice, we did not notice a significant improvement in their answers when compared to group S2. They did not perform noticeably better than the sighted participants in the same tasks.

This observation suggests that auditory stimuli do not provide any more superior information or stronger evidence for our assumptions than other sources. However, when provided with AD, the blind participants' performance improved.

This conclusion has important methodological implications for people working with the blind. The study provides evidence that blind children, being naturally eager to explore the surrounding world, have the potential to become attentive and fully able adult interpreters in everyday situations. Of course this is if they are provided with sufficient explanations, assistance and care from parents and educators. Although (as shown in this study) AD does not always guarantee success in the comprehension of utterances, it undoubtedly improves understanding in communication by providing blind people with valuable but usually inaccessible information. Being aware of this fact, AD should be used not only during theatrical performances, TV shows and in cinemas, but should be implemented into every-day communication e.g. by explaining to blind people what a new place looks like, what is amusing when people are laughing, or what a professor is doing during a lecture. This will give blind people a sense of security and comfort, as well as make them more confident in communicative situations.

Finally, the findings show that an insufficient amount of contextual cues rarely leads to the abandonment of the inferential procedure, as argued by Sperber and Wilson in Relevance Theory. The empirical data from this study indicates that in spite of the fact that some relevant information was inaccessible for the focus groups, they presented interpretations based on information available by utilising natural deductive mechanisms. Only in critical situations did the participants refuse to offer any answer, or give up the effort to recover any interpretation. This does not have to mean that they totally failed to understand what was being communicated, but for instance that they were ashamed to present dubious interpretations. As a result, it is more appropriate to think about the inferential process as individual and unique to every person, and as something which always leads to some kind of assumption, even if it is not wholly equivalent with a speaker's intentions.

In light of the study presented in this book, it is well-justified to assume that blind and sighted adults are not as different as many sighted people would think. In spite of the fact that blind people have limited or no access to visual information, we cannot regard them as any less competent reasoners than sighted individuals. If we go one step further, considering the difficulties and obstacles they face in the communication process, it would not be an exaggeration to say that their inferential abilities must be very well-developed if they are able to understand utterances on a par with sighted people, who have easy access to visual information and prior visual experience. This study shows that contextual information, not only visual but also derived from other sources, has an influence on effective comprehension, and the lack of this contextual material hinders the inferential process, both in the cases of blind and sighted people. However, the study also demonstrates that comprehension is a complex and intricate process which can be understood only if we look at it from an interdisciplinary perspective, and only then will there be a chance to explain the many aspects that have so far been failed to be explained. Thus, further and in-depth research in this area is necessary in order to establish the effect that visual impairment has on the development, cognition and reasoning of many people.

SUMMARY AND CONCLUSION

It is striking and at the same time thought-provoking that humans are most intrigued and attracted by what is unknown, inexplicable and, most of all, inaccessible. Among many phenomena which can be described as such, human comprehension is the one that, despite age-long scholars' concern, extensive research and immense progress, still remains mysterious. The inquisitive human nature provokes thinkers to ask still new questions, look for new answers and explanations, speculate, hypothesise and wonder how different our life would be if we were not equipped with the complex cognitive abilities which we have and utilise in any language activity. On contemplating that, Marty (1908:89) once inquired:

> "How would it be then if language was not an intrinsically necessary representation of the world of thoughts but an intentional one, for the purpose of mutual understanding, but randomly and unsystematically acquired [...]?" (Nerlich and Clarke 1996:191)

Silly and childish as the question may seem, it not only reflects the author's need to penetrate the nature of the human mind, but, most importantly, it indirectly diverts our attention to the effect of our experience and conceptual organisation on our understanding. It makes us realise that although normally we are not conscious of this, our comprehension is a perfectly-organised mental process, and not less complicated than our organism.

In this vein, we could ask a myriad of similar hypothetical questions concerning human comprehension and communication, such as:

- What would our comprehension be like if each concept constituted a separate entity unrelated with any other?
- What would happen if our mental capacities were finite, limited and ready to acquire new information until a specified number of items had been collected?
- How would we communicate if we were 'egoistic' listeners and speakers, taking into consideration only our own perspective and unwilling to help our interlocutors to recover our intentions?

- What would our communication be like if we all had exactly the same knowledge about reality and if we understood everything in exactly the same way?

These few representative questions would probably be among a thousand of more mentioned on this occasion, and each person would add new ones to the exceptionally long list. Among all of the individuals offering the potential questions which they would like to find answers to, there would surely be someone who would ask what effect visual impairment has on comprehension, and how their understanding would be different if they were blind. This is the question which we also found inspiring and which we aimed to answer in the work. Interestingly, all the questions mentioned above, reflecting the human need to understand the power of comprehension, coincide with the interest of Relevance Theory, which relentlessly attempts to explain how comprehension works and how it is possible in daily communication. Hence, in this work devoted to the study of the relation between comprehension, context and visual impairment, we provided evidence that the assumptions of Relevance Theory help us to understand the problem, offering reliable descriptions and explanations.

In this book we made an effort to substantiate the claim that context plays a decisive role in the comprehension process. In the first chapter of the work our intention was to show how, in the light of the pragmatic theory of relevance, comprehension is dependent on contextual cues derived from three main sources: perception, general knowledge and linguistic content. Revealing the interdisciplinary legacy of pragmatics and discussing various concepts, terms and examples (adopted partially or entirely from other disciplines to the model put forward by Dan Sperber and Deirdre Wilson), we aimed to put forward the arguments that only a holistic, multifaceted and interdisciplinary view could be successful in explaining the processes of human understanding. Discussing the relevance-theoretic assumptions about comprehension and context, and presenting analysis of explicit and implicit utterances, figurative language and problematic communication, allowed us to show that context is present at each particular moment of communication and undergoes constant changes as the communication proceeds. Contrary to how it is understood in alternative models and approaches, the context should not be described as a set of elements comprising communicative situations, but as a set of assumptions triggered in a hearer's mind and dependent on an individual's experience and knowledge. The dynamic nature of context requires from the hearer a constant monitoring and updating of contextual information in the comprehension process, this is driven by the constant search for contextually relevant information, and depends on the accessibility of the information.

The main aim of the present book was to examine the role of accessible contextual cues and the effect of visual impairment on comprehension. The analysis of available literature investigating the developmental and cognitive differences between blind and sighted people (which we presented in chapter two), allowed us to highlight the present state of research, and main research tendencies in the field, as well as to formulate appropriate hypotheses for the empirical study presented and discussed in chapter three. Relevance Theory provided us with the necessary tools to analyse the obtained results, which were a testament to the assumptions put forward in the theory. Examining the blind and sighted adults on their interpretation of the dialogues, presented as text, recording or film, we aimed to discover if the lack of certain contextual information (in the case of the text or recording) would have an effect on the participants' comprehension. Consequently, our intention was to find out if in natural communicative situations, blind and sighted people understand utterances differently due to the inaccessibility of contextual cues.

The first observation made on the basis of the findings was that, comprehension should not be interpreted as a binary category of total success or total failure. As we observed, even in the absence of certain contextual information, both blind and sighted people are able to interpret utterances according to the information which is available. Incoherent, ambiguous or incomprehensible parts of utterances do not stop them from guessing, stipulating or deducing meanings on the basis of general knowledge and other accessible contextual cues. Even if it is not exactly the intention which originally the speaker had in mind, the 'partially successful' interpretation is very often a sufficient substitute in communication.

Additionally, the very fact that the hearer is wrong or unaware about one thing, does not directly lead to misinterpretation as the knowledge of some concepts does not guarantee correct contextual assumptions. Since there is much more to failure or success in comprehension than only one false idea/thought/assumption, we should talk about a series of conditions which have proved unsuccessful, or have succeeded in leading to (more or less) favourable outcomes. Consequently, as we observed in the study, it is very difficult to describe any regularities or tendencies in the process. It applies to blind and sighted people's understanding of particular pragmatic tasks, based on a different amount of contextual cues. Since participants' success varied depending on the dialogue and tasks involved, it made us think that each natural communicative situation is unique as it refers to different concepts, and requires different configurations of pragmatic tasks. The fact that two utterances include, let us say, irony does not necessarily mean that they are comparable, which makes the analysis of comprehension in natural communication a challenge.

In addition to the observations listed above, the study provided confirmation of the relevance-theoretic assumption, that due to differences in conceptual knowledge (stemming from dissimilar experiences which each individual has), no two people arrive at exactly the same interpretation in a communicative situation. The discrepancies are more evident if the available contextual cues do not appropriately determine the intended interpretation. As a result, the people (blind and sighted) reading the text provided in the experiment, more frequently offered idiosyncratic interpretations based on weak assumptions, than people listening to the recordings or watching the films. Although the texts provided less contextual information than the recordings and even less than the films, it does not necessarily mean that the comprehension of the written text is by definition more likely to be unsuccessful than of recorded utterances, nor that a film provides all of the information necessary for interpretation.

Comparing the interpretations offered by blind and sighted people, we observed that the two groups did not differ significantly in the ways they interpreted the utterances. The only differences that occurred, did not result from developmental impediments or the cognitive inferiority of the visually impaired, but were the consequence of an insufficient amount of contextual information. Providing blind people with the necessary contextual cues or making up for the missing information (e.g. with audio description) allowed them to understand utterances at the same level as sighted people. The insufficiency of contextual information might not only affect the 'on the spot' interpretation of utterances, but might also have long-term consequences leading to the occurrence of gaps in blind people's conceptual knowledge. Although we did not observe the significant effect that these gaps have on comprehension (the power to hinder or prevent blind people from arriving at any interpretation), it should be kept in mind that the study was not directly aimed at exposing the gaps, which are particularly difficult to detect in adults. Beyond the shadow of a doubt, the issue calls for special attention and should be carefully examined in order to confirm if misunderstood or missing concepts really do affect comprehension and seriously obstruct communication.

The study allowed us to observe that comprehension was more effort-consuming (for both blind and sighted people) in the case of cognitively challenging tasks. Ambiguity resolution, establishing coherence, interpretation of irony and figurative language, were more vulnerable to failure or misinterpretation, and hence communicatively risky. At the same time, as predicted by Relevance Theory, they triggered much richer assumptions than explicitly communicated utterances, which might be more beneficial from the perspective of both the speaker and interpreter. Considering the comprehension of ambiguous, incoherent and ironic utterances, we did not notice statistically significant differences between blind and sighted people, if provided with a sufficient amount of contextual cues. This brings us to the final conclusion that blind and sighted people are equally competent reasoners, and that difficulties and impediments that the blind experience in childhood are successfully overcome, as reported by earlier studies on the cognitive abilities of blind people.

All in all, the book should be considered as a starting point for further and more detailed research in the fields and areas indicated in the study. In order to better understand the relation between comprehension and visual impairment, it is imperative that appropriate studies be performed on different age groups of blind children and adolescents, so as to specify at which point of their development various pragmatic difficulties are eliminated. We strongly believe that similar tools and procedures employed in the work, but obviously appropriately adapted to the age and competence of children, could be utilised, which may produce interesting results in the future and provide further insight into the mysteries of human understanding.

REFERENCES

Adams, P. (1972) Language in thinking. Baltimore: Penguin.

Adelson, E. & Fraiberg, S. (1974) Gross motor development in infants blind from birth. Child Development, 45, 1-126.

Akamatsu, T. (1987) The notion of 'degree of relevance' in phonology. La Linguistique, 23, 49-62.

Akmajian, A., Demers, R., Farmer, A. K. & Harnish, R. M. (2001) Linguistics, 5th Edition: An Introduction to Language and Communication. Massachusetts: The MIT Press.

Allen, G.D. (1983) Linguistic experience modifies lexical stress perception. Journal of Child Language, 10, 535-549.

Amedi, A., Raz, N., Pianka, P., Malach, R. & Zohary, E. (2003) Early 'visual' cortex activation correlates with superior verbal memory performance in the blind. Nature Neuroscience, 6, 758-766.

Andersen, E.S., Dunlea, A. & Kekelis, L. (1984) Blind children's language: resolving some differences. Journal of Child Language, 11(3), 645-664.

Andersen, E.S., Dunlea, A. & Kekelis, L. (1993) The impact of input: Language acquisition in the visually impaired. First Language, 13, 23-49.

Andrews, J., Resenblatt, E., Malkus, U., Gardner, H. & Winner, E. (1986) Children's abilities to distinguish metaphoric and ironic utterances from mistakes and lies. Communication and Cognition, 19, 281-298.

Ariel, M. (2002) The demise of a unique concept of literal meaning. Journal of Pragmatics, 34(4), 361-402.

Asher, R. (1994) The Encyclopaedia of Language and Linguistics. Oxford: Pergamon Press.

Asher, N. & Lascarides, A. (1995) Lexical Disambiguation in a Discourse Context. Journal of Semantics, 12(1), 69-108.

Ashmead, D.H., Wall, R.S., Ebinger, K.A., Eaton, S.B., Snook-Hill, M.M. & Yang, X. (1998) Spatial hearing in children with visual disabilities. Perception, 27(1), 105-22.

Assimakopoulos, S. (2003) Context selection and relevance. Paper delivered at the Theoretical & Applied Linguistics Postgraduate Conference. University of Edinburgh, Edinburgh.

Attardo, S. (2000) Irony as relevant inappropriateness. Journal of Pragmatics, 32, 793-826.

Attardo, S. (2001) On the pragmatic nature of irony and its rhetorical aspects. In E. Nemeth (ed.) Pragmatics in 2000. Proceedings from the 7th Pragmatics Conference, vol. 2, pp. 52-66. Antwerp: IPrA.

Attardo, S. (2008) Semantics and pragmatics of humour. Language and Linguistics Compass, 2(6), 1203–1215.

Austin, J. (1962) How to do things with words. Oxford: Clarendon Press.

Axel, E. S. (2003) Art beyond sight: a resource guide to art, creativity and visual impairment. New York: AFB.

Babbie, E. (2007) The Practice of Social Research. Belmont, CA: Wadsworth.

Bach, K. (1994) Conversational implicature. Mind & Language, 9, 124-162.

Bach, K. (2005) Pragmatics and the Philosophy of Language. In L. Horn & G. Ward (eds.) The Handbook of Pragmatics, pp. 463-485. Oxford: Blackwell.

Bach, K. (2009) Impliciture vs. explicature: What's the difference?. In E. Romero & B. Soria (eds.) Explicit Communication: Robyn Carston's Pragmatics. Basingstoke: Palgrave-Macmillan.

Bach, K. & Harnish, R. (1979) Linguistic communication and speech acts. Cambridge: MIT Press.

Barbe, K. (1995) Irony in Context. Amsterdam: John Benjamins.

Baron-Cohen, S. (2001) Mindblindness: an essay on autism and theory of mind. Cambridge: MIT Press.

Barrett, M. (1995) Early lexical development. In P. Fletcher & B. MacWhinney (eds.) The handbook of child language, pp. 362-392. Oxford: Blackwell.

Barry, A.K. (2002) Linguistic perspective on language and education. Westport: Greenwood Publishing Group.

Barsalou, L. (1999) Perceptual symbol systems. Behavioral and Brain Sciences, 22, 577 609.

Barth-Weingarten D., Dehe, N. & Wichmann, A. (2009) Where Prosody Meets Pragmatics. Bingley: Emerald Group Publishing Limited.

Beaugrande, R. de. (1980) Text, Discourse, and Process: Toward a Multidisciplinary Science of Text (Advances in Discourse Processes 4). Norwood, NJ: Ablex.

Becker, J.A. (1990) Processes in the acquisition of pragmatic competence. In G. Conti-Ramsden & C. E. Snow (eds.) Children's language, Volume 7, pp. 7-24. Hillsdale, NJ: Lawrence Erlbaum.

Bedny, M., Pascual-Leone, A. & Saxe, R. R. (2009) Growing up blind does not change the neural bases of Theory of Mind. PNAS, 106(27), 11312-11317.

Begum, S. (2003) Cognitive Development in Blind Children. New Delhi: Discovery Publishing House.

Belletti, A. (2004) Structures and beyond. Oxford: Oxford University Press.

Bendych, E. (1994) Badania nad rysunkiem dziecka niewidomego Cz. I. Szkoła Specjalna, 5, 276-287.

Berman, R.A. (2004) Language Development across Childhood and Adolescence. Amsterdam: John Benjamins.

Bezuidenhout, A. & Sroda, M.S. (1998) Children's use of contextual cues to resolve referential ambiguity: An application of relevance theory. Pragmatics & Cognition, 6, 265-299.

Bieglow, A. (1990) Relationship between the development of language and thought in young blind children. Journal of Visual Impairment and Blindness, 84(8), 414- 419.

Bigelow, A. (1995) The effect of blindness on the early development of the self. In P. Rochat (ed.), The Self in Infancy: Theory and Research, vol. 112, pp. 327-347, Amsterdam: North-Holland/ Elsevier Science Publishers.

Bieglow, A. & Bryan, A. (1982) 'The understanding of spatial prepositions 'in', 'on' and 'under' in blind and sighted preschool children'. Paper presented at the Canadian Psychological Association Conference, Montreal.

Blagden, S. & Everett, J. (1992) What colour is the wind?. Bristol: NSEAD.

Blakemore, D. (1992) Understanding Utterances: An Introduction to Pragmatics. Oxford: Blackwell.

Blakemore, D. (2001) Discourse and Relevance Theory. In D. Schiffrin, D. Tannen & H. Ehernberger Hamilton (eds.) The handbook of discourse analysis, pp.100-118. Oxford: Blackwell.

Blass, R. (1990) Relevance Relations in Discourse. Cambridge: Cambridge University Press.

Blaye, A., Ackermann, E. & Light, P. (1999) The relevance of relevance in children's cognition. In J. Bliss, P. Light & R. Saljo (eds.) Social and Technological Resources for Learning, pp. 120-132. Pergamon/Elsevier.

Blaye, A. & Bernard-Peyron, V. (1996) Une étude développementale des activités de catégorisation : Variabilité inter- et intra-individuelle des conduites. Communication presented to the Xiemes Journees de Psychologie Différentielle. Lorinet (France).

Bloom, P. (2002) Mindreading, Communication and the Learning of Names for Things. Mind & Language, 17(1-2), 37-54(18).

Bloom, P. & German, T.P. (2000) Two reasons to abandon the false belief task as a test of theory of mind. Cognition, 77, B25-B31.

Blutner, R. (2005) Pragmatics and the Lexicon. In L. Horn & G. Ward (eds.) The Handbook of Pragmatics, pp. 488-514. Oxford: Blackwell.

Blutner, R. (2007) Optimality theoretic pragmatics and the explicature/implicature distinction. In N. Burton-Roberts (ed.) Pragmatics, pp. 45-66. Basingstoke: Palgrave.

Bohus, D. & Rudnicky, A. (2008) Sorry, I didn't catch that! An Investigation of Non-Understanding Errors and Recovery Strategies. In L. Dybkjær & W. Minker (eds.) Recent Trends in Discourse and Dialogue, pp. 123-152, Dordrecht: Springer.

Bonvillian, J.D., Raeburn, V.P. & Horan, E.A. (1979) Talking to children: the effects of rate, intonation, and length on children's sentence imitation. Journal of Child Language, 6(3), 459–467.

Boroojerdi, B. & Cohen, L.G. (2003) Cross-modal reassignment of function in the human brain. In F. Boller, J. Grafman & I. H. Robertson (eds.) Handbook of neuropsychology, pp. 153-166. Amsterdam: Elsevier Science.

Bortfeld, H. and McGlone, M.S. (2001) The Continuum of Metaphor Processing. Metaphor and Symbol, 16(1&2), 75-86.

Bou-Franch, P. (2002) Misunderstandings and Unofficial Knowledge in Institutional Discourse. In D. Walton & D. Scheu (eds.) Culture and Power: Ac(unofficially) knowledging Cultural Studies in Spain, pp. 323-341. Berlin: PeterLang.

Bradsford, J. (2000) How people learn: brain, mind, experience and school. Washington: National Academy Press.

Brain, C. & Mukherji, P. (2005) Understanding child psychology. Cheltenham: Nelson Thornes Ltd.

Bredart, S. & Modolo, K. (1988) Moses strikes again: Focalization effect on a semantic illusion. Acta Psychologica, 67, 135-144.

Breheny, R. (2001) 'Meaning, communication and theory of mind'. Paper delivered at the 23rd Annual Conference of the Cognitive Science Society. Edinburgh, August.

Brewer, W.F. & Treyens, J.C. (1981) Role of schemata in memory for places. Cognitive Psychology, 13, 207-230.

Bromberek-Dyzman, K. (2010) Irony Processing – One Stage or Two?. In E. Wałaszewska, M. Kisielewska-Krysiuk & A. Piskorska (eds.) In the Mind and across Minds: A Relevance-Theoretic Perspective on

Communication and Translation, pp. 208-223. Newcastle: Cambridge Scholars Publishing.

Bruce, V., Green, P.R. & Georgeson, M.A. (1996/2003) Visual perception: physiology, psychology and ecology. New York: Psychology Press Ltd.

Bucciarelli, M., Colle, L. & Bara, B.G. (2003) How children comprehend speech acts and communicative gestures. Journal of Pragmatics, 35, 207-241.

Burkhardt, A. (1990) Speech acts, meaning, and intentions: critical approaches to the philosophy of John R. Searle. Berlin, New York: de Gruyter.

Burlingham, D.T. (1961) Some notes on the development of the blind. Psychoanalytic Study of the Child, 16, 121-145.

Bührig, K. & ten Thije, J. D. (2006) Beyond misunderstanding: linguistic analyses of intercultural communication. Amsterdam: John Benjamins.

Capone, A. (2009) Are explicatures cancellable? Toward a theory of the speaker's intentionality. Intercultural Pragmatics, 6(1), 55–83.

Carberry, S. (1986) The use of inferred knowledge in handling pragmatically ill-formed queries. In R. Reilly (ed.) Communication Failure in Dialogue, pp. 187-200. Amsterdam, North-Holland: Elsevier Science Publishers.

Carlson, G. (2005) Reference. In L. Horn and G. Ward (eds.) The Handbook of Pragmatics, pp. 74-96, Oxford: Blackwell.

Carston, R. (1998) Syntax and pragmatics. In J.L. Mey (ed.) Concise Encyclopaedia of Pragmatics, pp. 978-986. Oxford: Pergamon.

Carston, R. (2002) Thoughts and Utterances. Oxford: Blackwell.

Carston, R. (2004) Explicature and Semantics. In S. Davis & B. Gillon (eds.) Semantics: A Reader, pp. 817-845. Oxford: Oxford University Press.

Carston, R. (2005) Relevance Theory and the Saying/Implicating Distinction. In L. Horn & G. Ward (eds.) The Handbook of Pragmatics, pp. 633-656. Oxford: Blackwell.

Carston, R. (2009) The explicit/implicit distinction in pragmatics and the limits of explicit communication. International Review of Pragmatics, 1(1), 35-62.

Chandler, D. (2009) Semiotics: the basics. London, New York: Routledge.

Chapman, E.K. (1978) Visually handicapped children and young people. London: Routledge and Kegan Paul Ltd.

Chen, R. (1992) 'Ambiguity Can Be Pragmatic, and a Good Thing, Too'. Paper presented at the Annual Conference on Pragmatics and Language Learning, Urbana, IL.

Chevallier, C., Wilson, D., Happé, F. & Noveck, I. (2009) From acoustics to grammar: Perceiving and interpreting grammatical prosody in adolescents with Asperger Syndrome. Research in Autism Spectrum Disorders, 3(2), 502-516.

Chierchia G. (2004) Scalar implicatures, polarity phenomena and the syntax/pragmatics interface. In A. Belletti (ed.) Structures and Beyond, pp. 39-103. Oxford: Oxford University Press.

Choi, Y. (2003) 'Preschool Aged Children's Use of Prosody in Sentence Processing: The Cases of Korean Children'. Unpublished doctoral book, Duke University.

Choi, Y. and Mazuka, R. (2003) Young children's use of prosody in sentence parsing. Journal of Psycholinguistic Research, 32, 197-217.

Chomsky, N. (1965) Aspects of the Theory of Syntax. Cambridge, MA: MIT Press.

Chomsky, N. (1968) Language and mind. New York: Harcourt, Brace and World.

Christiansen, J.A. (1999) Relevance in the language production of aphasic patients. In First International Conference on Neuropsychology in Internet.

Clark, B. (2007) Blazing a trail: Moving from natural to linguistic meaning in accounting for the tones in English. In R.A. Nilsen, N.A. Appiah Amfo & K. Borthen (eds.) Interpreting Utterances: Pragmatics and its Interfaces. Essays in Honour of Thorstein Fretheim, pp. 69-81. Oslo: Novus.

Clark, B. & Lindsey, G. (1990) Intonation, grammar and utterance interpretation: Evidence from English exclamatory/inversions. UCL Working Papers in Linguistics, 2, 32-51.

Clark, E.V. (2001) Grounding and attention in Language Acquisition. In Proceedings from the Main Session of the 37th Meeting of the Chicago Linguistics Society.

Clark, E.V. (2003) First language acquisition. Cambridge: Cambridge University Press.

Clark, E.V. (2005) Pragmatics and Language Acquisition. In L. Horn & G. Ward (eds.) The Handbook of Pragmatics, pp. 562-575. Oxford: Blackwell.

Clark, H.H. (1996) Using language. Cambridge: Cambridge University Press.

Coulson, S. & Matlock, T. (2009) Cognitive Science. In S. Dominiek, J. Östman & J. Verschueren (eds.) Cognition and pragmatics, pp. 86-110. Amsterdam: John Benjamins.

Couper-Kuhlen, E.& Ford, C.E. (2004) Sound patterns in interaction. Amsterdam: John Benjamins.

Coupland, N., Giles, H. & Wiemann, J. (1991) Miscommunication and Problematic Talk. London: SAGE.

Cruse, D.A. (1986) Lexical semantics. Cambridge: Cambridge University Press.

Cruse, D.A. (2001) The Lexicon. In M. Aronoff & J. Rees-Miller (eds.) The Handbook of Linguistics, pp. 238-264. Oxford: Blackwell.

Crystal, D. (1999) Prosodic development. In P. Fletcher & M. Garman (eds.) Language acquisition: studies in first language development, pp. 174-197. Cambridge: Cambridge University Press.

Curcó, C. (2000) Irony: Negation, echo and metarepresentation. Lingua, 110, 257-280.

Curl, T.S., Local, J. & Walker, G. (2006) Repetition and the prosody-pragmatics interface. Journal of Pragmatics, 38(10), 1721-1751.

Davidson, D. (2000) What metaphors mean. In J. Stainton (ed.) Perspectives in the Philosophy of Language: a concise anthology, pp. 333-350. Toronto: Broadview Press.

Davis, M. (1995) Philosophy of language In N. Bunnin & E. Tsui-James (eds.) The Blackwell Companion to Philosophy, pp. 90-139. Oxford: Blackwell.

de Beaugrande, R. & Dressler, W. (1981) Introduction to text linguistics. London: Longman.

DeBeni, R. & Cornoldi, C. (1988) Imagery limitations in totally congenitally blind subjects. Journal of Experimental Psychology, Learning, Memory and Cognition, 14, 650-655.

De Brabanter, P. (2009) Uttering sentences made up of words and gestures. In B. Soria & E. Romero (eds.) Explicit Communication: Essays on Robyn Carston's Pragmatics. London: Palgrave.

DeCasper, A.J., Lacanuet, J.P., Busnel, M.C., Granier-Deferre, C. & Maugeais, R. (1994) Fetal reaction to recurrent maternal speech. Infant Behaviour and Development, 17, 159-164.

Dewey, J. (1931) Context and Thought. Philosophy, vol.12 no.3, pp. 203-224. Berkley: University of California Press. (reprint in Boydston, J.A. (ed.) (2008) John Dewey: The Later Works, 1925-1953 Volume 6: 1931-1932. Southern Illinois University Press).

Dews S. & Winner, E. (1999) Obligatory processing of literal and nonliteral meanings in verbal irony. Journal of Pragmatics, 31(12, 2), 1579-1599(21).

Dews, S., Winner, E., Kaplan, J., Rosenblatt, E., Hunt, M. & Lim, K. (1996) Children's understanding of the meaning and functions of verbal irony. Child Development, 67, 3071- 3085.

Dimcovic, N. & Tobin, M. J. (1995) The use of language in simple classification tasks by children who are blind. Journal of Visual Impairment & Blindness, 89(5), 448-459.

Donaldson, M. (1978) Children's Mind. Fontana: London.

Dromi, E. (1999) Early lexical development. In M. Barrett (ed.) The Development of language: studies in developmental psychology, pp. 99-131. Philadelphia: Psychology Press.

Drummond, K. & Hopper, R. (1991) Misunderstandings and its remedies: Telephone communication. In N. Coupland, J.M. Wiemann & H. Giles (eds.) Miscommunication and Problematic Talk, pp. 301-314. London: SAGE.

Dulin, D. (2008) Effects of prior experience in raised line materials and prior visual experience in length estimations by blind people. The British Journal of Visual Impairment, 26(3), 223-237.

Dunlea, A. (1989) Vision and the emergence of meaning: blind and sighted children's early language. Cambridge: Cambridge University Press.

Dunlea, A. & Andersen, E. (1992) The emergence process: conceptual and linguistic influences on morphological development. First Language, 12, 95-115.

Duranti, A. & Goodwin, C. (1992) Re-thinking context: language as an interactive phenomenon. Cambridge: Cambridge University Press.

Ekbia, H.R. & Maguitman, A.G. (2001) Context and Relevance: A Pragmatic Approach. In V. Akman (ed.) Modeling and Using Context, pp. 155-168. Berlin, Heidelberg: Springer

Erin, J.N. (1986) Frequencies and types of questions in the language of visually impaired children. Journal of Visual Impairment and Blindness, 80, 670-674.

Ervin-Tripp, S. (1970) Discourse agreement: How children answer questions. In J. Hayes (ed.), Cognition and the Development of Language, pp. 79-106. New York: John Wiley.

Ervin-Tripp, S. (1977) Wait for me, roller-skate!. In S. Ervin-Tripp & C. Mitchell-Kernan (eds.) Child Discourse, pp. 165-185. New York: Academic Press

Evans, V. & Green, M. (2006) Cognitive linguistics: an introduction. Edinburgh: Lawrence Erlbaum Associates.

Eysneck, M.W. & Keane, M.T. (2000) Cognitive psychology: a student's handbook. Hove: Psychology Press Ltd.

Fauconnier, G. (2005) Pragmatics and Cognitive Linguistics. In L. Horn & G. Ward (eds.) The Handbook of Pragmatics, pp. 657-674. Oxford: Blackwell.

Fazzi, D.L. & Klein, M.D. (2002) Cognitive Focus. Developing Cognition, Concepts and Language. In R.L. Pogrund & D.L. Fazzi (eds.) Early Focus: working with young children who are blind or visually impaired and their families, pp. 107-153. New York: AFB.

Finello, K.M., Hanson, N.H. & Kekelis, L.S. (1992) Cognitive Focus; Developing Cognition, Concepts and language in Young Blind and Visually Impaired Children. In R.L. Pogrund, D.L. Fazzi & J.S. Lampert (eds.) Early Focus: Working with Young Blind and Visually Impaired Children and Their Families, pp. 34-49. New York: AFB.

Firth, J.R. (1957) Papers in Linguistics 1934-51. Oxford: Oxford University Press.

Fodor, J. (1983) The Modularity of Mind. Cambridge, MA: MIT Press.

Foulke E. & Halten, P.H. (1992) A collaboration of two technologies. Part 1: Perceptual and cognitive processes: their implications for visually impaired persons. British Journal of Visual Impairment, 10, 43-46.

Foulke E. & Sticht, T. (1974) Review of research on the intelligibility and comprehension of accelerated speech. In N.J. Lass (ed.) Speech and hearing: selected readings, vol. 10, pp. 78-90. New York: MSS Information Corporation.

Fraiberg, S. (1977) Insights from the blind: Comparative studies of blind and sighted infants. New York: Meridian.

Frampton, M.E, Kerney, E. & Schattner, R. (1969) Forgotten children: a program for the mulihandicapped. New York: New York Institute for the Education of the Blind.

Fredsted, E. (1998) On semantic and pragmatic ambiguity. Journal of Pragmatics, 30(5), 527-541.

Freedle, R.O. (1977) Discourse Production and Comprehension (Advances in Discourse Processes 1). Norwood, NJ: Ablex.

Fretheim, T. (1996) Accessing contexts with intonation. In T. Fretheim & J.K. Gundel (eds.) Reference and Referent Accessibility, pp. 89-112. Amsterdam: John Benjamins.

Fretheim, T. (2009) On the functional interdependence of explicatures and implicatures. In B. Behrens & C. Fabricius-Hansen (eds.) Structuring information in discourse: the explicit/implicit dimension, pp. 17-32. Oslo: Oslo Studies in Language 1(1).

Fretheim, T. & van Dommelen, W.A. (1999) Building context with intonation. In P. Bouquet, L. Serafini, P. Brézillon, M. Benerecetti &

F. Castellani (eds.) Modeling and Using Context, pp. 463-467. Berlin: Springer-Verlag.

Friedman, J. & Pasnak, R. (1973) Accelerated acquisition of classification skills by blind children, Developmental Psychopathology, 9, 333-337.

Fromkin, V., Rodman, R. & Hyams, N. (2007) An Introduction to Language (8th ed.). Boston, MA: Thomson Wadsworth.

Garrett, M. & Harnish, R.M. (2007) Experimental pragmatics. Testing for implicitures. Pragmatics & Cognition, 15(1), 65-90.

Gazdar, G. (1979) Pragmatics: Implicature, presupposition and logical form. New York: Academic Press.

Gelman, R. & Greno, J. (1989) On the nature of competence: principles for understanding a domain. In L. Resnick (ed.) Knowing and learning: essays in honour of Robert Glaser, pp. 125-186. Hillsdale, NJ:Erlbaum.

Gentner, D. & Bowdle, B. (2002) Metaphor processing, psychology of. Encyclopaedia of Cognitive Science. London: Nature Publishing Group.

Gernsbacher, M.A., Tallent, K. & Bolliger, C.M. (1999) Disordered discourse in schizophrenia described by the structure building framework. Discourse Studies, 1(3), 355-372.

Gibbs, N. (1981) Reflections on visually handicapped children I have known. The British Psychological Society Division of Educational and Child Psychology Occasional Papers, 5, 48-50.

Gibbs, R. W. (1986) On the psycholinguistics of sarcasm. Journal of Experimental Psychology: General, 115, 3-15.

Gibson, J.J. (1979) The ecological approach to visual perception. Boston, MA: Houghton Mifflin.

Gibson, J.J. (1986) The Ecological Approach To Visual Perception. Hillsdale, NJ: Lawrence Erlbaum Associates.

Lawrence Erlbaum Associates.

Giora, R. (1998) Irony. In J. Verschueren, J-O Östman, J. Blommaert, & C. Bulcaen (eds.) Handbook of Pragmatics, pp. 1-21. Amsterdam: John Benjamins.

Giora, R. & Fein, O. (2007) Irony: Context and Salience. In R.W. Gibbs & H.L. Colson (eds.) Irony in language and thought: A cognitive science reader, pp. 201-215. New York: Lawrence Erlbaum Associates.

Givón, T. (1989) Mind, code, and context: essays in pragmatics. Hillsdale, NJ: Lawrence Erlbaum Associates.

Glucksberg, S. & Keysar, B. (1990) Understanding metaphorical comparisons: beyond similarity. Psychological Review, 97(1), 3-18.

Goldin-Meadow, S. & Feldman, H. (1977) The development of language like communication without a language model. Science, 197(4301), 401-403.

Goodluck, H. (1991) Language acquisition: a linguistic introduction. Oxford: Blackwell.

Gordon, R.A., Druckmann, D., Rozelle, R. M. & Baxter, J.C. (1997) Non-verbal behaviour as communication. In O. Hargie (ed.) The handbook of communication skills, pp. 73-120. London: Routledge.

Grassman, S. & Tomasello, M. (2010) Prosodic stress on a word directs 24-month-old's attention to a contextually new referent. Journal of Pragmatics, 42, 3098-3105.

Grice, P. (1957) Meaning. In P. Grice (1991) Studies in the way of words, pp. 213-222. Harvard: Harvard University Press (first published in The Philosophical Review vol. 66 (1957)).

Grice, P. (1975) Logic and Conversation. In R. J. Stainton (ed.) (2000) Perspectives in the Philosophy of Language: a concise anthology, pp.271-287. Toronto: Broadview Press.

Grundy, P. (2000) Doing Pragmatics: 2nd edition. London: Arnold.

Gualmini, A., Crain, S., Meroni, L., Chierchia, G. & Guasti, M.T. (2001) At the semantics/pragmatics interface in child language. Proceedings of Semantics and Linguistic Theory XI. Ithaca, NY: CLC Publications, Department of Linguistics, Cornell University.

Guenthner, F. & Schmidt, S. J. (1979) Formal semantics and pragmatics for natural languages. Dordrecht: D. Reidel Publishing Company.

Gumperz, J. (1978) The Conversational Analysis of Interethnic Communication. In E. L. Ross (ed.) Interethnic Communication, pp.13-31. Athens, GA: University of Georgia Press.

Hall, A. (1982) Teaching Specific Concepts to Visually Handicapped Students. In S. Mangold (ed.) A Teacher's Guide to the Special Educational Needs of Blind and Visually Handicapped Children, pp.10-19. New York: AFB.

Halliday, M. (1978). Language as Social Semiotic. London: Edward Arnold.

Halliday, M. & Hasan, R. (1976) Cohesion in English. London: Longman.

Hampson, P. & Morris, P. (1996) Understanding Cognition. Oxford: Blackwell.

Hancock, J.T, Dunham, P.J. & Purdy, K. (2000) Children's Comprehension of Critical and Complimentary Forms of Verbal Irony. Journal of Cognition and Development, 12, 227-240.

Happé, F. (1993) Communicative competence and theory of mind in autism: a test of relevance theory. Cognition, 48, 101-119.

Happé, F. (1995) Understanding minds and metaphors: Insights from the study of figurative language in Autism. Metaphor and Symbolic Activity, 10, 275-295.

Harris, M. (1992) Language experience and early language development: from input to uptake. Hove: Laurence Erlbaum Associates Ltd.

Harris, R. & Taylor, T.J. (1997) Landmarks in Linguistic Thought I: The Western tradition from Socrates to Saussure. London: Routledge.

Hatwell, Y. (1985) Piagetian Reasoning in the Blind. New York: AFB.

Hatwell, Y. (1993) Images and non-visual spatial representations in the blind. In D. Burger & J. Sperandio (eds.) Non-visual Human-Computer Interactions: Prospects for the visually handicapped, pp. 13-36. London: John Libbey and Company Ltd.

Haugeland, J. (1993/98) Pattern and Being. In J. Haugeland (ed.) (2000) Having Thought: Essays in the Metaphysics of Mind, pp. 267-290, Harvard: Harvard University Press.

Hayes, J.R., Waterman, D.A. & Robinson, C.S. (1977) Identifying the relevant aspects of a problem text. Cognitive Science, 1, 297-313.

Hebb, D.O. (1949) The organization of behavior. New York: John Wiley & Sons.

Heim, I. (1982) 'The Semantics for Definite and Indefinite Noun Phrases'. Doctoral book, University of Massachusetts, Amherst.

Heller, M.A. (1989) Picture and pattern perception in the sighted and blind: The advantage of the late blind. Perception, 18, 379-389.

Hellman, C. (1995) The Notion of Coherence in Discourse. In G. Rickheit & C. Habel (eds.) Focus and coherence in discourse processing, pp. 190-202. Berlin, New York: de Gruyter.

Hinde, R.A. (1972/1979) Non-verbal communication. Cambridge: Cambridge University Press.

Hinnenkamp, V. (2001) Constructing misunderstanding as a cultural event. In A. Di Luzio, S. Gunther & F. Orletti (eds.) Culture in Communication, pp. 211-244. Amsterdam: John Benjamins.

Hirsch, G. (2011) Redundancy, irony and humor. Language Sciences, 33, 316-329.

Hirschberg, J. (1985) 'A Theory of Scalar Implicature'. Unpublished doctoral book, University of Pennsylvania, Philadelphia.

Hirschberg, J. (2005) Pragmatics and Intonation. In L. Horn & G. Ward (eds.) The Handbook of Pragmatics, pp. 515-538. Oxford: Blackwell.

Hobbs, J.R. (1979) Coherence and coreference. Cognitive Science, 3, 27-90.

Hobbs, J.R. (1990) Literature and Cognition. Stanford: CSLI Lecture Notes.

Hoff, E. (2005) Language Development. Belmont, CA: Wadsworth.

Horn, L. (1972) 'On the Semantic Properties of Logical Operators in English'. Doctoral book, UCLA, distributed by IULC.

Horn, L. (1985) Metalinguistic negation and pragmatic ambiguity. Language, 61, 121-174.

Horn, L. (1989) A Natural History of Negation. Chicago: University of Chicago Press.

Horn, L. (2005a) Current issues in neo-Gricean pragmatics. Intercultural Pragmatics, 2(2), 191–204.

Horn, L. (2005b) Implicature. In L. Horn & G. Ward (eds.) The Handbook of Pragmatics, pp. 3-28. Oxford: Blackwell.

Horn, J.L. & Hofer, S.M. (1992) Major abilities and development in the adult period. In R.J. Sternberg & C.A. Berg (eds.) Intellectual development, pp. 44-99. New York: Cambridge University Press.

House, J. (1990) Intonation structures and pragmatic interpretation. In S. Ramsaran (ed.) Studies in the Pronunciation of English, pp 38-57. London: Routledge.

House, J. (2006) Constructing a context with intonation. Journal of Pragmatics, 38(10), 1542-1558.

Huang, Y. (1994) The syntax and pragmatics of anaphora: A study with special reference to Chinese. Cambridge: Cambridge University Press.

Hudson, J. & Nelson, K. (1983) Effects of script structure on children's story recall. Developmental Psychology, 19, 625-635.

Hudson, J. & Slackman, E.A. (1990) Children's use of scripts in inferential text processing. Discourse Processes, 13, 375-386.

Hymes, D. (1974) Foundations in Sociolinguistics: An Ethnographic Approach. Philadelphia: University of Pennsylvania Press.

Ifantidou, E. (2005) The semantics and pragmatics of metadiscourse. Journal of Pragmatics, 37, 1325-1353.

Imai, K. (1998) Intonation and relevance. In R. Carston & S. Uchida (eds.) Relevance Theory. Applications and Implicatons, pp. 69-86. Amsterdam: John Benjamins.

Inhelder, B. & Piaget, J. (1964) The Early Growth of Logic in the Child (Classification and Seriation). New York: Harper New York.

Ivanko, S.L. & Pexman, P.M. (2003) Context Incongruity and Irony Processing. Discourse Processes, 35(3), 241-279

Jaszczolt, K.M. (2001) Against ambiguity and underspecification: evidence from presupposition as anaphora. Journal of Pragmatics. 34(7), 829-849.

Jaszczolt, K.M. (2002) Semantics and Pragmatics: Meaning in Language and Discourse. Harlow: Pearson Education Ltd.

Jaworska-Biskup, K. (2009) 'Concept understanding by congenitally blind children. Implications for learning and teaching English as a foreign language'. Unpublished doctoral book. The John Paul II Catholic University of Lublin, Lublin.

Jodłowiec, M. (2008) Relevance Theory and degrees of understanding. In E. Mioduszewska & A. Piskorska (eds.) Relevance Round Table I, pp. 23-39. Warsaw: Warsaw University Press.

Johnson, M. (1987) The Body in the Mind: The Bodily Basis of Meaning, Imagination, and Reason. Chicago: University of Chicago Press.

Jorgensen, J. (1996) The functions of sarcastic irony in speech. Journal of Pragmatics, 26, 613-634.

Juricevic, I. & Kennedy, J. M. (2006) Looking at perspective pictures from too far, too close and just right. Journal of Experimental Psychology: General, 135(3), 448-461.

Jusczyk, P.W., Cutler, A. & Redanz, N.J. (1993) Infants' preference for the predominant stress patterns of English words. Child Development, 64, 675-687.

Kandolf, C. (1993) On the Difference between Explicatures and Implicatures in Relevance Theory. Nordic Journal of Linguistics, 16, 33-46.

Kaplan, D. (1989) Afterthoughts. In J. Almong, J. Perry & H. Wettstein (eds.) Themes from Kaplan, pp. 565-614. Oxford: Oxford University Press.

Kasper, G. & Rose, K.R. (2003) Pragmatic development in a second language. Oxford: Blackwell.

Katz, D. (1946) Hur tecknar blinda? (trans. How do blind people draw?). Nya Psykologiska Stroevtag. Stockholm: Stockholm Kooperativa Bokfoerlag.

Katz, J. & Fodor, J. (1963) The structure of a semantic theory. Language, 39, 170-210.

Kehler, A. (2005) Discourse Coherence. In L. Horn & G. Ward (eds.) The Handbook of Pragmatics, pp. 241-265. Oxford: Blackwell Publishing Ltd.

Kekelis, L.S. & Andersen, E.S. (1984) Family communication styles and language development. Journal of Visual Impairment and Blindness, 78(2), 54 - 65.

Kempson, R. (1975) Presupposition and the delimitation of semantics (Cambridge Studies in Linguistics). Cambridge, London: Cambridge University Press.

Kempson, R. (1988) On the grammar-cognition interface: The Principle of Full Interpretation. In R.M. Kempson (ed.) Mental Representations:

The Interface Between Language and Reality, pp. 199-224. Cambridge: Cambridge University Press.

Kempson, R. (2002) Pragmatics: Language and Communication. In M. Aronoff & J. Rees-Miller (eds.) The Handbook of Linguistics, pp. 394-427. Oxford: Blackwell.

Kennedy, J.M. (1980) Blind people recognizing and making depictions. In M. Hagen (ed.) The perception of pictures. vol. 2, pp. 263-303. Boston: Boston University Press.

Kennedy, J.M. (1993) Drawing and the blind: Pictures to touch (1st ed.). New Haven, CT: Yale University Press.

Kennedy, J.M. & Fox, N. (1977) Pictures to see and pictures to touch. In D. Perkins & B. Leondar (eds.) The Arts and Cognition, pp. 118-135. Baltimore: Johns Hopkins.

Kennedy, J.M., Fox, N. & O'Grady, K. (1972) Can "haptic pictures" help the blind see?. Harvard Graduate School of Education Bulletin, 16, 22-23.

Kephart, J.G., Kephart, C.P. & Schwarz, G.C. (1974) A journey into the world of the blind child. Exceptional Children, 40, 421-427.

Kintsch, W. & van Dijk, T. A. (1978) Toward a model of text comprehension and production. Psychological Review, 85(5), 363-394.

Klima, E. & Bellugi, U. (1973) Syntactic regularities in the speech of children. In C. Ferguson & D. Slobin (eds.) Studies of child language development, pp. 333-354. New York: Holt, Rinehart and Winston.

Knauff, M. & Johnson-Laird, P.N. (2000) Visual and spatial representations in spatial reasoning. In Proceedings of the 22nd Annual Conference of the Cognitive Science Society. pp. 759-765. Mahwah, NJ: Erlbaum.

Knauff, M. & Johnson-Laird, P.N. (2002) Visual imagery can impede reasoning. Memory and Cognition, 30, 363-371.

Knauff, M. & May, E. (2004) Visual Imagery in Deductive Reasoning: Results from experiments with sighted, blindfolded, and congenitally totally blind persons. In Proceedings of the 26th Annual Conference of the Cognitive Science Society, pp. 708-713. Mahwah, NJ: Lawrence Erlbaum Associates.

Kuczaj, S.A. (1990) Constraining constraint theories. Cognitive Development, 5, 341-344.

Kumon-Nakamura, S., Glucksberg, S., & Brown, M. (1995) How about another piece of pie? The allusional pretence theory of discourse irony. Journal of Experimental Psychology: General, 124, 3-21.

Labov, W. (1969) The Study of Non-standard English. Champaign: National Council of Teachers of English

Lakoff, G. & Johnson, M. (1980) Metaphors we live by. Chicago: University of Chicago Press.

Lakoff, G. & Turner, M. (1989) More than Cool Reason: A Field Guide to Poetic Metaphor. Chicago: University of Chicago Press.

Landau, B. (1983) Blind children's language is not "meaningless". In: A.E. Mills (ed.) Language acquisition in the blind child: Normal and deficient, pp. 62-76. London: Croom Helm.

Landau, B. (1995) 'Language and experience in blind children: retrospective and prospective'. Paper presented at the Mary Kitzinger Trust Symposium: Blindness and Psychological Development, 0-10 years, University of Warwick, UK, September.

Landau, B. & Gleitman, L. R. (1985) Language and experience: Evidence from the blind child. Cambridge, MA: Harvard University Press.

Langacker, R. (1987) Foundations of Cognitive Grammar, Volume I. Stanford: Stanford University Press.

Langdon, R., Davies, M. & Coltheart, M. (2002) Understanding minds and understanding communicated meanings in schizophrenia. Mind & Language, 17(1-2), 68-104.

Lecacheur, M., Desprels-Fraysse, A. & Blaye, A. (1999) Children's sensitivity to inductions of logical and schematic categorization. Enfance, 51(2), 157-170.

Leech, G. (1983) Principles of Pragmatics. London: Longman.

Lenneberg, E.H. (1967) Biological foundations of language. New York: Wiley & Sons.

Lessard, N., Paré, M., Lepore, F. & Lassonade, M. (1998) Early-blind human subjects localize sound sources better than sighted subjects. Nature, 395, 278-280.

Levinson, S. (1983) Pragmatics. Cambridge: Cambridge University Press.

Lewis, D. (1979) Scorekeeping in a Language Game. In P. Portner & B. H. Partee (eds.) (2002) Formal semantics: the essential readings, pp. 162-177. Oxford: Blackwell.

Lewis, V. (2003) Development and disability. Oxford: Blackwell.

Lightbown P.M. & Spada, N. (1999) How languages are learned. Oxford: Oxford University Press.

Livingston, N. (1998) Comprehension of irony in Schizophrenia. Cognitive Neuropsychiatry, 3(2), 127-138.

Locke, J.L. (1996) Development of the Capacity for Spoken Language. In P. Fletcher & B. MacWhinney (eds.) The Handbook of child language, pp. 278-302. Oxford: Blackwell.

Loukusa, S. (2007) 'The use of context in pragmatic language comprehension in normally developing children and children with

Asperger Syndrome / High-functioning Autism. An Application Of Relevance Theory'. Doctoral book, the University Of Oulu, Oulu.

Lowenfeld, B. (1981) Berthold Lowenfeld on blindness and blind people: selected papers. New York: AFB.

Lucas, S.A. (1984) Auditory discrimination and speech production in the blind child. International Journal of Rehabilitation Research, 7, 74-76.

Lueck, A.H., Chen, D. & Kekelis, L.S. (1997) Developmental guidelines for visually impaired infants: A manual for infants birth to two. Louisville, KY: American Printing House for the Blind.

MacDonald M.C., Pearlmutter, N.J. & Seidenberg, M.S. (1994) The lexical nature of syntactic ambiguity resolution. Psychological Review, 101(4), 676-703.

Malinowski, B. (1923) The Problem of Meaning in Primitive Languages. In C.K. Ogden & I.A. Richards (eds.) (2004) The Meaning of Meaning, pp. 296-336. New York: Harcourt, Brace and Co.

Mandler, J.M. (1992) How to build a baby II: Conceptual primitives. Psychological Review, 99, 567-604

Mann, W.C. and Thompson, S. (1987) Relational propositions in discourse. Discourse Processes, 9, 57-90.

Mann, W.C. & Thompson, S. (1988) Rhetorical structure theory: towards a functional theory of text organization. Text, 8(3), 243-281.

Manor, R. (2001) On the overlap of pragmatics and semantics. Synthese, 128, 63-73.

Marek, B. (1987) The pragmatics of intonation. Lublin: Redakcja Wydawnictw KUL.

Marek, B. (1999) A Blind Child in an English Language Classroom. Network. A Journal for English Language Teacher Education, 2(1) Omnibus & The British Council.

Marek, B. (2000) 'Does a stone look the way it feels?'. Paper presented at the Fifth European ICEVI Conference, Cracow, July.

Matsui, T. (1993) Bridging reference and the notions of 'topic' and 'focus'. Lingua, 90, 49-68.

Matsui, T. (1998) Pragmatic criteria for reference assignment: A relevance-theoretic account of the acceptability of bridging. Pragmatics & Cognition, 6, 47-98.

Matsui, T. (2000) Bridging and Relevance. Amsterdam: John Benjamins.

Mattingly, I.G. & Liberman, A.M. (1990) Speech and other auditory modules. In G.M. Edelman, W.E. Gall & W.M. Cowan (eds.) Signal and sense: Local and global order in perceptual maps, pp. 501-519. New York: Wiley.

Mehler, J., Jusczyk, P., Lambertz, G., Halsted, N., Bertoncini, J. & Amiel-Tison, C. (1988) A precursor of language acquisition in young infants. Cognition, 29, 143-178.

Mehrabian, A. (1972/2007) Nonverbal Communication. Chicago: Aldine-Atherton.

Menn, L. & Stoel-Gammon, C. (1996) Phonological Development. In P. Fletcher & B. MacWhinney (eds.) The handbook of child language, pp. 335-360. Oxford: Blackwell.

Mey, J. L. (2001) Pragmatics: An Introduction. Oxford: Blackwell.

McAlpine, L.M. & Moore, C.L. (1995) The development of social understanding in children with visual impairments. Journal of Visual Impairment and Blindness, 89, 349-358.

McCarthy, M. (1991) Discourse Analysis for Language Teachers. Cambridge: Cambridge University Press.

McNeill, D. (1968) On the theories of language acquisition. In T.R. Dixon & D.L. Horton (eds.) Verbal behavior and general behavior theory, pp. 406-420. Englewood Cliffs, NJ: Prentice-Hall.

McRoy, S. (1998) Preface-Detecting, Repairing and Preventing Human-machine Miscommunication. International Journal of Human-Computer Studies, 48, 547-552.

McTear, M. (2008) Handling Miscommunication: Why Bother?. In L. Dybkjær & W. Minker (eds.) Recent Trends in Discourse and Dialogue Vol.3, pp. 101-118. Dordrecht: Springer.

Miecznikowski, A. & Andersen, E. (1986) From formulaic to analysed speech: Two systems or one?. In J. Connor-Linton, C.J. Hall & M. McGinnis (eds.) Perspectives on language, Southern California Occasional Papers in Linguistics: Vol. 11: Social and Cognitive, pp. 181-202. Los Angeles: University of Southern California.

Millar, S. (1986) Studies on touch and movement: their role in spatial skills and Braille. The British Journal of Visual Impairment, 4(1), 4-6.

Millar, S. (1994) Understanding and Representing Space. Oxford: Oxford University Press.

Miller, K., Schmitt, C., Chang, H. & Munn, A. (2005) Young children understand some implicatures. In A. Brugos, M.R. Clark-Cotton & S. Ha (eds.) Proceedings of the 29th Annual Boston University Conference on Language Development, pp. 389-400. Boston: Boston University.

Mills, A.E. (1987) The development of phonology in the blind. In B. Dodd & R. Campbell (eds.) Hearing by eye: The psychology of lip reading, pp. 145–161. London: Lawrence Erlbaum Associates.

Mills, A.E. (1988) The language of blind children: normal and abnormal. In P. Jordens & J. Lalleman (eds.) Language Development, pp. 57-70. Dordrecht: AVT Publications.

Milner, A. D. & Goodale M.A. (1995/1998) The visual brain in action. Oxford: Oxford University Press.

Minervino, R.A., Martín, A. & Trench, M. (2009) 'Congenitally Blind do not Comprehend Better 'I Grasp the Idea' than 'I See the Idea': A Challenge to the Use of Sensory-motor Conceptual Metaphors in the Comprehension of Metaphorical Expressions'. Paper presented at the Annual Meeting of the Cognitive Science Society COGSCI, August.

Minsky, M. (1977) Frame-system theory. In P.N. Johnson-Laird & P.C. Watson (eds.) Thinking: Readings in Cognitive Science, pp. 355-376. Cambridge: Cambridge University Press.

Minter, M., Hobson, R.P. & Bishop, M. (1998) Congenital visual impairment and theory of mind. British Journal of Developmental Psychology, 16, 183-196.

Mioduszewska, E. (2008) On relevance of non-communicative stimuli: the case of unintentional obscurity. In E. Mioduszewska & A. Piskorska (eds.) Relevance Round Table I, pp. 67-76, Warsaw: Warsaw University Press.

Mirecki, P. (2002) Misunderstanding and communication failure in Relevance Theory - a problem revisited. In E. Mioduszewska & A. Piskorska (eds.) Relevance Round Table I, pp. 77-86. Warsaw: Warsaw University Press.

Mirecki, P. (2004) Communication 'failure' – a definition and classification within the Theory of Relevance. In E. Mioduszewska (ed.) Relevance Studies in Poland vol.1, pp. 67-89. Warsaw: Warsaw University Press.

Moore, C. & Davidge, J. (1989) The development of mental terms: Pragmatics or semantics?. Journal of Child Language, 16, 622-641.

Morris, C. (1938/1970) Foundations of the Theory of Signs. Chicago: Chicago University Press.

Muchnik, C., Efrati, M., Nemeth, E., Malin, M. & Hildeshimer, M. (1991) Central auditory skills in blind and sighted subjects. Scandinavian Audiology, 20, 19-23.

Mulford, R.C. (1981) 'Talking about seeing: some problems of semantic development in blind children'. Doctoral book, Stanford University, Stanford.

Murphy, M.A. & Vogel, J.B. (1985) Looking out from the isolator: David's perception of the world. Developmental and Behavioural Paediatrics, 6, 118-121.

Natsopoulos, D. (1986) A verbal illusion in two languages. Journal of Psycholinguistic Research, 14(4), 385-398.

Nelson, K. & Gruendel, J. (1986) Children's scripts. In K. Nelson & J. Gruendel (eds.) Event knowledge: structure and function in development, pp. 21-46. Hillsdale, NJ: Lawrence Erlbaum.

Nerlich, B. & Clarke, D. D. (1996) Language, action, context: the early history of pragmatics in Europe and America 1780-1930. Amsterdam: John Benjamins.

Newton, D.A. & Burgoon, J.K. (1990) Nonverbal conflict behaviours: Functions, strategies and tactics. In D.D. Cahn (ed.) Intimates in conflict: A communication perspective, pp. 77-104. Hillsdale, NJ: Lawrence Erlbaum.

Niemeyer, W. & Starlinger, I. (1981) Do blind hear better? Investigations on auditory processing in congenital early acquired blindness II. Central functions. Audiology, 20, 510-515.

Norgate, S.H. (1996) 'Conceptual and lexical functioning in blind, severely visually impaired and sighted infants'. Unpublished doctoral book, Warwick University.

Norgate, S.H. (1997) Research methods for studying the language of blind children. In N.H. Hornberger & D. Corson (eds.) Research methods in language and education, pp. 165-174. Dordrecht: Kluwer Academic Publishers.

Noveck, I.A. (2001) When children are more logical than adults: Experimental investigations of scalar implicature. Cognition, 78(2), 165-188.

O'Neill, D.K. (1996) Two-year-old children's sensitivity to a parent's knowledge state when making request. Child Development, 67, 659-677.

Padilla Cruz, M. (2007) Can irony be phatic? A relevance-theoretic proposal. In M. Losada Friend, P. Ron Vaz, S. Hernández Santano & J. Casanova (eds.) Proceedings of the 30th International AEDEAN Conference. Huelva: Servicio de Publicaciones de la Universidad de Huelva, CD ROM edition.

Pagliano, P. J., Zambone, A. & Kelley, P. (2007) Helping children with visual impairment: A review of the literature. British Journal of Visual Impairment, 25(3), 262-274.

Papafragou, A. (1998) The acquisition of modality: implications for theories of semantic representation. Mind and Language, 13(3), 370-399.

Papafragou, A. (2002) Mindreading and Verbal Communication. Mind & Language, 17(1), 55-67.

Papafragou, A. & Musolino, J. (2003) Scalar implicatures: experiments at the semantics-pragmatics interface. Cognition, 86, 253-282.

Papafragou, A. & Tantalou, N. (2004) Children's computation of implicature. Language Acquisition, 12, 71-82.

Papp, S. (2006) A relevance-theoretic account of the development and deficits of theory of mind in normally developing children and individuals with autism. Theory & Psychology, 16(2), 141-161.

Parke, K. Shallcross, R. & Anderson, R. (1980) Differences in coverbal behavior between blind and sighted persons during dyadic communication. Journal of Visual Impairment and Blindness, 74, 142-146

Patterson, M.L. (1995) A parallel model of nonverbal communication. Journal of Nonverbal Behaviour, 19, 3-29.

Peccei, J. S. (1999) Pragmatics. London: Routledge.

Perkins, M. R. (2007) Pragmatic impairment. Cambridge: Cambridge University Press.

Perkins, M.R. (2010) Pragmatic impairment. In J. S. Damico, N. Müller & M. J. Ball (eds.) The Handbook of Language and Speech Disorders, pp. 227-246. Oxford: Blackwell.

Perez-Pereira, M. & Castro, J. (1992) Pragmatic functions of blind and sighted children's language: a twin case study. First language, 12, 17-37.

Perez-Pereira, M. & Conti-Ramsden, G. (1999) Language development and social interaction in blind children. Hove: Psychology Press Ltd.

Perfect, M. (2001) Examining communicative behaviors in a 3-year-old boy who is blind. Journal of Visual Impairment and Blindness, 95, 353-365.

Peters, A.M. (1994) The interdependence of social, cognitive and linguistic development: evidence from a visually impaired child. In H. Tager-Flusberg (ed.) Constraints on Language Acquisition: Studies of Atypical Children, pp. 195-219. Hove: Erlbaum.

Pexman, P. M. (2008) It's Fascinating Research: The Cognition of Verbal Irony. Current Directions in Psychological Science, 17(4), 286-290.

Piaget, J. (1951) The child's conception of the world. London: Routledge.

Plunkett, K. & Schafer, G. (1999) Early speech perception and word learning. In M.D. Barrett (ed.) The Development of language, pp. 51-72. Hove : Psychology Press Ltd.

Politzer, G. (1993) La psychologie du raisonnement: lois de la pragmatique et de la logique formelle. Thèse de Doctorat d'Etat, University of Paris, France.

Preisler, G. (1991) Early patters of interaction between blind infants and their sighted mothers. Child: Care, Health and Development, 17, 65-90.

Preisler, G. (1995) The development of communication in blind and in deaf infants – similarities and differences. Child: Care, health and development, 21(2), 79-110.

Preisler, G. (1997) Social and emotional development of blind children: a longitudinal study. In V. Lewis & G. Collis (Eds.) Blindness and Psychological Development in young children, pp. 69-85. Leicester: British Psychological Society (BPS) Books.

Pring, L., Dewart, H. & Brockbank, M. (1998) Social cognition in children with visual impairments. Journal of Visual Impairment and Blindness, 92, 754-768.

Prizant, B.M. (1985) Toward an understanding of language symptomatology of visually-impaired children. In A. Sykanda, J.E. Jan, S. Blockberger, B. Buchanan & M. Groenveld (eds.) Proceedings of the Fifth Canadian Interdisciplinary Conference on the Visually Impaired. Vancouver: The Canadian National Institute for the Blind.

Puppel, S. (2001) A Concise Guide to Psycholinguistics. Poznań: Wydawnictwo Poznańskie.

Recanati, F. (1989) The pragmatics of what is said. Mind and Language, 4, 295-329.

Recanati F. (2003) Embedded implicatures. Philosophical Perspectives, 17, 1299–332.

Recanati, F. (2004) Literal Meaning. Cambridge: Cambridge University Press.

Recanati, F. (2005) Pragmatics and Semantics. In L. Horn & G. Ward (eds.) The Handbook of Pragmatics, pp. 442-461. Oxford: Blackwell.

Reddy, V. (1999) Prelinguistic communication. In M.D. Barrett (ed.) The Development of language, pp. 25-50. Hove: Psychology Press Ltd.

Rehbein, G. (2006) The cultural apparatus: Thoughts on the relationship between language, culture, and society. In K. Bührig & J. D. ten Thije (eds.) Beyond misunderstanding: linguistic analyses of intercultural communication, pp. 43-96. Amsterdam: John Benjamins.

Roberts, A. (1998) Coping with blindness: personal tales of blindness rehabilitation. SIU Press.

Roberts, C. (2005) Context in Dynamic Interpretation. In L. Horn & G. Ward (eds.) The Handbook of Pragmatics, pp.197-218. Oxford: Blackwell.

Röder, B., Demuth, L., Streb, J. & Rösler, F. (2002) Semantic and syntactic priming in auditory word recognition in congenitally blind adults. Language and Cognitive Processes, 18, 1-20.

Röder, B., Rösler, F. & Neville, H.J. (2000) Event-related potentials during language processing in congenitally blind and sighted people. Neuropsychologia, 38, 1482-1502.

Röder, B., Teder-Salejarvi, W., Sterr, A., Rösler, F., Hillyard, S.A. & Neville, H.J. (1999) Improved auditory spatial tuning in blind humans. Nature, 400, 162-166.

Rogers, S. & Puchalski, C. (1984) Social characteristics of visually impaired infants play. Topics in Early Childhood Special Education, 3(4), 52-56.

Rogow, S. (1982) Rhythms and rhymes: Developing communication in very young blind and multihandicapped children. Child: Care, Health and Development, 8, 249 -260.

Rosch, E. (1975) Cognitive representations of semantic categories. Journal of Experimental Psychology: General, 104, 192-233.

Rosch, E. (1977) Human categorization. In N. Warren (ed.) Studies in Cross-linguistic Psychology, pp. 1-49. London: Academic Press.

Rosch E. (1978/1999) Principles of categorisation. In B. Lloyd & E. Rosch (eds.) Cognition and Categorization, pp. 27-48. Hillsdale, NJ: Erlbaum.

Rowland, C. M. (1983) Patterns of interaction between three blind infants and their mothers. In A.E. Mills (ed.) Language Acquisition in the Blind Child: Normal and Deficient, pp. 114-132. London: Croom Helm.

Sacks, S.Z. (2006) Theoretical Perspectives on the Early Years of Social Development. In S.Z. Sacks & K.E. Wolffe (eds) Teaching Social Skills to Students with Visual Impairments: From Theory to Practice, pp. 51-80. New York: AFB.

Sadock, J. (2005) Speech acts. In L. Horn & G. Ward (eds.) The Handbook of Pragmatics, pp. 53-73. Oxford: Blackwell.

Sanford, A. & Graesser, A. (2006) Shallow processing and underspecification. Discourse Processes, 42(2), 99-108.

Sak-Wernicka, J. (2009) 'Blind learners' gaps in the knowledge-can Relevance Theory account for them?'. Paper presented at Relevance Round Table Meeting II, Warsaw University, June.

Sak-Wernicka, J. (2010) 'Context and humour: a comparative study of blind and sighted adults'. Paper presented at Interdisciplinary Humour Conference, San Zeno di Montagna, Italy, August.

Salthouse, T. (1991) Theoretical perspectives on cognitive aging. Hillsdale, NJ: Lawrence Erlbaum Associates.

Saussure, F. de (1916/1974) Course in general linguistics. (trans. W. Baskin.). London: Fontana/Collins.

Schank, R.C. & Abelson, R.P. (1977) Scripts, plans, goals and understanding. Hillsdale, NJ: Erlbaum.

Schiffrin, D. (1984) Meaning, Form, and Use in Context: Linguistic Applications. Washington, DC: Georgetown University Press.

Searle, J. (1969) Speech acts. Cambridge: Cambridge University Press.

Shannon, C. & Weaver, W. (1949) The mathematical theory of communication. Urbana: University of Illinois Press.

Shatz, M. (1980) Communication. In P.Mussen, J. Flavell & E. Markman (eds) Handbook of child psychology: Vol.3. Cognitive development, pp. 841-869. New York: Wiley.

Siegal, M. & Surian, L. (2009) Conversational Understanding in Young Children. In E. Hoff & M. Shatz (eds.) Blackwell Handbook of Language Development, pp.304-323. Oxford: Blackwell.

Slackman, E.A., Hudson, J.A. & Fivush, R. (1986) Actions, Actors, Links, and Goals: The Structure of Children's Event Representations. In K. Nelson & J. Gruendel (eds.) Event knowledge: structure and function in development, pp. 47-69. Hillsdale, NJ: Lawrence Erlbaum.

Smith, A. (1987) 'Training perceptual strategies inpatients with visual loss'. Paper presented at the Annual Meeting of the American Psychological Association, New York, August.

Smith, J.W. & Kandath, K.P. (2000) Communication and the Blind or Visually Impaired. In D. O. Braithwaite & T. L. Thompson (eds.) Handbook of communication and people with disabilities: research and application, pp. 389-403. Mahwah, NJ: Lawrence Erlbaum Associates.

Smith, P.T., Baker, R.G. & Groat, A. (1982) Spelling as a source of information about children's linguistic knowledge. British Journal of Psychology, 73, 339-350.

Snedeker, J. and Yuan, S. (2007) Effects of prosodic and lexical constraints on parsing in young children (and adults). Journal of Memory and Language, 58, 574-608.

Snow, C.E. (1999) Conversations with children. In P. Fletcher & M. Garman (eds.) Language acquisition: studies in first language development, pp. 69-89. Cambridge: Cambridge University Press.

Solska, A. (2005) Linguistically encoded contradictions in understanding verbal irony. In A. Korzeniowska & M. Grzegorzewska (eds.) Relevance Studies in Poland. vol. 2, pp. 125-138. Warszawa: Warsaw University Press.

Solska, A. (2008) Accessing multiple meanings: the case of zeugma. In E. Mioduszewska & A. Piskorska (eds.) Relevance Round Table I, pp. 109-122. Warsaw: Warsaw University Press.

Spencer, K.D. (2001) Broadening the units of analysis in communication: speech and nonverbal behaviours in pragmatic comprehension. Journal of Child Language, 28, 325-349.

Sperber, D. & Wilson, D. (1986/1996) Relevance: Communication and Cognition. Oxford: Blackwell.

Sperber, D. & Wilson, D. (2002) Pragmatics, Modularity and Mind-reading. Mind & Language, 17, 3-23.

Stainton, R. (2000) Perspectives in the Philosophy of Language. Toronto: Broadview Press.

Stalnaker, R. (1978). Assertion. In P. Portner & B. H. Partee (eds) (2002) Formal semantics: the essential readings, pp. 147-161. Blackwell Publishing Ltd. (from P. Cole Pragmatics (1978) New York: Academic Press).

Stalnaker, R. (1996) Pragmatics. In H. Geirsson & M. Losonsky (eds.) Readings in language and mind, pp 77-87. Oxford: Blackwell.

Sweetser, E. (1991) From Etymology to Pragmatics: Metaphorical and Cultural Aspects of Semantic Structure. Cambridge: Cambridge University Press.

Taboada, M.T (2004) Building coherence and cohesion: task-oriented dialogue in English and Spanish. Amsterdam: John Benjamins Publishing Co.

Tait, P.E. & Ward, M. (1982) The comprehension of verbal humour by visually impaired children. Journal of Visual Impairment and Blindness, 76, 144-147.

Taylor, T.J. (1990) Which is to be master? The institutionalization of authority in the science of language. In J.E. Joseph & T.J. Taylor (eds.) Ideologies of language, pp. 9-26. London: Routledge.

Tomasello, M. (1995) Joint attention as social cognition. In C. Moore & P. Dunham (eds.) Joint attention: its origins and role in development, pp. 103-130. Hillsdale NJ: Lawrence Erlbaum.

Tomasello, M., Call, J. & Gluckman, A. (1997) The comprehension of novel communicative signs by apes and human children. Child Development, 68, 1067-81.

Traum, D. & Dillenbourg, P. (1996) Miscommunication in Multi-Modal Collaboration. In Working Notes of the AAAI-96 Workshop on Detecting, Repairing, And Preventing Human-Machine Miscommunication, pp. 37-46, August.

Trevarthen, C. (1982) The primary motives for cooperative understanding. In G. Butterworth & P. Light (eds.) Social cognition: Studies of the development of understanding, pp. 77-109. Brighton: Harvester Press.

Troster, H. & Brambring, M. (1992) Early social-emotional development in blind infants. Child: Care, Health and Development, 18, 207-227.

Trueswell, J.C., Sekerina, I., Hill, N.M. & Logrip, M.L. (1999) The kindergarten-path effect: studying online sentence processing in young children. Cognition, 73, 89-134.

Turnbull, W. (2003) Language in Action: Psychological Models of Conversation. New York: Psychology Press.

Tzanne, A. (2000) Talking at cross-purposes: the dynamics of miscommunication. Amsterdam: John Benjamins.

Ungar, S. (2000) Cognitive mapping without visual experience. In R. Kitchin & S. Freundschuh (eds.) Cognitive mappings: present, past, and future, pp. 221-248. London: Routledge.

Urwin, C. (1981) Early language development in blind children. The British Society Division of Educational and Child Psychology Occasional Papers, 5, 78-93.

Urwin, C. (1984) Communication in infancy and the emergence of language in blind children. In R. Schiefelbusch & J. Pickar (eds.) The Acquisition of Communicative Competence, pp. 479-524. Baltimore: University Park Press.

Vanderveken, D. & Kubo, S. (1994) Essays in speech act theory. Amsterdam: John Benjamins.

van Dijk, T.A. (1977) Context and cognition: Knowledge frames and speech act comprehension. Journal of Pragmatics, 1(3), 211-231.

van Dijk, T.A. (1979) Relevance Assignment in Discourse Comprehension. Discourse processes, 2, 113-126.

van Valin, R. D. (2008) Investigations of the syntax-semantics-pragmatics interface. Amsterdam: John Benjamins.

Vedeler, D. (1991) Infant intentionality as object directedness: an alternative to representationalism. Journal for the Theory of Social Behaviour, 21, 431-448.

Vihman, M. (1996) Phonological development: the origins of language in the child. Oxford: Blackwell.

von Firsh, K. (1967) The dance language and orientation of bees. Cambridge, Mass.: Belknap Press of Harvard University Press.

Warren, D.H. (1994) Blindness and children: an individual approach. Cambridge: Cambridge University Press.

Warren, M. (2006) Features of naturalness in conversation. Amsterdam: John Benjamins.

Warren, D.H. & Hatton, D.D. (2003) Cognitive development in children with visual impairments. In S.J. Segalowitz & I. Rapin (eds.) Handbook of neuropsychology, 2nd Edition, vol. 8, Part II, pp. 439-458. Amsterdam: Elsevier Science.

Wedgwood, D. (2005) Relevance theory and implications for linguistic structure. In D. Wedgwood (ed.) Shifting the focus: from static structures to the dynamics of interpretation, pp. 41-74. Amsterdam: Elsevier.

Welsh, R.L. & Tuttle, D.W. (1997) Congenital and Adventitious Blindness. In J.E. Moore, W.H. Graves & J. Patterson (eds.) Foundations of rehabilitation counseling with persons who are blind or visually impaired, pp. 60-79. New York: AFB.

Wharton, T. (2003) Interjections, language, and the 'showing/saying' continuum. Pragmatics & Cognition, 11(1), 39-91.

Wharton, T. (2009) Pragmatics and Non-Verbal Communication. Cambridge: Cambridge University Press.

Widdowson, H. G. (1992/2004) Text, context, pretext: critical issues in discourse analysis. Oxford: Blackwell.

Wierzbicka, A. (2003) Cross-cultural pragmatics: The semantics of Human Interaction. Berlin: de Gruyter.

Więckowska, E. (2006) Nauczanie rysunku a rozwój wyobrażeń i pojęć przestrzennych dziecka niewidomego. Laski, 5/6, 102-113.

Wilson, D. (1970) If that. Linguistic Inquiry, 1, 369-373.

Wilson, D. (1994) Relevance and Understanding. In G. Brown, K. Malmkjaer, A. Pollitt & J. Williams (eds.) Language and Understanding, pp. 34-58. Oxford: Oxford University Press.

Wilson, D. (1998) Discourse, coherence and relevance: a reply to Rachel Giora. Journal of Pragmatics, 29, 57-74.

Wilson, D. (2000) Metarepresentation in linguistic communication. In D. Sperber (ed.) Metarepresentations, pp. 411-448. Oxford: Oxford University Press.

Wilson, D. (2005) New directions for research on pragmatics and modularity. Lingua, 115(8), 1129-1146.

Wilson, D. (2006) The pragmatics of verbal irony: Echo or pretence?. Lingua, 116, 1722-1743.

Wilson, D. (2009) Irony and metarepresentation. UCL Working Papers in Linguistics, 21, 183-226.

Wilson, D. & Sperber, D. (2005) Relevance Theory. In L. Horn & G. Ward (eds.) The Handbook of Pragmatics, pp. 607-628. Oxford: Blackwell.

Wilson, D. & Sperber, D. (2007) On Verbal Irony. In R.W. Gibbs & H.L. Colson (eds.) Irony in language and thought: A cognitive science reader, pp. 35-56. New York: Lawrence Erlbaum Associates.

Wilson, D. & Wharton T. (2006) Relevance and prosody. Journal of Pragmatics, 38(10), 1559-1579.

Winner, E. (1997) The point of words: children's understanding of metaphor and irony. Harvard: Harvard University Press.

Wittgenstein, L. (1953) Philosophical Investigations. (trans. G.E.M. Anscombe). Oxford: Blackwell.

Yule, G. (1996) Pragmatics. Oxford: Oxford University Press.

Yus, F. (1997) Grammar: Relevance-theoretic concerns. Revista Alicantina de Estudios Ingleses, 10, 235-248.

Yus, F. (1998) Irony: Context accessibility and processing effort. Pragmalingüística, 5(6), 391-411.

Yus, F. (2000a) On reaching the intended ironic interpretation. International Journal of Communication, 10(1-2), 27-78.

Yus, F. (2000b) Literal/nonliteral and the processing of verbal irony. Pragmalingüística, 8(9), 349-374.

Yus, F. (2003) Humor and the search for relevance. Journal of Pragmatics, 35(9), 1295-1331. Special issue on the pragmatics of humor.

Zwicky, A. and Sadock, J. (1975). Ambiguity tests and how to fail them. In J.P. Kimball (ed.), Syntax and Semantics, vol.4, pp. 1-36. New York: Academic Press.

Zwiers, M.P., Van Opstal, A.J., & Cruysberg, J.R.M. (2001) A spatial hearing deficit in early-blind humans. Journal of Neuroscience, 21(9), RC142/1-5.

Internet sources

http://www.who.int/mediacentre/factsheets/fs282/en/ (28.04.2011)

http://firr.org.pl/1/nasze-projekty/projekt-equal/tlo-projektu-4/sytuacja-osob-niewidomych-w-polsce.html (28.04.2011)

APPENDIX A

A Braille version of a crossword

A window with a computer application invented to enable blind people to solve crosswords – a screen print out

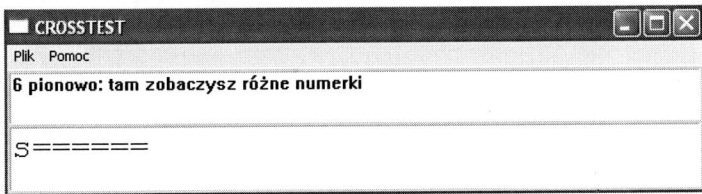

APPENDIX B

Woman: Honey, which bathroom tiles do you like more: the green ones or the ones with the subtle border?
Man: The ones with the border are ok.
Woman: Don't you think that the border is too subtle.
Man: The other ones, then.
Woman: I like them more, too. You see how well we understand each other.

1. What do you think the wife's intention was?
a) She wanted her husband to choose between the green tiles and the tiles with the subtle border.
b) She wanted her husband to confirm her choice of tiles.
c) She wanted to make sure how successful their marriage is.
d) Other intention (if so, suggest what)
e) I don't know.

2. On a scale of 1 to 5, rate husband's involvement in the choice of the bathroom tiles.

Lack of involvement				**Full involvement**	**I don't know**
1 ▨	2 ▨	3 ▨	4 ▨	5 ▨	▨

3 Which statement best describes the situation?
a) The wife is surprised that her husband shares her taste and they've chosen the same tiles.
b) The wife respects her husband's opinion and hopes they will choose tiles together.
c) The wife has already chosen the green tiles and she tries to suggest her choice to her husband.
d) Other statement (if so, suggest what)
e) I don't know.

Situation 2

Hannah: When did it happen?
Julie: About an hour ago.
Hannah: What kind of wine?
Julie: Burgundy.
Hannah: That's ok. We can deal with it. Is it cotton and silk?

1. What has happened?
a) Wine was spilled.
b) The wine has run out.
c) Julie has some problems.
d) Other (if so, suggest what)
e) I don't know

2. Hannah's last comment suggests that:
a) it will be difficult to remove the wine stain.
b) it is too late to find any shop open and buy the wine.
c) they will discuss Julie's problems.
d) Other (if so, suggest what)
e) I don't know

3. On a scale of 1 to 5, rate Hannah and Julie's attitude to what has happened:

	Deeply pessimistic				**Highly optimistic**	**I don't know**
Hannah	1 ▢	2 ▢	3 ▢	4 ▢	5 ▢	▢
Julie	1 ▢	2 ▢	3 ▢	4 ▢	5 ▢	▢

Situation 3

Joanna: I have two tickets for "Don Giovanni."
Tom: Who's he fighting with?
Joanna: It's an opera.
Tom: Let us meet later!

1 Joanna intends to:
a) boast about the tickets which she has managed to get hold of.
b) invite Tom to the opera.
c) tell Tom that she has bought tickets for the opera which they both wanted to see.
d) Other intension (if so, suggest what)
e) I don't know

2 Is Tom going to the opera?
a) definitely yes   b) probably yes   c) rather not
d) definitely not   e) I don't know

3 Which sentence best describes the situation?
a) Tom is too busy to talk with Joanna about the opera and he wants to meet later.
b) Tom doesn't feel like going to "Don Giovanni" and opera is not his cup of tea and he.
c) Tom would like to go to a boxing match.
d) Other sentence (if so, suggest what)
e) I don't know

Situation 4

Robert: What did you do on Saturday?
Martin: I went to the zoo with my kids.
Robert: Did you enjoy it?
Martin: The twins didn't give a damn about animals and were playing caps. Alli wanted to see a baby ostrich but it refused to come out of the enclosure. In the end all we saw was a cleaning lady.

1. On a scale of 1 to 5, rate Martin's satisfaction with the visit to the zoo.

Lack of satisfaction				Great satisfaction	I don't know
1 ▣	2 ▣	3 ▣	4 ▣	5 ▣	▣

2. How long was the family at the zoo?
a) not long because the kids weren't interested
b) not long because the kids were bored
c) until the kids finished playing caps
d) until they closed the zoo
e) I don't know

3. How many kids did Martin take to the zoo?
a) 2
b) 3
c) 4
d) I don't know

Situation 5

Wife: We need a new bedspread … and carpet …
Husband: If a carpet, then chairs, if chairs, then a mirror, wardrobe
and then our kids will hate us.
Wife: Why?
Husband: Because we will divorce.

1. On a scale of 1 to 5 rate how much Husband wants to buy new things
for the house.

Not at all   **Very**   **I don't**
                                                            much   **know**

1 ▣   2 ▣   3 ▣   4 ▣   5 ▣   ▣

2. The husband thinks that (circle the best answer):
a) their children will not approve of the exchange of old things for new
ones.
b) the choice of new things will lead to conflict between him and his wife
c) They can't afford to buy new things at present.
d) Other answer (if so, suggest what)
e) I don't know.

3. Is the husband really going to divorce his wife?
a) yes
b) no
c) I don't know.

Situation 6
Eve: What do you have there?
Arthur: I've bought Sting's new single.
Eve: Let's hear it.
(after a short while)
Eve: Pull the tab!

1. What does Arthur have a problem with?
a) playing the CD
b) opening the CD
c) nothing
d) other problem (if so, suggest what)
e) I don't know

2. Which sentence best describes Eve's behaviour?
a) Eve is impatient with Arthur's clumsiness
b) Eve tries her best to help Arthur
c) Eve expects Arthur to be able to do two things at once.
d) other sentence (if so, suggest what)
e) I don't know.

3. (Answer the question) What 'tab' is Eve talking about?

Situation 7

A: How're things?
B: Not good. Last weekend my parrot died. I'd it for 10 years.
A: Will you buy a new one?
B: Sure...after all it's only a bunch of feathers.

1. On a scale of 1 to 5, rate how much Mark was attached to his parrot.

Not at all   **Very**   **I don't**
                                                   much   **know**

1 🔲   2 🔲   3 🔲   4 🔲   5 🔲   🔲

2. What will Mark do?
a) He will buy a new parrot, although it is not worth much.
b) He won't buy a new parrot, because it is not worth much.
c) He won't buy a new parrot, because he misses the old one.
d) Other answer (if so, suggest what)
e) I don't know.

3. Mark's response suggests that:
a) Parrots are less valuable pets than dogs or cats.
b) Contrary to what Andrew thinks, his parrot can't be exchange for a new one.
c) Mark makes fun of the situation because he doesn't want Andrew to think he is sentimental.
d) Mark makes fun of the situation, but parrot's death has depressed him.
e) Other answer (if so, suggest what)
f) I don't know.

Situation 8

Woman: Dinner's ready!
(after a while)
Woman: This would be good for *Animal Planet*!

1. In the above utterance 'this' refers to:
a) dinner
b) something not mentioned that the mother can see
c) the behaviour of the family members
d) Other (if so, suggest what)
e) I don't know

2. What does the mother mean by saying 'This would be good for Animal Planet!'?
a) She means that vegetarians would be outraged if they saw their dinner.
b) She means that the family is misbehaving at the table.
c) She means that their house is infested with vermin.
d) She means that the family could make a career in television.
e) Other (if so, suggest what)
f) I don't know.

3. The mother says it with:
a) anger
b) pity
c) indignation
d) surprise
e) amusement
f) Other (if so, suggest what)
g) I don't know.

Situation 9

Woman: Have you called the neighbour to apologise to her?
Man: Just like you told me.
Woman: And did your world come crashing down?

1. Has the man called the neighbour to apologise?
a) yes
b) no
c) I don't know.

2. The dialogue implies that:
a) the neighbour is a difficult person.
b) it was difficult for the man to apologise to the neighbour.
c) something tragic happened to the man.
d) other (if so, suggest what)
e) I don't know.

3. What exactly is the woman asking by saying "And did your world come crashing down?"?
a) If the neighbour offended the man during the phone call.
b) If apologising to the neighbour was really that difficult.
c) If something tragic happened to the man.
d) other (if so, suggest what)
e) I don't know.

Situation 10

Man: Have you already chosen?
Woman: I don't want to make a fuss, but on the menu you've got
***Sodole* in the French wines' section.**
Man: I see. And for you, sir?

1.Which statement is true for the situation?
a) The woman is surprised that in the restaurant they serve one of her favourite and rarest of wines.
b) The woman tries to point out to a mistake on the menu.
c) The woman has come to the restaurant alone.
d) other (if so, suggest what)
e) I don't know.

2. How does the manr react to woman's utterance?
a) He takes the order.
b) He takes note of her remark.
c) He is embarrassed.
d) He is nervous.
e) other reaction (if so, suggest what)
f) I don't know.

3. On a scale of 1 to 5, rate the given emotions which the woman feels in the situation.

	Lack				**Great**	**I don't know**
a) surprise	1	2	3	4	5	
b) contentment	1	2	3	4	5	
c) indignation	1	2	3	4	5	

Situation 11

Woman: Darling, I've bought you a new sweater.
Man: Did you buy it in that shop for fat people? Do you always buy
clothes for me there?
Woman: It's also a shop for tall and well-built people. Besides, they
use very good fabrics.

1. On a scale of 1 to 5, rate how much the man is satisfied with the
present.

Not at all				Very much	I don't know
1 ▨	2 ▨	3 ▨	4 ▨	5 ▨	▨

2. Does the woman always buy clothes for the man in the shop for large
people?
a) yes
b) no
c) I don't know

3. The woman bought the sweater in the shop for large people because
(choose the main reason):
a) clothes bought in the shop fit the husband.
b) clothes bought in the shop are made of good fabric.
c) she wanted to make him look tall and well-built.
d) she wanted to make him nervous.
e) other reason (if so, suggest what)
f) I don't know.

Situation 12

Girl: Dad, I'm sick.
Man: You've seen the neighbour's cat!?
Girl: No, what's it doing?
Man: Lying on the street and pretending to be asleep.

1. Why does the father think that the girl is sick?
a) Because she looks ill.
b) Because neighbour's cat is disgusting.
c) Because the sight of the dead cat is disgusting.
d) Other reason (if so, suggest what)
e) I don't know.

2. What is the man not telling directly?
a) that he hates cats
b) that the neighbour's cat is disgusting
c) that the neighbour's cat has been run over
d) The man is not hiding anything.
e) Other thing (if so, suggest what)
f) I don't know.

3. The cat in the conversation is:
a) sly
b) lazy
c) dead
d) playful
e) Other feature (if so, suggest what)
f) I don't know

INDEX